Transforming Into Kingdom

Transforming Into Kingdom

Daughters of Zion Arise

MELANIE REMBERT

TRANSFORMING INTO KINGDOM DAUGHTERS OF ZION ARISE

iUniverse books may be ordered through booksellers or by contacting:

iUniverse
1663 Liberty Drive
Bloomington, IN 47403
www.iuniverse.com
1-800-Authors (1-800-288-4677)

ISBN: 978-1-5320-4261-4 (sc)
ISBN: 978-1-5320-4262-1 (e)

Library of Congress Control Number: 2018901298

Print information available on the last page.

iUniverse rev. date: 03/19/2018

DEDICATION

I dedicate this book back to Father God.

I am very appreciative of my wonderful and handsome husband Elder Jason Rembert and our beautiful children; Paris, John, and Asia.

*Special thanks to Paris who kept encouraging me saying these words: "Mom, finish the book."

INTRODUCTION

To follow after man is to follow after natural things man have. To follow after God is to follow after Spiritual things God has.

_Jesus Christ

I have great news! God, through divine design, instructed me to write down some of the things He's wanting to say to His daughters in this day and time when confusion has taken over the globe. With men wanting to be women and women wanting to be men our children are left in a confusing state _while the earth we eat from is getting sicker and sicker because of sin, demonic spirits, and powers running rampant through the land. How do we as daughters of God play our part in this major catastrophic case? Is it anything we can do besides passively stand by and hate what is going on around us? The answer is YES! We must turn back to our first love! We must turn back to prayer! We must turn back to the order God has instructed of us and also become virtuous. Who can find a virtuous woman, for her price is far above rubies! In this book you will find information the Lord has set aside just for you. By the leading of the Holy Ghost we must take this information and begin to pray with it. So many things taught and passed to us from civilization\ America has been wrongly delivered, but today we must take a stand and say no more! God put us here to be help meets to our husbands and to uplift Jesus name in worship! We are to become that kingdom God can live in. Imagine how harmonious it would be in our homes if we took a stand against regular America and said, "I'm going back to being the weaker vessel. I'm not equal to a man and I never desire to be. I am female and I enjoy the benefits God has given me. I am strong enough to be weak, because in our weakness is where God's strength is made perfect"! Often times I hear others tell me that I am such a strong individual. Many obstacles and trials that would have broken a normal person down and made them renounce the faith completely while never looking back only proceeded to make me taller and my faith stronger in Christ Jesus! God has revealed certain mysteries in this book and one of them is that His strength is made perfect when we are weak. Many ladies today choose to go the route of being equal to men but the sweetest rode is that of the weaker vessel! I get to see God flex for me everyday! The weaker vessel is spiritually STRONG, because she is in a place where strength is made PERFECT! (2Cor 12) All daughters whom has submitted to Father loves for Him to implement His strength in her everyday life! Let the weak say "I AM" strong! Father is the "I Am that I Am!" (Exodus 3:14) In our weakness His strength is made PERFECT! Do you know how beautiful it is, in all our femininity, to be weak before God? The "I Am" swoops in and causes you to appear supernatural! Are you in love yet? "I AM!!!" I am in love with the "I Am" who IS LOVE! He makes everything I'Mpossible! With Father we become just that _SUPERNATURAL! Let the weak say Father is strong! Do you have the strength to tell America that you desire no longer to be as strong as a man? With Father we embrace our weakness as the weaker vessel! It's simply wonderful! I encourage you to read and apply the material in this book. If applied you'll feel like that virtuous woman you've always wanted to become who is delicate, peaceable, harmonious, righteous, and Holy with wisdom. She is also a strategic warrior so don't let that pure smile she has fool you! She appears weak and vulnerable to the natural eye but she's packed with discernment and love(the strongest weapon ever) that is not of this world and,the Holy Spirit whispers secrets to her knowing she is loyal enough to keep and pray about them! She has no need to posses strength because the strongest one of all accompany her day in and day out. She has given up her vindictive ways so if you've wronged her, you won't feel the same wrath you would from a woman who hasn't submitted. But when she goes into her secret place of prayer YOUR NAME will be on her lips! Being that she's weak her strong God will accompany her in prayer. She will begin to tell Him to bless you and make your way prosperous! She'll ask Him to please open doors for you that will be a blessing to your life. God then begins His vengeance process because NOBODY gets over on His baby! Yes He answers her prayers but His vengeance is applied as well because He's found one who actually need and loves His protection. This book will teach us how to become this type of daughter! One who's meek and quiet in Spirit but vicious in prayer! One strong enough to slay demons but weak and submitted to the man of the house and to authority. Daughters rise up! Take your rightful places!

The very reason I am still alive, able to function, still wake up with a smile embedded in my face, and joy has taken over my soul is because Jesus Christ has never left me alone! He took me over the deepest waters of life and in His arms I soared as I heard ones telling me what I couldn't do and who I was not qualified to be! God took me in His arms and the negative voices became faint while His became clear in my ears. From that day forward I was never no more the same! I look in the mirror and I see a miracle. Here I stand a lady that should have been put away in a mental institute from detrimental trials and tribulations only God could have sustained me and my mind through. Demonic attacks of witchcraft tried to take me out _while a real demon literally took on human form and jumped on top of me beginning to war with me as I was laying upon my bed early early one morning trying to over power me in a form of rape, but the blood stained banner waved high as I clawed away at this demon scratching and warring feeling the flesh in my hands, about ten years ago, I began to try and call my master. However, the demon knowing what was about to take place began to choke me! I quickly regained the strength to say the name JESUS and the demon disappeared immediately! God said No! He didn't let that demonic force penetrate me! He allowed me to come into the reality that demons are very real and can take on human form. They are very vicious and have one goal in mind. To destroy you! He also showed me the true power of the name Jesus! Demonic forces are afraid of this name! We must stay covered under the blood ladies! That demon knew that I had a massive assignment and that is to make sure these instructions right here are able to reach across the waters and over the globe! This biblically based tool will help lead us back to our place of covering! With all the things I've been through the Lord allowed my heart to still love and be full of compassion, my faith reaching past limits, and having a surety knowing that I am a true genuine daughter of the King!

God gave me the material in this book, I was just the vessel writing and I take no credit for His Knowledge and Wisdom. To God be the glory.

Behind The Veil {Intro}
_Choose Life

One day a young man stumbled upon this beautiful lady and offered her five long stem roses as a token of his affection. The lady smiled and was delighted! To her surprise another gentleman stepped up to her and offered her five seeds to show his affection also. She looked upon the seeds while holding the roses and laughed profusely for surely the other had promised more beauty! She chose the prince of the roses without second thought! The other young gentleman ...well, he held out his hands and said

"Will their be another "?

One lady who was very flawed with many scars internally and outwardly from past hurts and disappointments whom felt she really didn't deserve anything stepped up in faith to claim the gentleman's affection and his seeds. He turned and looked her over very carefully and said
"You are the perfect one".

He offered the lady the seeds and his affection with great joy that she had made the right decision! She immediately went to find the things she might need to plant them to show her appreciation; a spade, rake, garden fork, water, slow release fertilizer, and a wheel barrow. While gathering these things she glanced at the window of the beautiful young lady and saw her long stem roses in a vase. *Just stunning*, she thought. Even still, without distraction, she began to work with these seeds she had which appeared to be rose seeds. She knew she had a lot of working and waiting ahead of her but was willing because she was just glad to be chosen!

Hours before planting she had to water them very good, while preparing her soil and using a spade shovel digging about 45cm wide and 30cm deep. Gathering her wheel barrow, soil and mix with compound she was ready for the challenge. After much preparation she placed the seeds in the ground. They didn't bloom until late spring, but when they came up they were the most majestic in town! While thankfully enjoying the view she happened to look down the street and noticed that those long stemmed roses the beautiful young lady had was long gone. The young lady even came by to admire what had now turn to be a huge rose garden and wished so badly that she had chosen differently.

(Www.vidiojud.com How to plant a rose bush)

The moral of the story:

God always gives things that are connected to life because He is life! Yes, it may take work to achieve what God has for you. Even tears may be cried, but in the end it's all worth it. Satan gives things that looks so promising and beautiful but dies over time every time because he promotes stealing, killing, and destroying. Choose life today!

The Lord gave us this particular scenario to show us that to many times we have been tricked by the enemy to believe we are getting something of great value. Have you notice that it does not last very long? The peace is short lived. The joy is short lived. The love is not experienced long. The enemy uses something shinny to us to distract us and to get us off the devine path God has set for us. God wants to offer us everlasting peace, joy, and love! This book will transform you from the spirit of Queen Vashtie who rebelled and chose not to come when being called, to Queen Esther who fasted and came without being called even if the penalty was death! Are you willing to be transformed into a necessity and not just a luxury? By placing investment in this book you have just realized that the change this world needs starts with you! I am Kingdom! I pray this book blesses you as it has me.

Contents

CHAPTER 1

The Heart Of A Child Gives You The Place of A King

America in all her glory has succumb to letting the weaker vessel, which are the ladies, begin to compete against men. We have left the mark that says we are to be feminine and have embrace a term called alpha female! The Alpha female runs the pack and makes even men bow to her. She's the one who pulls the attention in the business meetings by making all around her feel intimidated because no man can ever have authority over her. As a matter of fact, she is the boss point blank! She has no time for children so if a man does happen to snag her he had better realize that she has chosen differently for her body. No children will come through these loins and mess up what I have going on, she thinks! When we look around in today's society we see this type of lady more and more. She works so hard to prove she can do anything she desire to do and her gender has no say so in the matter! Is this you? Are you tired of being looked at as someone whom need a big and strong man to protect you and cover you from harm? Are you wishing for that change in this country where all men are literally created equal? Although this country is evolving in this very direction, I believe the joy we are truly waiting to experience won't be found in working harder in the industry. To gain a few more dollars and have equal pay as men is not the answer. We ladies lack something else, something deeper that hasn't reached the surface yet but is obviously disturbing our roots. We want to be seen as macho when honestly deep deep down within we still have the heart of a child!

We desire to please those closest to us. Even though we have grown and developed in many ways our hearts still long for that acceptance.

Let's take a look at the average child:

Children are our future, we always say! Such a joy and pleasure it is to be around a learning child bursting with energy. They are full of expectancy and faith. They believe that all they need is a good teacher and they can achieve being whatever it is they desire in life. Even words of encouragement go a long way with them. The average child seeks to please mother and father. If an incident occurs and the fault lie theirs, they become heavy hearted and immediately try to find ways to make things right again so that mother/father love can flow smoothly and without any hindrances again. Children are also quick to tell a trusted parent what's bothering them. They confess, they cry, they receive an encouraging word, and they then feel ready to conquer the world!

By actually stopping to address things that are important to God and actually caring when we offend Him, we take the correct steps to our purpose of being daughters in Christ Jesus! So step by step together we will remove the blinders off our eyes, strip away the clogs out of our ears, and allow God to lead us back home! Earlier I expressed to you that many women in America has taken on the spirit of wanting to be equal to a man. What we are about to discuss may seem contradictory! We have Ruth, Abigail, Deborah, Leah, Tamar and other ladies as well that we could have drawn conclusions from that the Holy Ghost could have given me lead way to write about in this opening chapter, but for some reason the Lord gave me Joseph! I believe with all my heart that He gave me Joseph for us to relate to because America has shifted our eyes into the direction of being capable of all! What better way to shift our eyes back to the place of consciousness, than to go right down the avenue where we have placed our eyes!(on man) The Lord in His infinite wisdom will show us how we can in fact relate to man! Not to the masculine testosterone of a man does He want us to relate, but to the heart of man. At the end of the day and when the dust settles forever, God will look at the heart of man.

> "Verily *I say unto you, except ye be converted, and become as little children, ye shall not enter into the Kingdom of heaven.*"
>
> **(Matthew18:3)**

Attention ladies...let's put this conversion in process and motion.

Let's examine Joseph. Yes Joseph! He may have been a man and I know how awkward this may seem but let's take a look at what the Lord wants to tell us. When the last trumpet sounds on that great day The bride of Christ, is what the Lord is coming back for! One body fitly joined together is what He seeks. We must make sure our half is ready so let's put on our spiritual mindset. This is the only way we will make it back to our rightful places!

> "*God is a spirit: and they that worship him must worship him in "spirit " and "truth""*
>
> **(John 4:24)**

The only way for us ladies to strip off and rid ourselves of all the ridicule since the start of time is to just be honest with God and get in the spirit of who He is and who we are supposed to be. So let's take a closer look at Joseph. Joseph, like us, had hard life circumstances that started when he was young. All he wanted to do was be accepted and loved by his family. A young heart is so precious. Most women today still have the young heart of a child, no matter how much lipstick, high heels, or different types of panty hose she has, the bottom line is she wants to be accepted and loved by those closest to her. Isn't this beautiful! God made us to grow and mature, but still have this magnificent heart of a child. This is totally okay but *only in the way of God* which is where we go wrong. A child's heart can't be trusted with everyone because it is to open and too pure! Father desires for us to have this child like heart toward Him and He then shows us how, when, and with who to use it in the earth realm! The bible says "*seek ye first the kingdom of God and all these other things will be added.*" So the things we desire naturally will draw close but first we must line up with the way God told us to be.

3

Are you willing to dedicate a child like heart to Father?

Let us examine Joseph's journey again: Joseph had such a great anointing on him until even he himself couldn't fully comprehend it at the time. He spoke out God given dreams and It caused conflict with those around him. They ended up plotting up a way to rid themselves of him. Joseph was later sold off by his brothers as a slave and ended up doing time in prison. (We ladies have been in prison way to long) Joseph, even in prison, excelled, kept an excellent spirit, and begin to gain respect from others. He utilized the gifts given to him by God interpreting dreams for the inmates. Even with his excellent spirit he saw other inmates by passing him and being relieved from prison.

Note : Never *get distracted by others success. God has a time and a plan for you. Just stay focused on what He told you to do.*

So Joseph's time finally came where he was brought before great men, the main man being the King. Know one in the king's house could interpret the King's dream and God allowed this to happen where what the king needed, Joseph was the only one who had it! My my my can you see the story unfolding? Pay close attention because this next part determines if we go back to jail or not.

What use is their to be relieved from a natural prison just to be held hostage in a spiritual one?

> "And *Joseph answered Pharaoh saying, it is not in me:*
> *God shall give Pharaoh an answer of peace." **(Gen 41:16)***

Wow! He was in the right place, at the right time, saying the right thing! It's not impossible. God wants someone who will not steal His glory. Joseph had been through enough so he walked softly to the ways of God. Even though he had grown into a man in statue his heart still longed to please God. Joseph's natural father was stripped away from him and he got to know God not only as the supreme being but God as his real Father. God desires us to view Him this way as well!

Now that Joseph has passed the test with God, he is then given an

OMG promotion. Joseph went on to use his excellence to prepare Egypt for a great famine. We all know the story. The famine entered and Joseph was the man to see in order for people all over to buy food! Low and behold look who shows up to buy food but the ones who sold him into slavery.

> "Joseph *knew his brothers, but they knew him not."(Gen 42:8)*

God, through trials and tribulations, had totally changed Joseph inside and out so to the point his own brothers didn't even recognize him. Father also wants to transform you too where your enemies wont recognize you anymore.

Question:

Do you know God, as Father?

What is hindering the process of transformation from happening for you?

Is it unwillingness to go through trials correctly?

Did you know that this is simply the method God chooses to take in order to change us from the inside out?

Look how much we have in common with Joseph the youngster sold into slavery. Our image to, was sold into slavery by the unrighteousness of Eve. She sold out the blessings we had for a chance to be like God.

Do we receive the fruit Eve has passed down to us for generations to equal authority or do we persist with and excellent spirit to find our rightful place in God?

Joseph learned the importance of having an excellent spirit while going through. He found no time for complaining which shows God we're not ready for the blessing. We must learn as well that complaining is a weapon of the devil! It slowly wraps around us like a snake until we're known as the complainer complaining about every single thing that goes wrong in our lives while creating terrible outcome. Those with a heart for God grow and mature but that one part of the heart should always remain a child. We should long to be accepted and loved by God. We should always cry out to Him and confess our short comings. With Joseph having a child like heart, God was able to afflict him and transform him into something uniquely wonderful. This doesn't mean that satan's evil ways wont come to try us still but that we have the victory. One evil way of satan that will keep us daughters from transformation is being *vindictive*! Let's grasp another look back at Joseph. In *(Gen 42:17-23)* we see the process of Joseph wanting to get revenge by throwing all his brothers in prison and only sending one back to gather the evidence he required, but after three days of the Lord dealing with him and in him loving the Lord he allowed the Lord to lead his emotions. He had mercy and enabled all the brothers to go back home but one. (God sees things differently than we do) In his obedience to reflect God's heart and mercy, a repenting heart came over his brothers for what they did to him. He not only allowed all brothers but one to return home, but he also returned their money to them. Now this is a great example of being a vessel for the Lord! When we can feed those who have persecuted us and show them kindnesses in return it is a big step in being lead by Father who taught this! It is not until after Joseph permitted God to come in that he began to show mercy. I am not concerned with how difficult it may seem, as long as we reach our goal. Being into God's will project His ways and way of doing things. It also brings true repentance, either from you to other people or from other people to you. Most of the time, both. Then just watch the transformation begin to take place! Joseph was well aware that he had to let the hurt and pain go. The heart of a child brings you to the place of a king! In *(Gen 42:24)* it tells that Joseph turned away from his brothers and wept. All that hurt of being stripped away from everything and everyone he knew was painful! Being torn away from his mom, his dad, and familiar surroundings caused his tears to not be restrained any longer. Tears are a sign of true strength. Exquisite! Be very aware that weeping is necessary in God.

How else will the soul release tremendous hurts and despair?

You ever felt real heavy or just burden down and you went off by yourself and let the tears flow?

How did you feel afterwards?

This step in deliverance and healing is very important not to miss. It's not a bad idea to implement a *"cry break"* in your schedule every now and then. You'll find yourself in the arms of Jesus Himself! Because of Joseph's willingness to go through his trials correctly and keep a child like heart toward God, God put him in the place of a king where even the king admired what he had to say and what he did! By learning our rightful place, which is to be a child, it throws us into the heart of the King! Our King of kings that is, King Jesus!!!

Behind The Veil
_*"Sold"*

Ever heard the term *"sold out "*? Often times this term creates fear in the minds and hearts of people .

> *"You must be sold out to Christ"*
> *"The item you so desperately need is sold out"*

Be not dismayed! This term was frightening even for the rich younger ruler who was told by Jesus to *sell all* he had and follow Him. *(Matthew 19: 16-24)* This man's countenance was sad after hearing this. We often time find comfort in our valuables. So much to the point that if we loose them *we* feel lost. Jesus wants us to view Him this way! If we loose HIM we feel lost. Being a follower of Jesus we must be willing to give up things and become *sold out*. Joseph's brothers sold him into slavery. They hated Joseph enough to want him gone. They plotted, they planned, they acted, and achieved what they had set out to do. In the end though, it was Joseph who achieved the relationship with God!

Question

<u>*Have you ever been plotted against?*</u>

<u>*Did you ever feel like someone wanted your job, husband, or certain skills you have?*</u>

<u>*How did you handle this situation?*</u>

Joseph had the trust of the king because he actually took his making without shying back.

In situations like these we must take the problem to the problem solver. This is the only way to come out on top!

Judas *sold* Jesus to the enemies who wanted Him dead. Jesus could have spoken and cursed these men using His power, but He went through the persecution and now know one can get to our Father but by the name of Jesus! He was *sold out* to the mission. We too had to be *sold* and not waver from the truth! After Jesus stopped by and paid the ultimate price, He bought us! It's like standing in line as a slave. Different masters are sizing you up, but the Good Master has His eye on you! (Thank you Jesus)The Master that wants to give you all power is looking at you! Even power to free your loved ones from the other task master's punishment. Either way a master will purchase you. Might as well have "The Good Master" and not one that drives you with terrible intentions. So those of us choosing redemption are *sold out, m*eaning we have nothing left. Nothing left of ourselves for sin, and nothing left for the demonic. One of the many beauties of being *sold out* to Christ is that He is responsible for our food.(He's glad about that)

> "*Give us this day our daily bread*"

Another great reason for being *sold out* to God is that He'll be responsible for your shelter, and your well being.

> "*You are my refuge and my fortress my God in you will I trust*"

I can't imagine having it any other way, because the state of America is rebellion. I think America is beautiful just like everyone else, but the girl is severely sin sick. This country actually allows homosexuals to try and take God's symbol of promise to never destroy the earth with water again and use it for naught. (The rainbow) Jesus spoke to me while in prayer one day concerning the homosexual behavior and said,

"I'm upset with their disobedience."

He said,

"They are not being who I told them to be and they're not acting like I told them to act."

Things are just that simple with God! I was stunned as I never thought of it this way before. He tells us how to act and who to be by the genital He gives us at birth. We then are to be raised in that way and obey what the bible says concerning our genital. I always thought that the sexual perversions of it was very wrong but disobedience never came to mind.

Disobedient people have no idea that fire is the next move of God. But each time they flash the rainbow symbol to show gay pride, they don't know it, but they are reminding God to bring fire and not water this time to consume them. I pray that many confused individuals are saved and washed in the blood before then. Notice how it's been a war on stripes every since God's rainbow, Joseph's coat of many colors, and it's no coincidence that America just happened to choose red stripes for the American flag! It is by Jesus stripes of blood that we were made healed and free and not from war in a country. We are on our way to becoming *Sold* out with no vacancy for the enemy! We shall be victorious with excellence!

CHAPTER 2

The Healing Mechanism In Tears

Life is so large and full of possibilities, potential, warfare, and exploration! We dwell on our capabilities, earned education, and self assurance to get us through to the next level in life. While all these exciting events and challenges take place we rarely take a look at something as simple as the benefit in tears although they are present as we travel through different phases in our lives. They end up being wasted on things and people like no good Jody from foot locker in the Mall.

The true meaning of wasteful is using or expending something of value carelessly, extravagantly, or to no purpose. *(of a person, action, or process)*

Capture a brief time to examine the human body. Isn't it amazing! We were made from the dust of the earth by God and He blew breath into us. Yes! People marvel at artist like Pablo Picasso, Leonardo da Vinci, and Jackson Pollack, but Jesus is the most artistic of them all! He is "the first artist" of all times. Just look at your body! Enormous, towering, short, plump, slender and/or all colors red, yellow, olive, orange, and brown all bodies are God's creation! We received everything we would require in order to function properly. From interior organs to our exterior eyelashes, nose hairs, and finger nails. I need to direct your attention back to tears. Tears are very precious to God and He's very observant how we utilize them. Often times people hurt us or life circumstances get the best of us and we feel it's to strenuous to bear. It is so taxing sometimes. Tears are a direct proof that life has it's ups and downs. Show me a person that chooses not to cry and I'll just have witnessed a very vindictive person. One that is unforgiving and one torn by hatred is what I'll behold because crying leads to healing! It all depends on me and how I choose to use my tears. Ladies, please refrain from ever wasting your tears again. God is not wasteful and neither should we be. What you choose to do during and after your state of releasing your God given arsenal of tears determine if you move forward in the things God has for you or not! Did you know this impelling information? Let's concentrate on Joseph again.

"And he turned himself about from them and wept and returned to them again and communed with them and took from them Simeon, and bound him before their eyes.

> *Then Joseph commanded to fill their sacks with corn, and to restore every man's money into his sack, and to give them provision for the way; and thus did he unto them."*
> **(Gen 42 vs 24-25)**

Joseph was a youngster sold into slavery by his brothers. He had a life of misunderstandings but maintained an excellent spirit! The brothers who treated him so badly now needed him to supply them food and Joseph is faced with what we all have been faced with at one point or another.

<u>Do I let the past go or do I stick it where it hurts?</u>

We notice that Joseph used his tears and then something beautiful happened. He shewed an act of kindness to those undeserving!

Awesome! It may seem like in this passage that Joseph was being unmerciful but this is not the case at all. Instead of Joseph keeping them all bound he only kept one. This was to ensure God's plan of action! By Joseph permitting God to have His way, his tears sprung him into another level of blessings and another realm spiritually. Joseph used his ordinance of tears and God's plan of action was a success. Real quick think of the last time you soaked up Kleenex really good with burning hot tears. Pay close attention.

Did you know that even through tears God gets the glory or satan gets the glory?

Yes, this is a fact. Even Jesus wept and He is our outstanding example! The last time you applied the healing instrument of tears were you:

complaining as this gold in liquid came rolling down your cheeks and stained your newly pressed blouse?

Were these thoughts on your mind or these words on your lips...

"I'll never have nothing"
"I'm always the one did wrong"
"Why am I always the go to girl"
"people never take me serious"
"I can't believe he cheated... that punk"
"I'm loosing my home and it's not fair"
"My life is moving no where, might as well grab a beer"
"I'm tired of fighting"
"What's the use, things will never change"
"I can't bare this obesity issue any more, I wish I would just die"
"I'm up to my neck in bills. Wish I could rob a store or maybe I should just sell me"
"They don't know who they messing with, I'll show them"

Sound a little familiar? All while God's instrument of healing is running down your face and mascara traveling down your pout like dark waters searching for the valley of despair! The evil one is not sitting back laughing at you. Oh no! He's playing god and very seriously excepting your praise since you choose to complain. The devil shows up and enjoys the praises you are giving him. He then rewards you with more things to complain and give him praises for. See, we have this misconception of satan being this capacious bad devil with tall red horns and a pitch fork that he likes to poke people with. Once they say *"ouch,"* he just giggles and rolls on the floor uncontrollably. Okay how can I say this? Never think this way again!!! Let me give you a new image to replace the old one. The bible says,

> "And no marvel; for satan himself is transformed into an angel of light."
>
> **(2 Corinthians 11:14)**

An angel of light is beautiful to look upon. Transform means; to make a thorough or dramatic change in the form, appearance, or character of. Now if satan was transformed this means he's not coming to you with a pitch fork and a red jump suit. He's coming as some one you feel you can relate to, or are attracted to. The devil is a very smooth operator that makes demons do his dirty work. We are at the climax of tears, but this subject at hand is in motion of need fully being addressed. So satan has his demons do his dirty work. He's the CEO. If you think about it, the manager is always clean. His suits are on tailor made and dry clean status. Anyone approaching from a far knows that must be the manager right there. Why? Because she or he is very clean and searching for loose ends in this corporation. Once they find it they appoint workers to do what it takes to fix the problem. Managers also look for ways to advance ahead of other establishments or companies. Their are shift managers, lead managers, regional managers, and CEOs. The devil is the CEO and often times while working in a factory, the big guy comes to town. He is surrounded by shift leaders, corporate/regional leaders as well as district, and he's giving all the people instructions during this big pow wow. We as people never hardly deal with satan himself yet because we have not mastered his demons or even ourselves yet. Once we deal with ourselves and get control through Jesus and the reading of His word then we war with our evil opponent. So CEO satan is walking through this corporation where you work and his demons and strong holds has the majority of the place on lock down but now clean cut, Armani suit wearing, swaged out satan sees you and he sees your "Jesus" light on. Now you are the very person, maybe the only person in this corporation that satan by passes his workers to say something to you directly! Most times we picture satan as this evil voice that says *"you better lust, hate, and lie or I'll kill you and your whole family"*, and then this is followed by evil laughing. No no no... Reprogramming in process. CEO, clean cut, great smelling, white teeth satan leans over your desk and says very smoothly

"I love your work."

He then turns back to his team and says

"See her gentlemen? This is what I call perfection! Move her to the top floor and give her the office with the big window. She's the best worker I've seen by far."

Then just like that a spirit of pride has come in and begin to grow in you! (All elevation is not of God.)

<u>With the utilization of God's healing instrument who do we glorify?</u>

If you don't fully understand how to tell then I'll ask you another question.

<u>Did you use this God given arsenal and then make a negative decision?</u>

Joseph wept and then turned and made a positive choice and his family was restored. Joseph allowed God to manifest forgiveness through him and even now we are still using him as an illustration! Consider those around you.

<u>Will they be able to use your life as a positive example?</u>

Let's untie God's hands. Let us be into Him like He's into us and we can then return unto the secret place of the Most High! (*Psalms 91*) Joseph could have perverted his God given instrument like many of us do today and turned around and placed his brothers in prison for life. He had the power to do it.

Often times the spirit of vindictiveness gets the best of people!

<u>What would this spirit have cost Joseph?</u>

Well, Joseph would have been just another Adam and Eve story. God being into man, man giving in to his own will, man causes the punishment of God on his life by choices "he" or " she" decided to make. I don't believe Joseph's brothers would have been given into the right repentance and the rest of Joseph's family like his dad and brother's families would have perish from starvation and a broken heart. Joseph would have also caused himself the punishment of God. Whew! I'm so glad he had a heart toward God and used his instrument of tears to make a change that God was able to bless and not curse. Tears heal the soul. When they are used correctly amazing results occur for you and those in connection with you! One should never base their healing on another person or how someone else may be acting towards you, or what they may be saying about you and what they may do. Even though Joseph's brothers had repentance because of God's mercy shown through Joseph, he didn't rely on how they acted towards him. It brought his family back together by this maturity right here!

Tears are an expression of the soul. They carry the explanation of happiness, joys, sorrow, and they define strength. You actually choose to cry instead of retaliation. This is a huge step towards the heart of God.

Dr. Bergman stated at the St. Paul Ramsey medical center in Minnesota, that "tears caused by simple irritants were being compared to those brought on by emotions." Researcher, Biochemist William Frey has spent fifteen years studying tears and found that stress induced tears actually remove toxic substance from the body. Volunteers were led to cry first from watching sad movies, and then from freshly cut onions. The researchers found that the tears from the movies, called emotional tears, Contained far more toxic biological by products! Weeping, they concluded, is an excretory process which removes toxic substance that normally build up during emotional stress. They also found that one of the most important of those compounds which removed tears was adreno corticotrophic normore (AC) one of the best indicators of stress. Suppressing tears increases stress levels and contribute to diseases aggravated by stress, such as high blood pressure, heart problems and peptic ulcers! My God. Another interesting fact researched by W.Frey is the important function of tears bathing your eyes in lysozyme, one of the most effective antibacterial and antiviral agents known. Lysozyme is the major source of the anti germ traits of tears. Amazingly, lysozyme inactivates 90 to 95 percent of all bacteria in a mere five to ten minutes. Without it, eye infections would soon cause most victims to go blind. This further concludes that our all supreme matchless Lord and Savior Jesus Christ is wisest! He gave us this golden tool and it must be utilized and properly. He gave us a healing mechanism in His infinite wisdom! The spirit of pride may in many cases stop some from crying, but now we see clearly prides intent on this end is to actually cause your body to be subject to more demonic spirits such as blood pressure low and high and also other infirmities God meant for us to stay free from! (God is about balance) Joseph let it flow and leaves us the example where now he found purpose in his trial.(Gen 45:5) Allowing God to manifest in him he found God's purpose for him! In order to get back to our first love we must move forward past vindictiveness and retaliating ways. They shall be behind us from this page forth in Jesus name!

Pray with me...

God, I come to you as humble as I know how. I fall down at your thrown of mercy. I come baring all the blame and admitting that I have done wrong in your eyes. Lord today I give you my vindictive ways. I renounce this spirit and I denounce it in Jesus name. I turn from this evil mindset. Lord I repent that I have fallen short of your expectations of me. Thank you for saving me and taking the spirit of being vindictive from me. Now Lord if it be pleasing to you, please fill that empty spot with more of what you desire for me to have from you. I open up as a willing vessel. Lord please help me to prepare my temple to carry the gospel of Jesus Christ. Amen.

Astonishing! I feel lighter, how about you? Yes, God has given His daughters direction to cry, talk to Him while doing so, and release toxins from the soul and body. When this is done we then *rise* and *turn*. This is the way back and also the way forward in God. Amen! By teaching our children to do this it'll place a major blessing on their lives. This is one of the very reasons God told us to correct our children. This is to cause tears to flow and then they are to rise and turn from ways of error and Ways that will cause them pain in adult hood.

> The *angel which redeemed me from all evil, bless the lads; and let my name be named on them, and the name of my fathers Abraham and Isaac: and let them grow into a multitude in the midst of the earth.* **(Gen 48:16)**

Hallelujah! Do you believe your today decision affect your children's tomorrow? Positively or negatively, it affects the next generation.

The way forward is back to our knees. The devil no longer gets glorified from us out of unconscious decisions of complaining. He doesn't get the credit for even the things we may think are bad, because God gets the glory in all things.

> In every thing give thanks: for THIS is the will of God in Christ Jesus concerning you.
> **(1 Thessalonians 5:18)**

Joseph learns and tells his brothers

> "So *now it was not you that sent me hither, but God: and he hath made me a father to Pharaoh, and lord of all his house, and a ruler throughout all the land of Egypt.*"
> **(Gen 45:8)**

Glory! Joseph allowed God to transform him and in this transformation God gave Joseph a new eye sight to see things on a different level! Yes, Joseph with his childlike heart was wanting so much to be excepted and loved by his brothers. God taught him through heart ache, tears, affliction, and betrayal that he should still see purpose. Joseph was one who naturally had the right to be upset and retaliative but putting on God's mindset and allowing God to do the work Joseph used his gifts and his tool of healing! He turned towards the reflection of God's heart. He showed mercy and God transformed him into someone even his enemies couldn't recognize! He stopped seeing trials as negative but started seeing them as God and purpose. This caused his father to leave great blessings on his children and Joseph walked in a realm with God as consequence to his correct action and for "know one" would Joseph leave this place.

> "And his brethren also went and fell down before his face;
> and they said, behold, we be the servants
> And Joseph said unto them, fear not: for am I in the place
> of God *(Gen 50 18:19)*

Praise Jesus! This is The perfect example of being in a place with God, that secret place, where you know for sure that it's only one God and only one King of kings! We can rise as well! We can turn from any situation and watch God move for us! We will be able to maintain high positions in the Kingdom of God while still having a child like heart and honestly offer everything back to God with pure motive! Where is that heart like a child?

> "And it came to pass in process of time, that the king of Egypt died. And the children of Israel sighed by reason of the bondage, and they "cried ", and their cry came up unto God by reason of the bondage.
>
> And God heard their groaning, and God remembered his covenant with Abraham, with Isaac, and with Jacob."
> *(Exodus 2 23-25)*

Groaning's don't mean getting in God face screaming, " you said you was gone do this, you said you was gone do that." The meaning for groaning is to *make a deep inarticulate sound in response to pain or despair, or to make a low creaking or moaning sound when pressure or weight is applied. Now this next verse is the kicker!*

> "And God looked upon the children of Israel, and God had respect unto them!!"*(vs 25)*

Do you see what I see?

God is showing us that He don't take it kindly for people in this day and age to treat Him like He is the criminal!

When you go to court and they put the prisoner on the stand they: question him, they interrogate him, they try and back him In a corner, and they start to scream, "but you said this, but you said that, and you're under oath so you can't lie!" Light bulb!

How many people treat Father this same way?

I'm speaking of people who are supposed to love Him. Those dealing in ministry everyday in their personal lives! The children are taught this method, and so generation after generation God, our Holy King of kings, get treated like dirt by us out of ignorance. Out of love and compassion God finds a reason to still love and bless us! But let us take our magnifying glass and look at *vs 25* again.

> "And God looked upon the children of Israel, and God had "respect" unto them." *(childlike heart)*

Why?

Well because they were not screaming in His face being disrespectful and treating Him like a liar on the stand by screaming "you said" and "you can't lie." Correction. ... "HE WONT LIE". God had respect not just love but respect because here was a people actually doing what He said to do,(cry unto the Lord) and acting the way He said act. (come unto me like a child) And they didn't scream at Him saying "remember you said this, remember you said that " the bible states *"And God remembered."*

God remembered because He actually had children acting like children. I have to say this next sentence because it must be said in it's entirety! Elohim is not slow, dumb, illiterate, mute, stupid, empty headed, or half baked! Wow that felt good!!! I shouldn't feel the need to say this but this is where "Christian folk" have drug the minds of those that are supposed to actually reverence God! This bad mentality and mind set has caused people to bleed in the brain causing spiritual blood clots. Now people actually think God can't really see what they do concerning their contrary ways against the gospel of Jesus Christ. This causes another clot because through actions by parents the children are taught the same way spiritually and naturally as well! We must come back to move forward to the point of tears, rising, and turning! You ever heard the term you must give respect to get it? Well, I know the children of Israel in the previous passage has proven this point for me. Lets not strive for respect from God, but lets yield and submit to the way God said to be and do. The respect thing just comes as a bonus of actually having the right motive, intent, and yielding of your complete soul to only please God! Let us focus on giving the word of God respect. Respect is not screaming "God you said and you can't lie". Respect is saying "yes Lord, whatever your will is Lord"! God has not one grain of salt problem "remembering" what He said. The problem is the way we choose to act.

> *"For God is not unrighteous to "forget" your work and labor of love, which ye have shewed toward his name in that ye have ministered to the saints and do minister."* **(Hebrew 6:10)**

Through tears we rise and we turn. The bible says *in all things give thanks!*

"Lord thank you for never leaving me or forsaking me."
"God thank you for being with me even until the end!"
It's not our job to contend with God! It's our job to be thankful!
God told Abraham He would destroy Sodom and Gomorrah.

> *Surly the Lord God will do nothing, but he revealeth his secrets unto his servants the prophets.* **(Amos 3:7)**

In this case he revealed this to Abraham. Abraham could have cried rose and turned but Abraham contended with God and asked God many questions concerning sparing the righteous. (His family was there)
God did agreed to spare Lot and his family.*(Gen 18 23-32)*
Lot's wife ended up dead anyway for disobedience and turned into a pillar of salt. Lot ended up in a cave being the father of his own grandchildren. Abraham learned a great wisdom from this, as well as

I, that God's way is the best way! Just cry, thank the Lord, rise and turn from the way you may see it. After then God spoke to Abraham. He told Abraham to go and sacrifice his own son. *(Gen 22 vs 2-8)* This time Abraham chose the right method. He did not contend with God, he did not ask questions, he definitely did not say

"God remember you said we would have this boy, now you want me to sacrifice him? You promised him to us and you can't lie".

No, Abraham learned from the past and he got up in belief that whatever God's will was was exactly what he would do. He even made his son carry his own cross by making him carry his own wood, and nobody can tell me that Abraham didn't shed tears on the way to do this. He loved his son but he loved God more! I know he used God's tool of tears and turned from the thoughts of telling God no. God honored Abraham and placed such a huge blessing on him and the bonus was that he got to keep his son too! God promised Abraham that:

> *"He would multiply his seed as the stars of the heaven and as the sand which is upon the sea shore; and thy seed shall possess the gate of his enemies"(Gen22:17)*

Even after this great promise, it's not recorded that Abraham kept God in check by screaming "God you said….now where is my many sons "? It is however recorded that:

> *"Abraham staggered not at the promises of God through unbelief; but was strong in faith, giving glory to God And being fully persuaded that, what he had promised, he was able also to perform!(Romans 4:20)*

Abraham Abraham Abraham!

> "And *so after he had patiently endured, he obtained the promise*"!*(Hebrew 6:15)*

Many people treat God with disrespect concerning their promise because of lacking two things: *patience* and *endurance*. Abraham was about a hundred and his wife was old to. Her womb was dead. *Abraham* though, *"staggered not at the promise of God through unbelief; but was strong in faith giving glory to God "(**Romans 4:20**)

With each cry we get closer and closer to our healing and our breakthrough. Use this beautiful God given instrument and experience great results! Lets give our King respect and behave towards Him like children. He deserve every ounce of it! Let's use our tears wisely and experience true healing while watching Him be matchless in our lives!

Behind The veil
_"More Than Toenail Polish"

You ever just took time to sit and think of the many ways Jesus loves us? Cheek this out! Father loves us so much that He gave our *fee(+)* a chance to be washed by the blood of the lamb on the cross. The way we walk normally is by placing one *foo(+)* before another. Babies don't jump in two *fee(+)* at a time when learning to walk. This is not so. One by one they take steps! Has your *foo(+)* come by way of the cross? *Foo(+)* without the cross(+) turns to *foo(l)*. Has each foo(+) been washed in the blood of the lamb? Two *fee(+)* can't walk together unless they agree. If our fee(+) has truly indeed been washed then our strides should be righteous. The places we go should not lead to ungodly mischief.

> *"My son, walk not thou in the way with them; refrain thy foo(+) from their path: 16) For their fee(+) run to evil, and make haste to shed blood."(**Proverbs 1 15-16**)*

Any way that is not the way of the cross is foolish because its destination is not God's Kingdom. The foo(+) that has not surrendered to the cross has become foo(l),and fools never like to be foolish alone. Now we have two fee(+) that has not surrendered to the cross! From foo(+)we get foo(l) and from fee(+) we get fee(l).Fools feel that they will find another way to make it to heaven without submitting to Jesus. Do you have fools feet? Believe it or not your feet are vitally important. Without feet we wouldn't be able to stand upright.

> *"Thy Word is a lamp unto my feet and a light unto my path." (**Psalms 119 vs105**)*

Without God's word being a lamp and light to our feet how can we see where to go in the dark? This equals fools feet. Fools feel around in the dark knocking things over, people over, relationships over, and opportunities over because they can't see it for what it really is!

> "And your feet shod with the preparation of the gospel
> of peace."
> *(Eph 6:15)*

Our fee(+) by way of the cross, must have peace.

> *"And the eye cannot say unto the hand, I have no need of*
> *thee: nor again the head to the feet, I have no need of you.*
>
> *Nay, much more those members of the body which seem to*
> *be more feeble, are necessary!"(1Corinthians 12vs21,22)*

So our fee(+) are for more than just toenail polish. God pays close attention to them. Has your fee(+) been washed? Marching forward we must be careful the path our fee(+) tread upon!

CHAPTER 3

The 1/2 Baked Bread

Many Americanized people despise humble beginnings. A great number also hate the process of development. The reasons being- *Television, Social media, magazines, news papers, peer pressure/influence, being a self idol, and pride of I'm supposed to be* somebody take our beautiful eyes off of the main one that actually gave life for us. Do we realize that in Genesis God made Eve *after* He made Adam to fall into a deep sleep? Have you ever put your children to sleep and then went to take a long bubble bath? You had time to think about what you would do when you got out, what bills to pay and plans for the near future. You didn't have someone pulling on your coat tail begging for cookies or to go outside or to the market. That was your time of meditation. Well God had Adam in this sleep so He could take His time with us. He wanted us to be perfect when He presented us to the man as a gift. Yes ladies, we are God's gift to men!

> *Neither was the man created for the woman but the woman for the man. For this cause ought the woman to have power on her head because of the angels.*
> **(1Corinthians 11:9)**

When you're created for somebody, it means the very thing about you makes them tick! It makes the blood come alive in many areas of the body. It awakens the nerve endings and causes the testosterone to journey through their bodies! Being created by the perfect creator insures that we are *exactly* what is desired. Not off by a 1\2 mile, or an inch or gram but *exactly* what he wants! Now exactly how much power is this? How much power do we give the devil to use when we are not submitted to Father and His Word? God strategically made us and built us to be help meets! To help our men become what God has put inside of them to be is what we are to do.

> Whoso *ever findeth a wife findeth a good thing and obtaineth favor of the Lord.*
>
> **(Proverbs 18:22)**

Notice He never said whoso ever findeth a *woman* finds a good thing because any female is called woman but a wife is someone who is *already* married! She is Married to God and seeking to please Him. In seeking to please God we will keep what He said in His word about how we are to respect our husbands. With us being already married to the Lord when our husbands find us he finds a *good* thing! Even now with us choosing to move everything out of that first seat in our hearts, we allow our King to take His proper seating in our hearts.

Side Note If putting God first is not already in practice in your home then with much love and respect toward your husband, God will show you how to have balance while making this transition. Not just kicking that man to the curb but still spending quality time with him_only now also setting aside time for God and only God during a designated time. It's like making kids eat vegetables. Sometimes they don't like it but it is because they don't see the benefits of what it can do for their physical bodies. Us choosing to make this plan an action allows our husbands to obtain favor with the Lord!

What is favor? (Eee.biblestudytools.com) Favor means *gaining approval, acceptance, or special benefits or blessings.* Another definition is *an act of kindness beyond what is due to usual.* In this case your husband will obtain favor with/ from the Lord. Why? Because he has a daily relationship with you (plus his own relationship with God) and by us having this relationship with God he gives us instructions on how to treat the king of our home, our priest. He chooses to help us navigate on His word despite maybe being treated unfairly by our spouses or what has been said that hurt our feelings. We cry to God, we rise, we turn and forgive and treat it as if it never happened!(2 Chronicles 7:14) This is where the word "unusual" and the word "blessing" comes in on favor!

Do you have the beautiful knowledge that a man is truly blessed to have a wife who actually lets the past mistakes be the past without bringing it up upon every uncontrolled emotion?

This is not of God and our spiritual bread will never ever get done this way! We will always be stamped as undone by God because half done still equals undone per Jesus Christ. Let's level up. We cry and pray, we rise, we turn with forgiveness! We must draw closer to God's thrown allowing this favor upon our husbands.

In order for us to get spiritually done we must go through Godly fire! God sometimes choose the closest person to us to refine us. Often times we feel we are ready for great platform in ministry or marriage and Sure while we were in the fire some parts of us do(did) in fact get done, But for 60% to still not be done the baker labels that bread as undone. For 20 % or 10% being undone the baker still labels the bread undone.

Why?

Well, because they don't want to make anyone sick!

Why do we have sick marriages?

Why do we have sick ministries?

The only way to get done is allowing the Lord to use whomsoever He will to refine us and also by navigating on the word of God through every situation! Believe it or not the heat of the oven will find you because the devil hates when you keep God's word of treating people right even though that co worker is evil to you.

*Note None retaliation allows God to turn the oven up on you!

Why would God turn the heat up on me?

........Well you want to get done don't you! When God sees that you are keeping His word through your daily trials He then knows you can stand a little more heat! This means you have leveled up! Congratulations!! Anyone that cooks knows you will next to never get bread done if the oven is set on 20 degrees and your family is starving! Unlike regular bread, God in His infinite wisdom don't start us out at 350° *Thank you Lord.* He gradually increase the temperature for us because He loves us. Those who have not leveled up from 20° and 30°,your family has been starving to death. This is a warning from God to us. We will be without excuse and will be held accountable as to why our husband, children, co workers and others were not able to take part in our spiritual bread. People should be able to spiritually eat off of our life and gain life. This is another way we glorify God by becoming ambassadors/a living example. Being undone does not have a good end. Our daily prayer is supposed to be for God's Kingdom to come and His will to be done in earth as it is in heaven! *(Matthew 6:10)*

How can God's Kingdom come in us if we are undone?

God is looking for a vessel willing to *go through the process to get the promotion/ promise. After *God's Kingdom comes and His will be done in earth as it is in heaven,* then *(vs 11)* He *can give us this day our daily bread*! As God gives us bread, we should and are supposed to *become* bread for someone else. Not stale bread saying and doing the same old thing but daily bread! You ever had the opportunity to smell fresh bread from the bakery either while passing or actually stopping by to pay a visit? The smell of that bread reaches far and wide and it speaks without speaking. "Whomever is hungry and need nourishing, I bid you come"! When you are holding the true light people will come from far and near to take part in your God given bread.

Vs 12 of *Matthew 6* says; *And forgive us our debts as we forgive our debtors.*

After people come to take part in our bread some will actually get offended because they see you have leveled up to another realm and dimension in God. Some make the decision to press in to God because they want this beautiful experience while others may do everything in their power to make sure you mess up, stop praying, fasting, reading your bible or try to prove you imperfect to others. They will take this as a full time job opportunity!

Note: Truth is -a lot of people have not become perfect because they are to busy trying to prove that YOU are not.

This is where your forgiveness is very important. This determines if we get all the way done or not. We must forgive those who persecute us!

Vs 13 states *And lead us not into temptation but deliver us from evil.*

<u>*Are you aware that being vindictive is very evil?*</u>

Being vindictive is designed to make sure we never get done! Vindictiveness keeps one going around in a cycle of circles their whole life. It also makes that same person anti Christ! People who have that "get back" spirit, are the same church people talking about, "When *the mark of the beast hits the land I'm not going to take the mark because that's anti Christ. The devil is a lie if he think I'm taking part in that!"*

(((NEW FLASH))), (((FLOOD WARNING))); Your house is full of water and you're in the bed sleep! Being vindictive makes that same person anti Christ.

<u>*How?*</u>

Jesus Christ came for forgiveness. If our daily life screams anything other than truly forgiving others then we are working on the side of the wicked one without knowing it! On the way to hell while saying Hallelujah! On the way to hell while holding important positioning in church! Glory anyway right? We only posses this attitude because we and our families have not met the lake of fire yet. We lead them right to damnation with second hand hatred. Father allowed it to be explained best in His word:

> *And every spirit that confesseth not that Jesus Christ is come in the flesh is not of God; and this is the spirit of an'-ti-Christ, whereof ye have heard that it should come; and even now already is it in the world.(**1 John 4:3**)*

I know what our mouth is saying. For God I live and for God I'll die, but:

<u>What exactly is our spirit confessing</u>?

<u>What are my actions?</u>

<u>Did you know withholding sexual pleasure from our spouse is being vindictive because we didn't get our way?</u>

<u>Are we aware that not cooking or doing our duties are vindictive ways causing us to be labeled anti Christ?</u>

> Ladies, thee banner over us should be love. *(**Song of Solomon 2:4**)*
> *Ye are of God little children.(**1 John 4:4**)*

We are addressed as little children because little children do what they are told! You ever punish your child for wrong doing to another child and then made them go apologize? *"Now hug their neck"*, you may say. They immediately do as told! And when you look up ten minutes later they are playing again. They are the very opposite of anti Christ, so be careful how you treat kids. They actually forgive and let go like Christ instructed us to do. They are very close to the heart of God. They don't renounce the very reason Jesus came *(which is for forgiveness)* until they are taught by parents to do so.

*Ye are of God "little children" and have overcome them:**Vs 4***

<u>*Overcome who?*</u>

We overcome those of the world and even in the church. Those ones who smell that fresh daily bread you have and want a bite so bad but are filled with things of the flesh - so they try to sabotage you, your name, your character, and your influence because they have not the courage to actually take the steps to get in the oven so the Lord can start to process them. "You" little children have overcome "them". The plots, the lies, the sewing discord, and trying to prove you imperfect. They turn into the accuser of the brethren! How dangerous! Of coarse revelation may still come to them from time to time, but their father the wicked one still gets to attend meetings in heaven too. That doesn't make him any less the devil.

"Because *greater is He that is in you, than he that is in the world*"! *Vs 4*

God is in us and we have overcome them! Now when they try to attack us with words or with actions, they don't have the realization that they are actually *scraping and fighting around our ankles* because we are so tall in Christ! It's like a little baby trying to beat up a teenager...... like........what are you doing little fella!?

We ask God to let His Kingdom come in us. God always honor His word. It is very tempting to get back at people, that's why we pray in

> *(Matthew 6:13)* *"lead us not into temptation but deliver us from evil. For thine is the Kingdom".*

(I am yours Lord. You let your kingdom come in me and their is no room for evil. Yours is the Kingdom. I am yours)

> *"For thine is the Kingdom and the power"* *(Matthew 6:13)*

<u>*...Power?*</u>

"Let *this mind be in you which was also in Christ Jesus".*
Philippians 2:5

> "For *God has not given us the spirit of fear; but of power, and of love, and of a sound mind*".
> **(2 Timothy 1:7)**

(These 3 work together as one)
1)A sound mind and love= power
2) real love and power = sound mind
3) With a sound mind and power= love must be present
*Note *:Only those in Christ have a "true" sound mind!*

> *These have one mind, and shall give their power and strength unto the beast. These shall make war with the Lamb, and the Lamb shall overcome them.(**Revelation 17:13**)*

Wow! How powerful it must be to have one mind! Two can't walk together unless they agree. Same mind. We whom are actually in Christ can have one mind in Christ who is the ultimate of all!!!! How powerful would WE be with also being sound!

> "*That ye put off concerning the former conversation the old man, which is corrupt according to the deceitful lusts; And be renewed in the spirit of your "mind". And that ye put on the new man, which after God is created in righteousness and true holiness*"!
> **(Ephesians 4 vs 22-24)**

> "*I beseech you therefore brethren, by the mercies of God that ye present your bodies a living sacrifice, holy, acceptable unto God, which is your reasonable service. And be not conformed to this world; but be ye transformed by the renewing of your "mind", that ye may prove what is that good and acceptable, and perfect will of God*"!
> **(Romans 12 vs 1-2)**

> "*For they that are after the flesh do "mind" the things of the flesh; but they that are after the spirit the things of the spirit*".
> **Romans 8:5**

"For *to be carnally minded is death; but to be spiritually minded is life and peace. Because the carnal mind is enmity against God: for it is not subject to the law of God, neither indeed can be. So then they that are in the flesh cannot please God. 14th vs says, for as many as are led by the spirit of God, they are the sons of God".* (**Romans 8:6**)

What am I saying?

It's simple.... *for thine is the Kingdom and the power* (our minds)
"Behold *I give you power over all the power of the enemy!"*
Luke 10;19

Satan whispers through and to the mind. This is his power tool. He fights the mind, suggest things to the mind, fools the mind and his power tool is the mindset. Guess what God's power tool was from the first beginning until even now..... The mind!!!(*let this mind be in you which was also in Christ Jesus)* satan copies God or tries to. The only way we will defeat the enemy *is through Jesus.* "*For thine is the Kingdom* (our bodies as temples) *the power*(our minds, how can we serve God without His mindset) *and the glory forever amen."*

"We are meant and purposed for the glory of God! To whom God would make known what is the riches of the glory of this mystery among the Gentiles; which is Christ in you, the hope of glory": (**Colossians 1;27**)

Christ "hopes" for glory out of our lives! Will they give me the glory or will they take it for themselves? He's in you just *hoping* that you'll make the choice to do something that gives Him glory! He's *hoping* that you'll live a life that will give Him glory! He's *hoping* that we'll keep watching and praying that we enter not into temptation. Watching? Watching who? Watching our own flesh and keeping it under subjection instead of pointing fingers at our brothers and sisters! Christ is *hoping* for glory.

One day I had to sing and I went up in the front of the church and begin to sing. In an instant I was literally on the inside of my own body like I was sitting down, and I could hear myself just singing and singing, but it wasn't me! The Holy Ghost had stood up in me! God's Kingdom is my body, His power concerning me is my mind. I do what He says to do, go where He says to go', and He leads my mind. That's the most power you can have over one's physical body. (An idol mind is the devil's play ground) God uses our vessels, our bodies as His kingdom in the earth, our minds to control what we do, where we go, and how we think and in conclusion He gets the glory! These three work together as one. The Kingdom the power and the glory. We must give Him all three to be effective! I am one body and God has all three of these things in me because I yield my body (His kingdom) my mind (His power)and complements and accolades from gifts God has invested in me, I give them back to God and this is *one form* of His glory. This is the process of great smelling, looking and tasting bread that will never spoil and will feed many many people far and wide but first starting with home!

Have you yielded your members to God yet?

Have you allowed God to transform you?

Do you give God control of you?

Do you give God the glory?

> *"Whether therefore ye eat or drink or whatsoever ye do, do all to the glory of God".(**1 cor 31**)*

> *"But if a woman have long hair, it is a glory to her. For her hair is given her for a covering "!*
> **1Corinthians 15)**

Yes Lord, our hair is our glory! Praise God! Our husbands are the head of our homes/the head of the woman and our hair is given us for a covering.

"But I would have you know, that the head of every man is Christ; and the head of the woman is the man; and the head of Christ is God.

Every man praying or prophesying, having his head covered, dishonoureth his head.

But every woman that prayeth or prophesieth with her head uncovered dishonoureth her head: for that is even all one as if she were shaven. (*Do we pray or prophecy in public places besides the church and home?*) For if the woman be not covered, let her also be shorn: but if it be a shame for a woman to be shorn or shaven, let her be covered.

For a man indeed ought not to cover his head, forasmuch as he is the image and glory of God: but the woman is the glory of the man.

For the man is not of the woman: but the woman of the man.

Neither was the man created for the woman; but the woman for the man.

[10] For this cause ought the woman to have power on her head because of the angels. **(1 Corinthians 11 3-10)**

So the man is the complete image of God! But the woman is the glory of the man. We came from the flesh side of man so we must beware because of the angels! There are actual angels that *guards the flesh* to make sure the flesh act like flesh and do some unbelievable things! Also all this talk of heads makes me think of what's inside the head? (The mind) So God thinks for Christ and Christ thinks for man and man thinks for woman(being that every decision made in the home is lastly his final decision with Him being the head that possess the mind spiritually.) In obedience we then should all be connected to the mind of Christ that brings all our minds in unity to One mind. (Let this mind be in you that was also in Christ) This brings harmony and flow of blessings!

Does our flesh continue to control us assisted by the angels of flesh that watch over it?

Doesn't the bible teach us with our renewed and transformed mind that all the glory belongs to God? Christ in us the hope of glory?

So ladies should we offer our hair back to God and watch He bless it and multiply it? This is just a question to think about. Me personally, I made a personal *choice*,after being suggested to do so, to offer my glory (my hair) back to God and my life has never been the same! I do so by keeping my head covered with scarves and wraps ECT while in public places and most often times at home too! Some ask me why do I keep my head covered. I guess in some ways it's odd and maybe uncomfortable for us to not know how a person's hair actually looks. I've seen a cartoon where the character kept a hat on all the time.....it was kind of frustrating for me as a child because I wanted to just see what his hair looked like. This is funny but we as humans have things that bother us that sometimes we don't even realize! In many cases this may even cause a distrust because I'm not able to observe every part of you when I want to. I've ran into very few who were actually offended with me and started using terms like Muslim and things to this nature! I've ran into those whom has treated me like I was holier than thou, and I've even ran into one lady who told me my husband was my covering. Then there are those who thinks it's wonderful and have been inspired to do it as well while not understanding the blessing behind it! There are those who treat me no differently and that's a blessing! With all the other negativity though Honestly I still lack the understanding of why it was so important as to get me to STOP doing it? It doesn't harm anyone and I don't believe that I act any differently...so why the warfare? It's because God asked me to do something that would cause persecution and I said yes! He asked me to do something naturally that steps on the enemies turf spiritually! Not all, but some are secretly afraid of things they don't understand and so there's a spiritual fight and attack that goes on spiritually and sometimes manifest naturally. Needless to say I still cover my head because God asked me to and I told Him YES end of story. I knew I would face being looked at differently and maybe being talked about by some but it came down to how bad did I want to please God vs having others wonder about me! I never gave it a second thought! I'm going to attempt to explain everything God has shared with me concerning this matter! I'll use words like "us", "our", "we", but just know as you continue reading that covering every day is something God suggested/asked me to do and I said yes. If you feel lead to do so then by all means. This DOES NOT determine if you are hell bound or not. Let's proceed!

So I chose to give my glory back to God! How is this done? It's the same way we give our bodies to God. We give our bodies to God by placing healthy things inside of it, because honestly and truthfully speaking, God doesn't want to invest Himself in a vessel that's not going anywhere for Him spiritually. If we keep choosing to pour cool aide and hazardous drinks and foods and substances in our vessels God knows this way of living does not promise long Gevity. We give our bodies to God also by covering it so only our husbands should joy in the majestic sight of our supernaturally crafted art work! God is not a wasteful God and so He will invest in those that are actually investing in themselves. Like the story so wonderfully told about the talents the master had given before he went on his long journey! All but one invested their talents and got more but the one that did not invest had his talent removed!

(Matthew 25 14-30) If a woman's hair is her glory and we give "all the glory to God" like we say then we should do nothing but healthy things for and to our hair. Right?

> *"But if a woman have long hair, it is a glory to her: for her hair is given her for a covering."*
> **(1 Corinthians 15)**

We prayed in *(Matthew 6:13)*

> *"And lead us not into temptation, but deliver us from evil:*
> *For thine is the kingdom, and the power " and the glory*
> *"for ever. Amen"*

We gave our loving savior the glory -all glory. Don't let this shock you but- He wants your hair, because it's the glory of the woman!

Somewhere we got confused of what we were supposed to be doing and how we were supposed to look.

> *"And Rebekah lifted her eyes, and when she saw Isaac, she lighted off the camel. For she had said unto the servant,*

> *what man is this that walketh in the field to meet us? And the servant had said, it is my master: therefore she took a vail, and covered herself."* **(Gen 24 vs 64-65)**

This was done as a sign of respect towards this man!

The way forward is back. The glory belongs to God. So ladies why do we continue to use our own glory for ourselves? We ask God to let His kingdom come, and His will be done. We are to become God's Kingdom that He may come and dwell in earth, in us. (We are made from earth; dust) And lead us not into temptation, but deliver us from evil. For thine is the "Kingdom" the "Power" and the "Glory".

Do you believe that it is evil to take glory for ourselves?

Is this taking back on the prayer, thine is the power and glory?

Look at this then....

> *Neither was the man created for the woman; but the woman for the man. For this cause ought the "woman to have power on her head" because of the angles.*
> **(1 Corinthians 11 vs 9-10)**

Ladies we MUST have the mind if Christ! He does continue to hope for glory! Glory out of us and our lives.

We give Jesus the Kingdom, Power, and Glory.

Do you believe it's evil to take this power/glory and use it in our own hands for our own personal motive?

Do you believe this ladies, when all the glory belongs to God and power to! For centuries we have day after day took this power and glory and used it for our own selfishness! Instead of dedicating our glory back to God, we for hours, days, and sometimes even months contemplate on hairstyles that will cause the Broadway show to pause, the actors to stop in mid sentence with mouth wide open gazing at us in awe- and for the crowd to then turn around and see what in heaven is going on just to turn around and spot us- then start to applaud because we look just that appealing!!! This is true. We think of ways "we" can get glory out of our glory. We think up styles that may get the attention of every man, even married men, we usually don't care, because when you have someone who has no wisdom on how to use glory, you typically get the example of women of folly! Folly meaning; lack of good sense; foolishness. Definition two reads *"a costly ornamental building with no practical purpose!"*

Does this explain some of the ladies you know?

Instead of stepping into our purpose of being Kingdom for God to use us mightily and allow the power and glory to be His, we settle for being an "ornamental building ". (A beautifully decorated building with no purpose once so ever.) My God. The women of folly act this way and perceive life this way. We spend so much time thinking of a show stopping hair style that will grab the *lustful* eye of man and the *envious* eye of women. STOP! Must we continue to sin with something that simply does not belong to us? Satan does enjoy this because this is a way that women error everyday. Owning glory and using it to glorify the devil's ways isn't good! God is ready to partake of fresh bread. He's ready to share you- This freshly baked and well done bread. He's ready to put you on the table of many men, women, and children so they can take part in Him, but He can't do this if we stay half baked! If He shares us with people while we are half baked this will make people sick and have half cocked views. Although God is actively and has used many beautiful spirit filled ladies that may not have chose to come to the point of total covering He is still looking for those ones who would dare to say yes too! Let's shake ourselves loose from what people say we ought to be, do, and look like!

> Be *not thou envious against evil men, neither desire to be with them. For their heart studieth destruction, and their lips talk of mischief. Through wisdom is an house builded: and by understanding it is established. And by knowledge shall the chambers be filled with all precious*

and pleasant riches. 5) A wise man is strong; yea, a man of knowledge increaseth strength. For by wise counsel thou shalt make thy war: and in multitude of counselors their is safety. Wisdom is to high for a fool: he openeth not his mountain the gate. He that deviseth to do evil shall be called a mischievous person. The thought of foolishness is sin: and the scorner is an abomination to men.

(Proverbs 24 1-9)

Many times in my life I remember going shopping with peers and having conversations like:

"I want a hair style that screams wild and free and ready to have fun, or I need a style that will absolutely make me look so stunning until memories of me will burn holes in his mind!" Firstly it's typically single women or those in adultery that still have these conversations. A woman trying to get back at a husband she has separated from may qualify in this conversation also. My point is that this from point one is not of God. If it promotes lust it's wrong. While I'm trying to burn lustful holes into one mans scull I'm talking foolery to my girlfriends because all the guys are trying to talk to me.

"I don't want them."

"I can't believe he came over here. He gets on my ever loving nerves, uggggghh!"

Simply no wisdom.

Common sense says if you're trying to cause sinful lust to flourish in one man for you, other men will see your same sinful plot and it will cause this same lust to jump! But because we try to use a glory and a power that we have no business using in the way that we do, now this power has us thinking unclear while releasing poisonous words of despair and degrading other men that bit after bait that "I" threw in the water. Sound familiar?

"Well I'm not attracted to him like that."

"He need to get out my face."

"Uuughh you need a breath freshen, please keep it moving!"

Women using illegal power. But it was me the one chatting with friends saying girl I need a style that will make every man drop to the knees! Then when every man come we attack some and receive the phone number of those we deem worthy of a little worthless conversation from us. To be honest we have nothing to say because we are still in the stage of not realizing in the entirety who and who's we really are. So we continue for decades to use this illegal power. We find creative ways to use the power of our minds and the glory of our hair to accomplish what we need done. OH yes!

"Let's see, I want to look like a lonely sexy librarian tonight, so I'll put my hair up in a ball with glasses and a white collard blouse."

"Tonight I feel freaky so when I go out I'll look like a countryside stable girl putting my hair in two ponytail braids."

Do I need to go on? All while finding ways to please the flesh and misuse what is supposed to be God's glory we continue in our ways that are oh so destructive.

These are things we do to God's glory while trying to use the glory for ourselves:

We spray perfume on it full of chemicals, trying to get a reaction out of the opposite sex. We utilize an electric hair brush, overly use curling and waving irons that burns the hair over time, perms that burn the hair overtime, hair dryers with damaging heat, we place damaging dye in our hair also, all to appear younger. Some wash the hair every single day and while the hair smells good, the proper volume comes from day two and day three of hair being unbothered with (8 ways you're damaging your hair www.m.webmd.com)(7 things French women never do to their hair by faith Hue)

High light, chemical straightening and all these things can lead to split ends, lack of luster, or hair (glory) breakage! The more we style our hair with hazardous chemicals the more we change the natural makeup of our hair. "If the cuticle of the hair is damaged as a result of over styling, the inner coir is exposed causing dryness, a lack of luster, and static ",says

Paradi Mirmirani, MD, a staff dermatologist at the Permanente medical group in Valley California. "Bleaching your hair penetrates the cuticle with chemicals and removes your natural pigment ",Mirmirani says. Bleaching, drying, and styling is a recipe for damaged glory. Mirmirani also says "heat causes temporary changes to the hydrogen bonds that hold hair together and that makes the (glory) look dull. Over time, the temporary changes can lead to more permanent damage if you tend to blow dry or iron on a daily basis! "Ponytails, and braids can cause hair to break, especially if your style is pulled tightly, and wearing it everyday can cause permanent hair damage to occur. Braiding or putting your hair in a ponytail when it's wet can cause damage sooner because wet hair is more fragile, she says! "Over brushing your hair can cause split ends and breakage. Over-shampooing can wash away your hair's natural moisture that helps the hair to appear healthy. "Extensions and weaves are a lot like ponytails and braids ",Mirmirani states, "over time they can leave your hair broken and brittle. The difference is the damage is at the roots where it is harder to cut out. Worse, traction alopecia is a serious hair loss condition caused by wearing tight hairstyles like extensions for too long a time period."

Mirmirani also gives the wisdom of whether it's heat, chemicals, dyes, or styling, it's all doing some degree of damage and a good rule of thumb is, the less you do to your hair, the better". Are you overwhelmed yet? Don't be. I have a little more information about your glory to share with you!

From best ways to protect your hair from sun damage: Cleveland clinic, health essentials states that -using hats, umbrellas, and the right conditioners helps to protect you. (Note: we all know by now that in most right conditioners lies at least one harmful ingredient so when does the madness end?) More on the article says "we all know that the sun's rays can damage your skin, but did you know the sun also can damage your hair? Hair having prolonged exposure to the sun, UVA and UVB rays can damage the outside cover of the hair strand called the cuticle. "Signs of damage to your (glory) include discolorations, dry and brittle strands, broken or split ends, thinning and fizziness. Damaged hair has a dry look and feel. It is unmanageable and wont hold a curl and also dries quickly.

Your hair is particularly vulnerable to sun damage if it's fine or light colored. They also stated that" you're more at risk for hair damage from the sun if you are African American due to the flat and coiled shape of hair." They left us with good news though ladies so cheer up! We can take precautions to protect our glory from the sun!

Why do this?

"The suns' rays act very much like bleach on hair," says dermatologist Wilma Bergfeld, MD. "Bleach reacts with the melanin in hair and removes the color in an irreversible chemical reaction. Making matters worse, hot flat irons, rollers, and chlorinated water in swimming pools are lightening your hair making it more vulnerable to the summer stress of heat and sun. All of these damage your hair's keratin" she says. Dr. Bergfeld offers tips and one of them was to wear a hat or cover yourself with an umbrella. (Protect your hair from sun damage with these four tricks www.mind body green.com Josh Rosebrook)

"There is not a cosmetic product out there that acts like a sun screen for your hair. Another article by Josh Rosebrook implies, their is way more to the hair on our heads than just adorning our physical appearance. Hair also protects us from UV radiation. Since it acts as a barrier between our skin and the suns rays our (glory) follicles can take on a lot of damage if not properly protected. On down in the article he states that "over exposure to the sun effects the protective barrier of natural oils we all have on our scalps by causing blood vessels to dilute and become inflamed sometimes resulting in hair loss!" He urges instead of chopping all your hair off, why not avoid sun damage all together? He says to "try updating your look with a hat". He named three more ways and one was applying sunscreens to the hair. My point is yes, God gave us a covering of hair to cover our scalps to protect us. Also he said it's our glory.

So the hair protects the head but what protects the hair?

Many people never stop to realize the demonic devices of Satan! Most weaves, wigs, and sew ins in America are formulated after Idol gods and goddesses. Does the names Indi, Isis, or Onyx remi ring a bell? Indian hair types, Malaysian hair, Eurasian hair, Brazilian hair and all these different weaves, extensions, and hair types have spirits linked to them and causes one to act certain ways! The enemy is so subtle. Did you know that a great deal of hair extensions are offered up to idol god's? It's sad but true. We feel that we are acting as usual after getting these extensions put in but with more self worth and esteem! This is simply not the case. We actually take on the spirits of what we choose to wear! Like putting on trashy clothes makes one act trashy. It's not the person but the demonic realm working through our choices! We can choose to think evil of someone and the demonic thrives through this by taking the next step of whispering to you to sew discord because misery loves company! So our feminine nature makes us want to look fresh but through wisdom we must make sure the cost of fresh is not damming to our souls!

> *Neither was the man created for the woman; but the woman for the man. For this cause ought the woman to have power on her head because of the angels.* Because women were made for men, the bible states that we ought to have power on our head because of the angels.
> **(1 Corinthians 11:9)**

• What I am about to say may seem a little harsh, but it is true! All angels are NOT natural angels of light ! This scripture is talking about demonic angels that have the knowledge that women were created for men, so they ride the glory of the woman to make her use it for lustful, sinful, envious things and whatever you use your head for, your body will follow. So now that the angels are riding the glory of the woman (her hair) now she wants to be "sexy" with more than just her naughty hair but clothes that are supposed to be a "cover" to other areas of the body that is sacred, start to come off little by little. Watch out for those demon angels. They will keep you at half baked! We should have power on our heads "because" of the angels! Watch out! My question to you is, what covers your glory? (If the answer is nothing then I'm sure the natural side affects is a real burden to bare with the destroying of the hair and the styling and burning and cutting.. the list is to long) but did you know that theirs a spiritual list as well? Their is a "Yes Lord" in God where Your glory will become God's glory and God's glory is always protected and covered! The demon angels will cover your glory if you don't get it covered!

- *What does your glory say about you?*

- *Do we still use it to flirt and get attention flipping the hair at every man we see ?*

- *Is it used to be seductive, attractive, business like?*

- They say the first thing you notice about people is their hair and our shoes. It's almost impossible to go through the day with men seeing our glory uncovered and our feet still be in the preparation of the gospel of peace!(hair, shoes) Even the bible states when putting on the whole armor of God that we should utilize" the helmet of salvation. *(Ephesians 6:17)* God wants us to be covered. Too the bible plainly specifies- because the woman was made for the man for this cause ought the woman to have power on her head because of the "angels". I ask again is all your glory given to God? If so, is His glory covered? God always covers His glory. Did you know that the miss use of glory causes idols to form! You ever just sat back and looked at commercial after commercial where women flaunted the hair color, texture, style, and length of their hair? We sit back and say " *man I wish I had that color or that length.* Idolizing someone else's glory and steady killing, frying, and dyeing our hair trying to get what someone else "appear" to have. (the devil is smoke in mirrors) We don't see envy and idolness but it's there! These are symbolic that the devil is at work in our lives. The idol made might be you yourself. You may have achieved the best hair in your circle of people (with expensive cost to hair health) and now you think your glory is the stuff and so you actually come to the place where you let people idolize your glory -In the market place or in the mall. Even with extension weaves and styles we have to get the ones that will attract lust from men causing them to idolize us and causing women to be envious! These are those demon angels in *(1corinthians 11:10)* because we have not taken upon ourselves to give God the glory and make sure God's glory is covered. The demonic angels have taken the position to cover our glory and now we use it, by the control of them, for corrupt and evil things we believe to be normal. Bottom line, our glory will be covered one way or another ladies. This information is not to make you fearful, but it can't be said that you never knew about this revelation! God gives us revelation because He wants walking this life to be as easier for us! It's up to us to choose the easier route He gives or go the way we know right ladies! We won't go to hell for not choosing to cover, but we sure go through it more intensely because of the demons we allow to access us! God is ready for us to come back home. His arms are opened wide!

- Do you think it is not a coincidence that women all across the world are going into protective mode when it comes to the health of the hair? They don't even know why. It's because God is calling us back. Not because of some fad. We think it's because we are tired of damaged over processed hair and unknowingly we are tired of not having a purpose, so we try to cover our glory with other coverings to regain strength of the hair like covering it with a wig or with extensions but these are in fact the wrong coverings! They do nothing but strip the hair even more and often times reseed the hair line which leads to baldness. The position we have found ourselves in is being left with lifeless glory. With the demonic angels watching over our glory, that we hate to give to God, we continually, with our glory, attract the same doggish man year after year instead of a man of God finding us! We also stay in the same cycle of no good friends who find every opportunity to stab us in the back. The same cycle ran by the same demon angel we allow to claim and cover our glory.

I know this throws many of us for a loopy loo! This isn't the way we were taught and this is something we have never heard! My question is;

Have what you were taught by peers and unsaved parents worked?

Look around! God is calling His daughters back so we can march forward in victory! He wouldn't have exposed this revelation to us if He didn't deeply care and was ready to see us walk in the fullness! Fresh baked bread! Those humble enough are being called into the deep. It's the only way Peter got to Jesus was to step outside the boat. Nobody else wanted to step out but Peter wanted to experience change bad enough! Tired of the same old cycle. God always covers His glory!

> *By the multitude of thy merchandise they have filled the midst of thee with violence and thou hast sinned: therefore I will cast thee as profane out of the mountain of God: (devoted to that which is not sacred or profane) And I will destroy thee "O covering cherub from the midst of the stones of fire.(**Ezekiel 28:16**)*

Wow! Satan is a covering!

> *Thou art the anointed Cherub that "covereth"; and I have set thee so; thou wast upon the holy mountain of God; thou hast walked up and down in the midst of the stones of fire. (**Ezekiel 28 vs 14**)*

This verse is for my religious people.

Can you see that every anointing is in fact not an anointing to glorify Jesus ?

Every thrill and chill felt does not necessarily mean we are next to the heart of God! The bible didn't say "*thou was* " the anointed cherub that covereth. God said "*Thou "art"* the anointed cherub that covereth!

God kicked his dusty behind out though. He's still anointed and he is still seeking to cover the glory that is supposed to belong to God and Him alone. *(Matthew 11:12) And* from the days of John the Baptist until now the kingdom of heaven suffereth "violence" and the violent take it by force. *(Ezekiel 28:16)* By the multitude of thy merchandise they have filled the midst of thee with "violence". Lord let your Kingdom come and your will be done in earth. (In me!) We are to be God's vessel ladies. Our bodies should be living sacrifice holy and acceptable unto God which is our reasonable service *(Romans 12:1)*

> *Again* for this cause ought the woman to have power on her head because of the angels.*(1corinthians 11:10)*

This anointed cherub is looking to cover our glory and to have us all fleshed out and using our glory to cause feelings of lust, hatred, mummers, and jealousy.

> There fore I will cast thee as profane out of the mountain of God! *(Ezekiel 28:16)*

> "Profane" meaning that relating or devoted to that which is not sacred.

Have you ever thought of your hair as sacred?

Me either. When the Lord first started to lead me to cover up, my husband was supportive but would every now and then suggest I wear my hair out or down on different occasions. Although it was tempting sometimes the Lord helped me through kind persuasive words to hold the standard of staying covered when out and about! My husband was very understanding and he supported what the Lord wanted to do though me in the earth. A few months ago my husband actually voiced to me that he has grown to appreciate me even more covering my hair. He said that my hair has become sacred to him and that it shines and is glory! He says he would be offended if I walked out exposing what God has challenged me to only let him indulge and take part in. I thought.... wow!! Is this the same man? We must, through knowledge, rid ourselves of the profane one and cover ourselves! The bread is smelling so good and in great process of getting done and being uniquely shareable. We must go back and forward in the things of God!

What is covering your glory?

Have you made the choice to give it to God?

Some may ask,...well why would God give us beautiful hair if He wanted us to find something to cover it up all the time? (Of coarse allowing our husbands to indulge in our hair when in the secret chambers of our homes) Great question! I'll answer this question with a series of questions.

- *How has it worked out so far with us doing emotional things to our hair to kill hair health and seduce men?*

- *Ever felt an emotional need for change and Just wacked it all off or put a loud funky color in it?*

- *Is it your desire to have long healthy hair?*

- Covering our glory allows this healing to take place in our souls as well while Healing from demonic angels surrounding your head and penetrating poison. Healing from self destructive acts is needful in this day and time. Covering God's glory allows you to gently plat or braid your hair and let the healing begin. I normally leave God's glory plated and moisturized for a week without even bothering it sometimes. My husband calls me his little Indian lady.(No offense to Indians as I am part Cherokee) Letting the hair actually heal properly from all the years of destruction in ignorance is what our glory needs. My hair has grown considerably and is healthier than ever because I made the choice after God suggested I do this. I was pleased to submit to His will for me. He gave me this revelation of demon angels covering after I told Him yes! So I cover my hair with a scarf or things like this all while being creative me! I have learned through scripture, trial, and error that I am to protect God's glory, Keep it away from the hazardous elements, and also self destructive chemicals and much heat. When I took this great turn my life began to change ! I gave God the glory and the enemy had no more access to live in my mind. When the enemy does still try to penetrate my mind, the Holy Ghost kicks Him out faster than he could land. I feel safe/sacred and covered by God's grace. It's a new look which brings on a new attitude that hey, I am worth something and God is now allowing me to see His will for me. He's allowing me to see everything as good like in the garden of Eden before Adam and Eve failed. God has since then given me a healthier way of eating and He talks with me on a daily basis. (Daily bread) W*hy*- Because God is looking for at least one that would be willing and obedient and will step out from the crowd and from peers and say *"God if you want me this way, then you don't have to ask twice.*

- The men that I come in contact with in public as a result to my obedience, have such a look of reverence and respect for the most part. It is not I but Christ that dwells in me. God has added great abundance to my life for my obedience. When we decide to let the ways of being treated and talked to like trash go we can recognize that we are royalty! When the man holler's at you about how fat your fanny looks, this is NOT a compliment. When we pull off that old slave mentality that us daughters aren't worth much, we can then see ourselves how God sees us! Not so long as those demon angles are covering your glory day and night!

- Anything precious to God, He covers! Even so much as Himself, He dwells in thick darkness. God wants all the glory! Let's cover up!

- *You ever seen the reaction of a man who has seen a naked lady?*

- It does something to their insides because the woman was made for the man. Just like your favorite food do something your insides when it's prepared just the way you like it! So yes, like our hair, our bodies are wonderfully made, but God wants us to cover up our private parts! Our breast and other areas exposed causes men to lust and think sexually of us-Our thighs!

- *How can God use you as a witness when your stuff is hanging all out and so tight you can't breath?*

- When used properly, our hearts are beautiful! So why would God waist this beauty by putting it on the inside of our bodies where nobody can see it? Should it not be exposed? God placed the heart and it's beauty on the inside because being exposed to the outside elements of life would cause the beautiful heart to very quickly stop beating due to unsanitary situations. God knows best! What about baby? The steps of how a baby changes rapidly in mommies tummy is to precious a beauty! Why would God allow this to be covered by thick layers of skin and fluid? Should not the world see the stages of baby's growth? God covers things treasured by Him! Just like we wouldn't let random men see us naked ladies we should be the same way about God's glory, our hair. Just like our hearts, God never meant for our hair to suffer from element or for us to dye and fry and dip it in sunscreen! God gets all the glory! This is not to twist your arm or make you feel that God is not with you if you don't cover up 24/7. People will claim you're scaring them by all the talk of spiritual dark angels but they go spend money at the movies to be scared on purpose for entertainment. I lack understanding about that. There are many powerful ladies that go forth and are used mightily by God! This place and revelation is where God led me as an individual too. We all have different assignments in life that leads us down different roads. For those of us willing to say yes to this great but beautiful sacrifice; now is time to see do we really mean what we have been saying to God for years. God gave Sampson directions concerning his hair because God had given him a special power of strength. Delilah tricked him and cut all his hair off! No strength. God has given us power within our hair! We are not supposed to expose our hair to every and anybody. This remains a true fact and we have become powerless. So we stoop and settle for being "sexy" to compensate for the power we once had. Those really desiring to please God and get back in right standing with him may take heed to these words. Rebecca covered herself in the presence of her new husband! Once we turn back and return into the ark of safety and let God do what He needs to do to process us and give our glory to Him, then we wont mind staying covered! Covering ourselves would be a delight because we will then be daily walking in the presence of God day and night. You must cover yourself in the presence of your King according to Rebecca.

- He that dwells in the secret place of the "Most High " shall abide under the shadow of the Almighty. **Psalms 91**

- Under the shadow means you're close to Him, cover up in the presence of royalty. I will say of the Lord He is my refuge and my fortress: my God in Him will I trust! Fortress means a heavily protected and impenetrable building, or a person or thing not susceptible to outside influence or disturbance. (This must mean we are inside somewhere right) Is God, though our obedience, our fortress or is the angel that covereth and got kicked out our fortress? The choice is ours.

- *Every wise woman buildeth her house: but the foolish plucketh it down with her hands. (**Proverbs 14 vs1**)*

- We all know that we have a natural house and a spiritual house. This passage goes for both! Let's not continue to pull down our spiritual houses strand by strand while allowing satanic angels to be our covering! *(Proverbs 14:33) says wisdom resteth in the heart of him that hath understanding.* We must understand that it's God's will for us to have long glorious hair, but to go our own way we hardly never healthily obtain this because of the demon angels creating the appearance that it's okay to use our bodies to sin. God's way was not for the elements and heat and demons to tare away our roofing leaving the house for full exposure of termites. But for us to have glorious hair and give it back to Him! You may not be in a place in your spirit to submit to this revelation and all men must work out their own soul salvation with fear and trembling! So you seek God about what He wants. And remember everything that is cherished is covered! Uuuummmm this bread has taken a major turn and is smelling so fine! !! A daughter of God's hair is her glory. With fasting and much much prayer let's grab courage and ask God for His wisdom. We give that glory back to God. He's the only one who knows how to use it properly!!

- **Behind The Veil**

- **_Give Me The King**

- *I'm not your average female. Let me assure you. Complication to the carnal mind describes me. My eyes observe that which nature can't perceive and my ears hear words not uttered with human vocal cords. While a gentle touch is inviting I intensely feel the words that are spoken to me and over me more sustaining. I smell the sweet scents of good motive, consciousness and truth while tasting the winds of change ever before me. I learned this way of life by watching the King! Eve's first encounter was with God! So a lady knows her genuine place is in the heart of a king. The King of kings that is! Nothing else fully appeases her appetite but to have ...well...Him. I have been through to much to short change myself. I won't settle for anyone else- not even the King's friends. ...I'm just not that type of lady. You know. Those that run with the King? They are mighty in statue, speech, and anointing, special indeed. They walk like Him, they have the same language and even certain mannerisms they make shows a reflection of Him. Sometimes I win a glimpse of Him while in their presence(Teachers, preachers, evangelist, apostles, Prophets) and it rattles my heart but still my soul yearns to be touched by Him who's not accessed by all. Experiencing those whom carry*

His glow is very nice to see and tempting to just stop right here at man I can see and smell at will- and true they smell so sweet with that Godly Oar scent of heaven, like honey nectar in the spring time, they speak from the well of truth and life! These men of God are very powerful and influential too because they roll with the King. Yes, I respect them greatly But I need that one on one. I won't stop until I'm the center of God's heart. I must be the one He thinks of when He needs something done. It must be me that He looks for everyday at a specific time to share communion with. So even though He's surrounded by His friends, I pursue Him in silent settle feminine ways until He notices me. I watch Him....the way He walk and talk...mostly the things He say, while it melts my heart I still find strength to meditate. I start to mimic His speech and things He does. I watch and learn things about Him so that I'm ready when He actually does notice my body language is towards Him! (Not just my words) I'm on my knees or laying prostrated letting Him know that only HE will do. While watching and preparing myself I learn that He takes every word to heart so my words, I make them few and I incline my ear to the beat of His heart. My words must line up with what He agrees with. I don't just speak anything but I'm careful what I express. Cautious not to "off"end Him because I don't want to "end"off causing Him to feel angry, annoyed, or resentful toward me. (He's all I have) so I have to make sure my spirit is real quiet too because He dwells in the secret place! I would never and would rather die then expose His secret dwelling ...our secret dwelling place! I desire His protection so much. He's my mighty strong tower! Rapunzel may let down her hair to escape that tower but only because she had the wrong refuge. With God Being my refuge and habitation I don't need a knight in shinning armor because in this strong tower my King keeps me from danger. I have no desire to ever leave the place of safety. After all, He's the only one never ever defeated and I'm driven near Him. I give Him all of me and everything I have. I'm just that into Him! Any time, any where, any day I'm on call. The Lord is my light and my salvation and I pleasure in things He tells me to do even though my flesh thinks it's hard. So every day I wait, watch, and listen with expectancy for the King Himself to say this word "Come", and I run as hard as I can with tears in my eyes and my cares having no choice but to strip away from me, leaving the past the past I run into the arms of the King! Aaaahhh now I'm safe, now I'm secure, now I'm never letting go!! (John 6:) No man can come to me, except the Father which hath sent me draw Him: The Lord is my light and my salvation; whom shall I fear? The Lord is the strength of my life; of whom shall I be afraid? (Psalms 27:1) Give me the King! I'll take nothing less.

CHAPTER 4

The Then and The Now

It was once true that many people knowing you well knew how to push your buttons. They knew how to raise your elevator all the way up to the top at the drop of a hat! This was before we gained the knowledge that God has given us a supernatural way of escape!

Now?

Now that God has revealed His heart of loving us through giving us a silent weapon of tears, we should become more in love with Him than anything else and see don't ladies of every creed and color launch forward into what God has for them! Watch how our emotions become covered under the blood of Jesus! We will forgive and we will let go quickly because being into God requires this. We will constantly watch ourselves transform where people close to us wont even recognize us! As we constantly use our instrument of tears telling God everything then rising up with forgiveness and mercy and turning to do positive things watch God remake us right in front of our own faces. Wow! I am excited for our future!

Let's start this chapter by discussing the meaning of tear and tear. Then we will further focus on God's double edge sword in action.

Tear means *a drop of clear salty liquid that is secreted by the lacrimal gland of the eye to lubricate the surface between the eyeball and eyelid and to wash away irritants.*

Definition two: *To make (an opening) in something by pulling it apart or by accident.*

Definition three: *to separate forcefully.*

> *Thou tellest my wanderings: put thou my tears into thy bottle: are they not in thy book? When I cry unto thee, then shall mine enemies turn back; this I know; for God is for me.*
>
> **(Psalms 56 8-9)**

My God! It's ironic that tear and tear has different meanings naturally, but spiritually they go hand in hand. If we consciously offer our tears to the Lord no matter the circumstances, then God begins immediately tearing things away from our lives that need not be! Enemies, frienemies, bad relationships, bad habits, but most times we unconsciously and unknowingly get up after using this instrument, and turn back into or to the very thing God tore away from us while on our knees crying. In the Greek we refer to it as "Da'kry" meaning tear. From this word they originated the word "dacryadenitis" meaning an inflammation of the lacrimal gland. A decrease or lack of lacrimal gland secretion is the leading cause of aqueous tear deficient dry eye syndrome (DES) Secretion- meaning a process by which substances are produced and discharged from a cell. It has been suggested that DES is an inflammatory disorder that affects the ocular surface and the lacrimal gland. Aqueous meaning of or containing water, typically as a solvent or medium.

<u>Do you still possess your cry?</u>

We see here that tears are important for a serious variety of reasons (Experimental eye research, Author manuscript HHS public access, Driss Zoukhri www.nebinlm. nih.gov) It's time out for the way it has continually been. That was then. This is now. God is a spirit.

How can we be into God but not by spirit first?

> *God is a spirit; and they that worship him must worship him in spirit and in truth.* **(John 4:24)**

God gave us our tears as a spiritual weapon against the enemy as a way to rid our bodies/ vessels of toxins, and as a way to start a healing process that we rise from and turn. Tears are an expression of your soul "to God".

Have you ever found yourself crying in the company of someone, only to gain comfort, or to stop him from leaving or maybe just tears in plain manipulation?

These, my friend, are direct examples of using this amazing gift God has given us for fleshly purposes where God gets no glory and where God get no glory it means satan is getting it. No in between. Tears are meant to tear. When using this weapon correctly God begins to tear those things not like him, and not good for you away from your body, soul, and spirit. What good is this weapon if we use it, then rise and go back to the very same foolishness? It's like constantly cutting yourself in the same place, while each time expecting no blood to come pouring out, and after a while we stop and look at God like, why are you not hearing me? Why are you not delivering me? "I'm waiting on God, " we say. "Lord is it something I've done?" Yes!!! The answer is yes. It's something you've done and keep doing. Put the knife away.

> *The weapons of our warfare are not carnal, but mighty through God to the pulling down of strong holds.* **(2 Cor 10:4)**

When utilizing our tears correctly, God will be able to proceed and grow you, pulling down everything around you that's keeping you from full focus on Him. God has been ready and willing for years to tear down things that depress and hinder us, but the enemy being so slick tries to begin with us from infant stages using our tears to manipulate and control those around us, only to get what we are seeking for at that moment and time. Crying and screaming for candy is one example. Yes the candy is pleasant, but it leads to wanting more candy and before we know it, over the years we have a mouth full of toothaches and cavities/ fillers and we use our tears for manipulation purposes again. "God my mouth is in pain please rescue me. Where are you God"? Once God allows finances to flow -you get that one tooth taken care of and who's back at the candy store? Loving God means we should trust everything He put in His word and His will should be our desire which is to please Him. God is so ready for us to come back until He gave us a weapon so powerful and you don't even have to purchase it! Just meditate and allow this beautifully designed weapon to flow! RISE AND TURN! Watch GOD ALMIGHTY with His strong and mighty ways get to tearing stuff up around you.

What is your tear status?

Now that we have our weapon of tearing down the enemy, tears flowing smoothly, and more frequently we move to God's shield of protection.

> *Above all, taking the shield of faith, where with ye shall be able to quench "all" the fiery darts of the wicked.* **(Ephesians 6:16)**

Us being the fabulous daughters that we are with the working, cooking, cleaning, taking care of the family, teaching children at church, participating in your children's teacher meetings, doing your wifely duties, and grocery shopping all while trying to maintain an open, honest relationship with God and achieving time to gather yourself and your thoughts- even though we thank God for our husbands sometimes we feel unprotected. All that our husbands go through with daily life shows us that they cover us the best way they can, but it seems as if another area may fall short. I'm here to tell you that this happens, not because our men are not men enough, they are. Fact is, God does not want us to forget that it is Him that hold it all together with no strain and while it's great to have our husband's protection, God is given us the whole armor of Himself! The shield of faith being one of the amazing parts of this armor! With life going at the speed of a race car our shield makes everything going on seem so small and minute because we know above all God's will be done.

<u>*What is a shield?*</u>

1) It's a broad piece of metal or another suitable material, held by straps of a handle attached on one side, used as a protection against blows or missiles
2) protects someone or something from a danger, risk, or unpleasant experience.

So God has given us this protection in place! This shield is designed mainly to keep us from ourselves and Also the enemy. You may be a little shocked that God would want to keep us from us but this is true! One of the main ways the enemy loves to attack the church is through people who claim they are down for the church. They are the ones who tend to sew the most discord among brothers. They step on some to get to others with purposes of gaining ungodly influence.

They rape and step over the weak along with those they have flattered using so many false statements having the wrong motive all while laboring in the church -only to get pastor to see he really needs them at all cost because if they leave the whole thing will come crashing down along with weak minded individuals following them out the door to destination super dead end. When the truth of the matter is those that are often looked over are anointed to do their jobs and to do them ten times better and with a right motive. The shield of faith! Faith keeps us believing that God is the source no matter what happens no matter who leaves!

*Let this mind be in you which was also in Christ Jesus (**Philippians 2;5**)*

<u>*Do we believe God wants us to have two minds?*</u>

Of coarse not! This is where (*James 1:8*) talks about "a double minded man is unstable in "all" his ways". God expects us to have one mind! His mind! The end. Our minds are no good.

> *"So then because thou art lukewarm, and neither cold nor hot, I will spue thee out of my mouth."* (**Revelation 3:16**)

Breaking it on down, you simply have no salt and so God spits out nasty food. The Lord loves His food hot and well seasoned! How can we be the salt of the earth without having the very mind of Christ? God forbid.

> *Ye are the salt of the earth: but if the salt have lost his savor, wherewith shall it be salted? It is thenceforth good for nothing but to be cast out and trotted under the foot of men.*
> (Like lukewarm unsalted food)
> (***Matthew chp5 vs 13-16***)

The shield of faith keeps us with our eyes in the right direction and our beliefs will line up to what our eyes see. We must see God in every situation and know that all things work together for good to them that love God, to them who are the called according to his purpose! Then: we thought our purpose was what we were suppose to be doing. Now: we know that HIS will is what matters! Not what we want to do but what He wants us to do. Amen!

You ever heard of a study called "resistant starch"? (By Kris Gunnars, BSC) This study shows that Most of the carbohydrates in the diet are starches. Starches are long chains of glucose that are found in grains, potatoes and various foods. But not all of the starch we eat gets digested. Sometimes a small part of it passes through the digestive tract uncharged! In other words it is resistant to digestion. This type of starch is called resistant starch, which function's kind of like soluble fiber. Many studies in humans shows that resistant starch can have powerful health benefits. This includes improved insulin sensitivity, lower blood sugar levels, reduced appetite and various benefits for digestion. To make a long story short, eating certain foods with starch in them at room temp causes these foods to go through the body uncharged because the body can't properly digest them at that temp. While this is great health wise naturally, spiritually God can not use the nutrients of our spiritual fruit when we are lukewarm/ room temperature. None of the nutrients is useful and others we witness to won't be able to digest one word we say because we are simply not the right temperature. The only way God gets the glory is when we come correct with a ready mind to be digestible!

Then: We used to come and go any old kind of way!

Now: We know that it is a correct way to come before God wanting to be hired by Him.

We must be digestible taking on the whole armor of God allowing it to tear away all ungodly residues.

- *Behind The Veil_*

  _Sexy Enough To Destroy A Son
  High minded, low minded, thicker than a can of butter milk biscuits or thinner than a flag pole- we all attract the opposite sex! This power comes with great price and many of us are still paying! Think about these questions:

- *What is the price of being "sexy" in this day in age?*

- *While we do the things to acquire this "sexy" who or what pays for it?*

- The answer to these questions are, our children pay, our relationship with God pay, and our men of God pay! Our children because they have a close up view to watch how "sexy" destroys our character and our integrity. They see close up how Mr. Shawn, who's married by the way, can't take his eyes off our behind as we walk past in our short spandex skirts! They see our breast hanging out freely to attract the eyes of those who's willing to show us the attention we are definitely begging for. We blur the lines in our daughters eyes that this is what I must become. We blur the lines for our sons to think this is what I must achieve in a wife. We set our children up for failure as daughter in law will attract eyes and succumb to cheating on our sons with other men who sees what she has to offer and for son in law to stay with charges drawn on him because daughter has him fighting over her all the time! What type of life is this? "Sexy" stands tall claiming generations with deception. Our relationship with God pay because this "sexy" completely goes against what He teaches us to be! Don't trade the Savior for your sexy!! The Lord says we are to be with a quiet spirit but "sexy" is LOUD! We are to be submissive to our own husbands, wear modest apparel, and shy away from men's faces. (1 Timothy 2:9)

- *Is "sexy" worth our relationship with Father?*

- *Is it worth being disobedient?*

- What about the men of God? Those left here to lead us by example weigh In the balance of living a double life! While he tried to be the God man that he is he can't help noticing the enormous amount of jiggling that's going on in our see through pants and tops! Headed home he tries to shake the memories because he actually does have a wholesome wife waiting home for him. Over time we find marriages busted up and destroyed in the church and "sexy" stands on the scene lurking with confidence of never being discovered the problem while in plain sight. We've been taught to appeal to the man's Eyes without acquiring the information that the eyes get tired after a certain point and goes looking for something more new and exciting which is a great reason God deals with the Heart! We as well should deal with the heart of man, the heart of our children, the heart of God! "Sexy" sells itself without ever telling us that it leads to destruction. Our biblical example is Sampson and Delilah. She used her "sexy" to destroy his strength and today while maybe not fully intending to, the enemy uses our desire for "sexy" to destroy men of God!

- Who will lead our daughters and sons if we destroy the influence of man being capable of leading?

- Our sons will be just another punk to ladies and daughters rebellious against authority. It's up to us to call "sexy" out! We can't ignore that we have beautiful bodies made by the First and best Artist ever! Our curves are stunning even on a bad day, however;

- *How do we channel the attractiveness God has blessed us with?*

- Let's look at these ladies <u>Esther</u> and <u>Vashtie</u>

And how similar they were!

- **Similarity**

Both were ladies of coarse.
They both were married to the king.
Both were beautiful .
They both disobeyed orders of the king.

- One was told to come before the king and his friends to show herself, her beauty, and her body but she refused. I guess she was tired of being a slave to "sexy" and it caused her title of Queen. Ever heard the term trophy wife? Sexy huh? She's sported as a lifeless trophy that get's dusted when time to be shown to friends. When it's time to make him look good her purpose comes into play. If this same lady gains weight she feels worthless and sometimes he helps her to feel this way. Allowing "sexy" to rule our lives subliminally puts us in a box that we bring nothing else to table. I mean sure we are made to "think " that we do but bottom line in that "sexy" holds the strings. Think I'm kidding? Gain weight while attached to a man that married your "sexy" and see what happens. Many women have already found out what happened sadly. Choose today not to be a slave to "sexy" any more.(S- E- X- Y• him wanting to experience new "SEX" appeal is "Y" he left me) Sexy is a slave term that we are free from starting today! Look at how our, once beautiful minds, have become so twisted. When a guy in passing relates the message that he finds us "sexy" we are to flattered for words! In old times any stranger walking up to a real feminine lady and vocalizing a word with sex in it would have gotten him a hot fire slap on the cheek!!! She then says "I'd never," and turns and walks abruptly away! We on the other hand thinks this is a reason to give this man our digits. While disturbed at the disrespect I cant be mad at men simply because a man will only respect a woman who requires it.

- Look at Esther who was stunning as well. She disobeyed the king to. She was told never to come before the king without being called first but she did. So one refused to come and one came without being called! One woman, a slave to "sexy" got dismissed by the king never to stand before him again and the other (not a slave to "sexy") got the kings heart to grow more fond of her through this Devine act of coming without being called.

- How?

- What was Esther's secret?

- Her secret was that she believed is someone other than herself and her ability to appeal to mans flesh. She believed on God and requested the people do a fast before this Devine happening took place of her going in before the king without being summoned! She was unselfish even though she was in a place to not be affected from the killing of her people. Her beauty or body curves wasn't what she relied on but it complimented the substance she had on the inside of her! When beauty compliments what God has placed on the inside of us the results are endless! Our sons and daughters discover a fighting chance to be what God has called for them to be. Our men of God can focus and lead us as God leads them and our relationship with God becomes sweeter and sweeter as the days go by because we have come obedient to the way He said we are to be. If she would have depended on the curves of her body she would have been a dead one because how many curves can the king see upon request?

- Answer these questions to see if you have the trophy wife mentality!

- **Questions:**

1) **Do you apply perfume to yourself only so that others may enjoy it as you pass?**
2) **Do you purchase items thinking of how others may perceive you?**
3) **Do you plan goals of losing or gaining weight to gran the attention and affection of men?**
4) **Do you make it a conscious habit to check how good your butt looks in the mirror?**
5) **Does a man passing by while calling you "sexy" make your day special?**
6) **Have you recently purchased a book, read a blog, google searched, how to make a man fall for you?**
7) **Do you hold your appearance higher than your salvation?**
8) **If being caught dead would you rather have make up and hair in place so when your body is found for the press to take photos of you're still looking stunning?**
9) **Does daydreams of being the attraction of the room at public events cloud your day?**
10) **Do you constantly think of ways to adorn the outward appearance ?**

- If you answered yes to more than five of these questions you must pray that God strip you of this trophy wife mentality! Ask God to make you what HE thinks is beautiful. He will then start from the inside and work His way out!

What's curves without finesse? It's a bunch of hills and valleys with no cause for greatness once so ever! From this day forward our beauty shall compliment our substance and we have no need for "sexy" because being submissive to the word of God is the most attractive of all*!*

CHAPTER 5

Brokenness Leads To Selflessness

- The average female in America today believe that feeling broken is a low place! We tend to feel misunderstood like the weight of the world is on our shoulders. Brokenness is not a terrible thing. It's actually easier to rebuild something that's broken then trying to remake a structure still standing. Many men and women found themselves in a broken place in the bible but something beautiful happened afterwards! What better example to set our eyes on than Jesus? Jesus did so many wonderful things! Healing the bedridden, casting out devils, destroying the territory of the enemy, and rebuilding self worth but one of the things that drew Jesus's heart in was when it came time to be crucified.

- *Then cometh Jesus with them unto a place called Geth-sem-a-ne, and saith unto the disciples, sit ye here, while I go and pray yonder. And he took with him Peter and the two sons of Zeb'-e-dee, and began to be sorrowful and very heavy. Then saith he unto them, "My soul is exceeding sorrowful, even unto death; Tarry ye here, and watch with me. And he went a little future and fell on his face, and prayed saying, "O my Father, if it be possible, let this cup pass from me. Never the less not as I will but as thou wilt. The 40th verse says And he cometh unto the disciples, and findeth them asleep, and saith unto Peter, " what could ye not watch with me one hour "? Watch and pray that ye enter not into temptation;*

*the spirit indeed is willing, but the flesh is weak." He went away again the second time and prayed saying "O my father if this cup may not pass away from me except I drink it, thy will be done And he came and found them asleep again: for their eyes were heavy. And he left them, and went away again, and prayed the third time saying the same words.(**Matthew 26 36-46**)*

- As I have shared with you verses out of KJV bible you see where Jesus prayed three times about the same matter. He was heavy and in agony. He needed, at that moment, God to move in His favor. Jesus was totally broken in this moment. In this beautiful moment of being broken Jesus says *"nevertheless, not my will but thine be done."* Only though true brokenness can perfect love be shown.

- Jesus said, *Father forgive them for they know not what they do. And they parted his raiment, and cast lots.(**Luke 23:34**)*

- True brokenness " will allow us to think of others even while they persecute us. In *Matthew 26 and 50* Jesus called Judas friend.

- Through brokenness, miracles can happen. Most often time when the Lord strategically place a devil around you it is only for you to know where the devil is and at what point he's up to! We misread the assignment and blow the mission most often. We move to fast and are left blind to the fact of the enemy's plan. A you that you never knew before can come forth and demonstrate the true love of God. You can demonstrate being a true air to the King of kings, but not a moment sooner of being broken. Being broken is never easy, but it is very much so necessary. The master manipulator satan knows this. Why else would *Matthew chapter 26 vs 36- 46 (666)* be his regret? God sees things way different than we do. The devil sees things different than we also. So while we as humans constantly beat up on ourselves by past regrets and things we should have done different, satan uses his past regret as a remembrance. It's nothing ironic about

Matthew chapter 26 vs 36- 46 with 6 being the last numbers in sequence to the three double digit numbers the enemy uses as his representation. He uses this to symbolize his regret, and also his false success to you and I.

- **Question**: *what does The enemy regret in Matthew 26,36-46?*

- *What is his false success?*

- *Why does he use the term "do what Thy wilt " among his satanist?*

- Truthfully, one thing the enemy regrets is the spirit of sleep on the disciples. Look at these words closely *and He saith unto Peter, " what could ye not watch with me one hour "?*

They were all sleeping but he came and addressed Peter! This simply says he loved them all but he had a particular rather closer connection with Peter spiritually! We learn while being taught but some of us exceeded others because our capacity and willingness to learn is greater! The enemy could have easily used manipulative words from Peter to say "hey man of God, God just spoke to me and said flee, you don't have to die". Their are saved people who will lie on God in a heart beat. Once Peter corrected Jesus and was told, "get the behind me satan." Satan could have easily done this again through Peter in Jesus's moment of toiling with destiny. Peter was also a man of war. He could have easily been thinking of a plan to slay those men coming for Jesus, I mean wasn't he told by Jesus to "watch!?" Sometimes when we watch, it is so we don't get caught! (Sometimes) Thank God for the spirit of sleep! Glory!! Sometimes we think a spirit of sleep comes from the devil but it doesn't. We experience a spirit of sleep every night to get refreshed for the next day! However the enemy will use, when allowed, the spirit of sleep to be sent to you at the wrong "timing" like while about to read the bible or behind the wheel of a vehicle. Satan regrets this spirit of sleep on these boys. If someone is sleep, they can't distract you! Sometimes in our weak moments we look for distraction subliminally because we don't want to face the music of what's really at hand. He regrets the three times Jesus prayed, three being a Devine number, and one of the greatest things satan regrets is Jesus's attitude.

Jesus prayed, *"never the less not as I will, but as thou wilt."*

- Now this really burned the devil. These few words Jesus spoke captured satan's attention. He hated Jesus and envied Him at the same time. These words and this attitude had such a huge impact on the enemy until he demands this attitude from those serving him. He even adopted Jesus words to use for his Satanist groups but the words are *"do what thou wilt, meaning don't consult God about anything! If it feels right to you then do it!* The devil's weakness is his regrets. Only because in his regrets lies the fact that we can now be forgiven for sin, and we have a fire example of how to seek God's will even if it means death for us and Also that his destination is hell because he has already lost the battle. The enemy has a false success in these sequence of scripture as well that he likes to use smoke in mirrors on; His false success to those who are blind is to plant fear in the minds of people to make them think he can do what he wants when it comes to killing you, stealing from you, destroying you. Truth is, God allowed this wonderful thing to happen and this was one of the most important reasons Jesus came to the earth. The enemy thinks he had one of his as an undercover agent (Judas) but God allowed Judas to be there. This had to happen.

- *Jesus answered them, Have not I chosen you twelve, and one of you is a devil?*

- **John 6 vs 70**

- The enemy used Christian people to do this to Jesus. The very ones that was supposed to believe on God did this, but Jesus turned right around and forgave them and paved the way where they could continue to get forgiveness. Out of all Jesus went through, He could have went the easy way out but brokenness led to selflessness and Jesus finished it! Praise God! Further on down we look at another false achievement of the devil which is that Peter, a man Jesus loved, would deny Him three times. The reason this is an illusive success is because Jesus had already prayed for Peter! Not that Peter wouldn't deny Him, but Jesus was praying for the after math which is what satan wanted to capitalize on. Once Peter had done this thing Father let Peter grab life and more abundantly. Peter took the trial he went though and ran hard for Jesus. This gave him the ammo to finish the work faithfully. Sometimes we try and pray people out of situations, but it's God will that they go through the trial, It'll give them strong reason to finish, like Peter. The enemy uses the term "do what thou wilt "to side step what Jesus did! Many so called Christians male and female follow after this phrase with their speech, their emotions, and their actions. The law of the devil is do anything "you" want to do. If it feels good then do it, but God's will is not allowed only yours....which is his. How many of us so called believers today are demonstrating satan's main motto? How many people are serving God on the outside but on the inside the heart is far from Him because your "own will " is in motion? This is the only law of satan. People by the droves, follow his law to the letter. Ladies this is why we must stay broken before the Lord. Brokenness leads to selflessness which leads to God's will.

- Another example of selflessness is in *(Judges 16:4))*(Sampson) *And it came to pass afterward that he loved a woman in the valley of So- 'rek, whose name was De- li'- lah. And the lords of the Phi-lis' - tin es came up unto her and said unto her, entice him, and see where in his great strength lieth and by what means we may prevail against him, that we may binde him to afflict him and we will give thee everyone of us eleven hundred pieces of silver.*

- She did as directed and accomplished the goal. Sampson loved and trusted this woman and she crushed him to his soul. Now even Sampson experienced selflessness through brokenness. They cut Sampson's hair and put his eyes out making sport of him. Sampson's whole man hood was built upon being strong, and now he's broken from being strong to weak. Sampson went From seeing to being blind and from loving strange women who used their powers to break him down to purposing to destroy the Philistines even if it meant him too. Brokenness caused Sampson to go from seeing and being blind to being blind and now seeing clearly his mission! Can you see with the eye of Christ? Once we become blind to the way we see things destiny takes shape.

- We as ladies choose death over life a lot of times because we are built up on emotions. We feel that heart break is the end of the rope for us. Sampson chose to make his weakest moment count for his strongest. Once satan knows our weak spots, he sends a trap in that same direction and if God let it come to pass it's only to bring us to a broken state of selflessness Where we give our very lives up spiritually to follow Him! It's only then unconditional love will prevail.

- *Now the house was full of men and women. And All the lords of the Philistines; and there were upon the roof about three thousand men and women that beheld while Sampson was made sport. And Sampson called unto the Lord and said o Lord God. (Calling God "Lord" means a submission.) Remember me, I pray thee, and strengthen me I pray thee only this once. Sampson bowed himself with all his might; and the house fell up on the lord's and upon all the people that were there in, so the dead which he slew at his death were more than they which he slew in his life.* **(Judges 16 28)**

- Amen. Spiritually speaking, God has purpose for your heart break. God's purpose for our soul is to slay more demonic forces in our spiritual death than we did when we were fully alive to our flesh!

- *Ever went through something so horrific and you thought, I'd rather be dead then feel this pain?*

- This is the very state where we should choose to look to the Father and choose selflessness. With the choices we make we set ourselves up for heart break after heart break until we see God as the "Lord God" ruler of all. Sampson didn't feel worthy of God's mercy so he prayed according to how he felt. Sampson chose a natural death, but God being so into us wants us to know that it is a spiritual death He desires of us and only through this will unconditional love flourish. Only though this will selflessness take place, and we will begin to be able to slay demonic spirits left and right by bearing the fruits of the spirit. After God sent Jesus to the earth Jesus died to Himself followed by a physical death and then was resurrected and all power was given to Him. Because of God through Jesus, now we are only required one spiritual death and one spiritual resurrection! After this process and the receiving of the Holy Ghost, God gives us the power to tread over scorpions and serpents.*(Luke 10:19)* And we are in charge through Jesus, of making our own flesh bow down to the will of God. We are then In charge to speak the word and the word only with all authority through Christ Jesus and demonic forces must submit not to us but to the word of God in us. Satan and his demonic forces only obey the word of God. This is why we experience the baptism. This symbolize Jesus' death (going under the water) and his resurrection (being lifted out of the water) The spiritual death and resurrection happens through baptism to the cross. This death was for you and I. To show us what we must do. We must die that spiritual death from sin and ways of the flesh, and be resurrected again through Jesus Christ all while bearing our cross.

- *The like figure whereunto even baptism doth also now save us (not the putting away of the filth of the flesh, but the answer of a good conscience toward God) by the resurrection of Jesus Christ. (Colossians 2:12) buried with him in baptism, wherein also ye are risen with him through the faith(spiritual) of the operation of God, who hath raised him from the dead. And you being dead in your sins and the uncircumcision of your flesh, hath he quickened together with him, having forgiven you all trespasses:* Amen! *(1 Peter 3:21)*

- The bible says *they that worship me must worship in spirit and in truth.* How can we worship in spirit unless we have died the death of brokenness to selflessness and put on the spirit of God. The spirit of truth. While going through spiritual death people will talk about you, laugh at you, lie on you, persecute you and push very hard to uncover your nakedness all while showing the "act" of caring for you. It would appear like they are offering you water to others who really thinking that it is, but they are putting vinegar in your mouth burning the open wounds of broken flesh and the hot tears coming down your face because it too, is burning the very wounds God allowed them to cost you. Do you come down off the cross and save yourself? Do you endure as a good solider knowing that Jesus is your reward and your spiritual resurrection will be full of grace, truth, mercy, and juicy fruits of the spirit -they will not only feed you, but your kids, neighbors, and all that comes in contact with you. Jesus comes that we may have life and have it more abundantly. This can't happen if we don't follow the way of Jesus Christ! A brokenness will lead to selflessness! It is No other way around it. A lot of people are dead while they yet breath. Those reborn in Jesus are living while yet breathing. Never to die again. To be absent from the body is to be present with the Lord! Praise God! Most of us still deal with the natural death of Jesus, because we are in a natural state of mind. 80% of the time natural and 20% of the time we are spiritual and this time is spent in church listening to a preacher. The true divine beauty in brokenness is that God can put us back together again any way He likes. We become a recreation and some pieces God may even decide not to use. We become a more beautifully defined us in Christ Jesus! To be broken is to be whole in God. The more broken we become, the more God gives us a touch of Him, the more of a master piece we will transform to be for Him. Brokenness is not easy but it is very necessary. This is a great way to show ones submission to God. Ever heard of generationally cursed? These curses must be broken off of your life. These curses will make sure you don't have a chance at experiencing freedom even from birth, so this brokenness is needed and necessary to even break these curses while in the process. From these broken pieces, God is closest to us. In this place we can very easily level up on our tears and cleanse our souls as well. Next time someone asks you how you feel, reply "broken". This is a beautiful thing.

- ***Signs of being broken:***

  The feeling of being alone with know one to talk to about how you actually feel and what you're going through.

  The feeling that the world is crumbling down around you and you have no stable ground to stand on.

  The feeling that you may loose your mind from being in situations that you have not bargained for and have no control over.

  The feeling that those you love the most continually let you down.

  The feeling that even though others are around, you'll always be alone.

  The feeling of being helpless and hopeless.

  The feeling of no way out .

  The feeling that God is really the only one you have.

- These are feelings that let you know brokenness is taken place, and if we go through this critical phase correctly, selflessness follows shortly after, and we become closer to Jesus because now we can actually relate. Flesh will have us to believe that being broken is horrific, but our spirit man needs this in order to prevail and allow God to get glory out of us. When going through brokenness, allow your mind to picture you already out and on your way to being a more beautifully made effective you. This to will give you strength to travel the journey of being transformed into selfless. True sons and daughters of God desire to level up to where Jesus was when He walked on the earth. Many believers only want to level up to where the pastor is. This is only because they may still be able to see sin on the leader and this makes them more comfortable with where they are in sin in their own lives. True pastors encourage people to reach and be like Jesus...not them. The truth is, Jesus is coming back and we must meet the standard no matter what or no matter who doesn't, "you have too", because God has commissioned us. From brokenness to selflessness to a more beautiful, effective, and sold out you!

Behind The Veil
_What Time Is It

Time is something we all relate to just about every day! We have scheduled times for shopping, work, football games, dental appointments, dance classes, etc.

What time was your baby born?

What time is the wedding?

Time to eat everyone!

Have you ever thought that maybe God is into time as well? Of coarse!! He's the inventor of time! Time is of God. It should never be a day that we don't look at our watch and see Jesus. Or have a set time to do something for Him besides our church schedule every week.

Ever tried to be in a relationship with someone without spending time with them?

What happened is you grew apart. Making quality time for God is one of the most important things we can do as children of God! *"I never knew you,"* is definitely not the words we are looking to hear from our savior! *Do you have specific prayer times through the day set aside for God?*

Just times to say something sweet to Him is a blessing. He looks forward to hearing that you need Him, or hearing/seeing that you cared enough to memorize something He said. God has feelings!!! How do you think it makes Father feel when millions of people believe on Him, who don't believe on Jesus, but they consistently pray around the clock to Him? Unfortunately He does not accept the prayers because they are not in Jesus name. Here "we" are being His sons and daughters yet not offering up prayers to Him because we don't have time. It's like having so many beautiful houses to live in but the Realtor wont let you bring your children with you. The houses that does allow you to bring your kids are run down. Sometimes the water is working…sometimes the lights are on and sometimes not. The run down houses relate to the prayer life and dedication of Christianity as a whole. The beautiful well maintained houses relate to other belief systems that are dedicated and sold out to God but do not believe in Jesus. We to can offer God a well kept place of habitation where His son is not only welcomed but we pray in His name as well! I believe and pray that God will save many that are not of the fold because their dedication is beautiful!

> **16** And other sheep I have, which are not of this fold:
> them also I must bring, and they shall hear my voice;
> and there shall be one fold, and one shepherd **John 10:16**

You ever wanted someone to spend time with you but they were always to busy and when they finally did come to spend time, they rushed through it with a world of other stuff on their mind?

Doesn't feel to good.

"See then that ye walk circumspectly, not as fools, but as wise, 16)Redeeming the time, because the days are evil. 17)wherefore be ye not unwise, but understanding what the will of the Lord is. 18)And be not drunk with wine, wherein is excess; but be filled with the spirit. 19) speaking to yourselves in psalms and hymns and spiritual songs singing and making melody in your heart to the Lord. 20)Giving thanks always for all things unto God and the father in the name of our Lord Jesus Christ;

*The Lord wants us to indulge in Him! It's really not to much to ask I mean after all, He does give us breath everyday to do so!" (**Ephesians 5 15-20**)*

"To every thing their is a season and a time to every purpose under the heaven: A time to be born, and a time to die: A time to plant, and a time to pluck up that which is planted; A time to kill, and a time to heal; a time to break down, and a time to build up; A time to weep, and a time to laugh; a time to mourn and a time to dance: a time to cast away stones, and a time to gather stones together, a time to embrace, and a time to refrain from embracing; a time to get and a time to lose; a time to keep, and a time to cast away. a time to rend, and a time to sew; a time to keep silence, and a time to speak: a time to love and a time to hate; a time of war and a time of peace." **(Ecclesiastics 3 1-8)**

Wow! The Word of God has established all these times, and how we reflect on our own lives.

<u>How often do we look at the clock to make sure we are not late for a personal agenda concerning God?</u>

I've gotten to where I set my alarm clock for prayer times to say sweet words to God. Jesus looks forward to these conversations! God wants to fellowship more with you!

What time or times are you willing to give him everyday?

He looks forward to connecting with those who loves when He bring His child with Him!!!

CHAPTER 6

The reassurance of Silence

Ever took a major test that made or broke your grade?

In this testing room you would have more or less seen one teacher with many students around taking the same test with the same number two pencil and the same bubble answer sheet with similar questions as yours. Even though you may have been nervously sweating the quietness in the room reassured you concentration and also that you were on testing grounds. Even though the reassurance of quietness was not something really discussed it was just something you expected to happen. No bright teacher would allow you to use the excuse that you made a bad grade because the class was to noisy and you couldn't concentrate during test time. Their would be no talking except to the teacher.

Have you ever taken a major test with your whole class loud and playing music?

I would think not.

Silence gives us the ability to concentrate and to focus. Another example of silence being golden is when you were younger do you ever recall asking your parents are guardians something and they gave you an answer you did not care to hear? So you went back in faith again a little later and you got the same answer? Then you decided a couple of hours later to go back one more time in hope for a different answer by a miracle and something unexpected happens this time. This time when you went to ask the same question to the same person this unique moment you got "silence". You receive no answer and this reassurance of silence let you know you had better go with the last answer received. This thing is all to familiar to our Lord and Savior Jesus Christ! As He went through the same thing with our Father which art in heaven. That reassurance of silence let Jesus know to go with the last answer He had received concerning this matter. Taking a glance at *(Matthew 26 vs 29,42,44)*

> *Jesus asked oh my Father if it be possible let this cup pass from me. Nevertheless not as I will but as thou wilt.*

Jesus prayed this prayer for the third time and got the reassurance of silence letting Him know that the last answer He received concerning this matter was still in effect.

How many of you are going through a test today and you keep asking God the same question but you're getting that reassurance of silence?

It's only to let you know to be still and go with the last answer God has given you. God loves you so much, but Just like when you're taking a test in class the teacher, like God, is silent. Often times this confuses the believer. They wonder why God is not verbal in the center of their crisis. It's because He is the teacher in our trial and He wants to see what you will do without direction. Have you taken notes from what He has been teaching you? Have you studied to show yourself approved? What God is looking for during this sabbatical is to see if you tell the enemy what is written like Jesus did on the mountain or will we try to fight the devil with flesh and blood. This is why God's word and the reassurance of silence will show us what level we are on and what grade we have made every time.

What grades are you making concerning these spiritual test?

If you just take a few minutes to look back on some of your major testing in life it felt like God was not present to our prayers /rants that go a little like this;

*"Lord why wont you talk to me or answer me? I need you,
I need direction! I need answers! Why have you turned
your face from me?"*

<u>When the truth of the matter is, what good teacher you know personally
that gives out all the answers during a test?</u>

I'll wait........ The whole point of a test is to see what you have learned
and what lessons need to be reassigned to you. When you think of
taking an actual test most authentic teachers will allow no talking. They
don't talk to you either allowing you to focus on your material and they
monitor you paying close attention to you to make sure of no cheating,
talking, or file play. So while God is so close to us during our testing
times He monitors us but often we don't understand the process so we
keep failing the test because of complaining and using our instrument
of tears to glorify the devil by saying God must not care or He would
be helping us or coaching us but what *have we learned is the question?*

What you have learned will 100% out of 100% show up in testing
scores! God is ready to take us higher but we must stop failing the same
coarse. The next time you desire to commune with God and you get that
reassurance of silence, look around and check to see if you're in a test.
If so then pass it with flying colors. Make sure moves and sure strides.
Always utilize all tools necessary because this is an open book test.
Gather all the knowledge and wisdom and even what you have learned
and you will ace this test.

> *Study to shew thyself approved unto God, a workman
> that needeth not to be ashamed, rightly dividing the word
> of Truth!*
>
> ### (2Timothy 2:15)

In a test we must be prepared and forever knowing that our teacher is
very close monitoring our actions, words, motives and comprehension.
Yes, and important part of the test is comprehension. We must
understand what it was or is that we're going through in order for God
to get the glory through our testimonies and witnessing to others about

how He brought us out. Without understanding our trials We repay God with many complaints of what's not fair. But when we understand the wisdom of the trial, then we go through it with complete confidence and with praises to our Kingdom Father! The testing process must be understood by those confessing Jesus Christ! Sometimes the Lord test us then other times the Lord allows the enemy to test us.

Are we pulling out spiritual grade up?

Let's not be flunking students because we choose not to study the book. Like with Jesus, the spirit of God led Him to the wilderness to be tested of the enemy and God is always close by to record your grade and your final answer should be *"It is written."* Now you see 10s all across the board! Anything outside of the word is a failing grade. The Lord allowed Job to be tested of the enemy and God was close by with that reassurance of silence at first to show that Job was righteous and faithful. It's time to ace these test and go higher in God because God is about elevation. When you're in that place of that quietness just know that it is on and popping and the spot light of the Holy Spirit **IS..... ..ON........ YOU!** Sharpen your pencils, buckle down, and start with "It is written!"

- **Behind The Veil**

  _Inspect The Fruit

A worm nesting inside an apple did not have to crawl inside it to make the apple it's habitat. This worm was born their. The apple is not only worm's home, but its supermarket as well. Nasty, I know!!! Here's how it all happens.

During the summer, small fruit flies can be found buzzing around orchards. These are called apple maggot flies. Each female finds herself a sweet smelling apple that is ripening and lands on it. Using a small, sharp, hollow tube on the under side of her body, the fly stabs a small hole in the fruit. Then she releases her eggs, which slide down that hollow tube into the apple. Soon afterwards, the eggs hatch into tiny white worms, in no way resembling their mother. These worms are called "railroad worms". All during the summer and into the fall, the "always hungry " worms nourish themselves by munching tunnels in the apple. When the apples are ripe in the fall and drop from the tree, the worms crawl out and burrow into the ground. Their, a hard outer skin develops on each worm's body. This hard skin becomes a winter home for the worm in the ground. It is inside this winter home that the worm becomes an apple maggot fly.

The following summer, the fly breaks open the skin, emerges, and begins to fly about the orchard. Then the entire process begins all over again!(Broadenme.tumblr.com)

- When God trust us with spiritual fruit, He also expects for us to maintain the up keep on it. If we choose to allow fruit flies to hang around our orchard we must expect worms to be apart of our harvest! We must become expectant of contamination to be transferred to others when we teach, preach, and prophecy goes forth because our fruit is sweet but it's tainted. Sometimes we don't feel like our gossiping friend or thieving lying associates are maggot flies laying eggs in our fruit because they are our friends, but these eggs are indeed laid. We look to have a promising harvest, and we think our fruits of love, joy, and peace is fine not knowing that, always hungry, worms are feasting on it and when we need to use peace in a chaotic situation we either can't find it, or because it's not pure anymore, we demonstrate peace but inwardly we have taken sides against someone else. This is ought against someone. This is tainted peace. You can look at people that seem to posses beautiful fruit but step on their toes and watch the explosion and the draw backs! Tainted joy is when worldly things can pull you down in the dumps. Tainted long suffering is when you only exercise longsuffering with your maggot fly friends and know one else. We must Be a fruit inspector but make sure we inspect our fruit first because it will depend on whether God chooses to use us or not! God is looking for someone who actually have fruit that is sharable and can transform someone else's life. This is how He receives the glory!

CHAPTER 7

Downsizing In Order To Upsize

- With all the daily life struggles, noisy interstates, coworkers on our jobs buzzing by in laughter, some on

- telephone calls, some with swearing on their lips, phones ringing, loud speaker announcements, children crying, men joking around with excitement, husband furious or wanting some quality time, wife disturbed about things of life, the smell of bread burning in the oven, the house smoked out, fire detector sounding off, home work help is needed for the kids, clothes need to be washed, dried, and put away- your car is turning into a second home' stuff is everywhere and just then you remember the cat hasn't eaten in three days! With all these things that go on in our noisy lives we grab the conception that God is supposed to be noisy also. I can see why we get so distraught and uncomfortable sometimes when two people are in a room and it's just silence. A lot of times we complain and mummer because God doesn't fit in our busy loud world but this was never the reason we were sent to this earth. We were sent to glorify God in the earth realm and to fit into His plan by praying the Lord's prayer that His kingdom would come in the earth as it is in heaven. We were to fit into His plan not He into ours, of making a life and running after earthly things then getting multiple jobs to pay for these earthly things. We shouldn't expect God to become noisy like the rest of our lives, but we as ladies should take the time out and turn aside to a peaceable quiet place and allow God to replenish us. Allow God to speak and give direction for the day. Allow God to show you the plan He has for you. How do we do this you might be wondering. Let's look closely at Peter and Andrew in *(Matthew 4:19)*

- Jesus saw these two men working for they were fishermen, and Jesus said follow me and I will make you fishers of men.

- *(Matthew 4:19)*

- Peter and Andrew did this supernatural thing of leaving their job to follow Christ.

- *Is this supernatural?*

- Well, it's not natural these days to leave your place of making money just like that, to follow someone you hardly know. These days you may get one in a million to do this but this person "has" to have a heart after God and leans on the scriptures for dear life. Like scriptures containing to

- *But seek ye first the kingdom of God, and his righteousness; and all these things shall be added to you. (Matthew 6:33)*

- These men downsized in natural things in order to upsize in the Kingdom of God. Of coarse Peter and Andrew didn't have their flesh burning for a Lexus jeep with factory rims, a Monticello, a house to make the neighbors envious, shoes that just hit the shelves this morning; the latest high tech electronics and things to this nature, and because of this they were able to make such a kingdom investment until their names are still ringing on the lips of people today!

- *What are the reasons today that our Kingdom investment is small and sometimes none?*

- It's because satan has waved his deceitful lust of the eye in front of people and now because we have taken part in this demonic attack and influence, we have to work ourselves to a pulp just to make ends meet for things we have acquired. We try to keep the items our flesh so lust after, therefore making less time to turn aside and be in the place God has called us to be in. Allow me to give an example of how this works.

- Ex: *Ashley and Tara arrived at work at the same time. Luckily Ashley had already paid the meter up for the week so she stepped out her beautiful vehicle in a rush when Tara stopped her and said, "wow....I can't feed the meter for looking at your designer heels. I must have a pair. How much did they cost?" She asked with her eyes dancing. "Did they set you back?" (Both ladies start to giggle not knowing truly that things like this does set you back) Ashley replies, "oh just 350.00. They were actually on sale ", she boasts. Both ladies enter the workplace. Tara purposing in her heart that the next 350.00 she receive is already accounted for.*

- Ladies when will the madness end? It's past time for us to realize the devices of satan that causes us to work like slaves in order to achieve things our flesh wants. Job had an excellent spirit and his heart was upright toward God. Job was also a rich man because of this. God was even able to allow the enemy to test Job and everything he had. His body, his kids, his wife, but Job stayed faithful and God restored everything back unto Job plus some. These days we look at the bible and even know the miracle of sacrificing for Jesus but we refuse to relate to it. We truthfully passively think, wow, that was a great story for that time and era, and we rejoice when this is preached but who actually allow this to be written on the tables of their heart and say God not another day will things I want replace you. Just think of somethings you could sacrifice for the Lord and I promise you, this will give you more time to turn aside and turn into purpose. I'm not telling you to quit your jobs, no. But I am saying their are things that can be done like:

- #1 down sizing our cable packages,(and those who are really serious about getting God's attention, even get rid of your favorite channel too) lust of the eyes is one of satan's main cards that he use. Who else do you know can beat generation after generation with only three playing cards?

- #2 Do we really need to get the most expensive vehicle in town when we can't afford it?

- #3 Designer purses are very nice, but honestly are you buying it because it has safe padding inside to keep your valuables from getting broken 100% money back guaranteed, or are we purchasing these items knowing we really can't afford to? Do you have to pick up extra shifts or cut short another bill because we can't wait to see the look on others faces that you actually have the bag they wanted? Or do you just have to have the bag first now everyone will want to run out and get one?

- The saddest excuse I've heard so far is, *"I'm a daughter of the King, the Lord wants me to look good and have nice things."* My question to us is, are we sure? Another question is;

- *Why would God want us to look good when we barley spend time with Him?*

- *Why would your husband or man friend want to bedazzle you with fine things and finances to be looking ever so debonair when you're not going to be spending any time at all with him?*

- *Why does "God" want your nails done?*

- *Why would "God" desire you to sport designer clothes?*

- *Please a lot the reason "God" loath for you to obtain and contain the latest technology available, and the most fad rad car out?*

- *Have you ever just tune your ear to those who highly speak of the way God wants them to have the finer things in life?*

- The only reason God would bless one is to glorify Himself and to show what He is capable of or because of one's fatefulness and sacrifice to and for Him (this includes sacrificing for one another) are we sacrificing for Jesus by feeding the hungry and serving the ill?

- *Are we much more sacrificing one bill to get our hair, nails and feet done?*

- *Are we sacrificing by taking our boats out on the beach's because young George Trailer the lll is graduating and the celebration we will throw will cause a couple thousand dollars?* Somewhere between us ladies holding our homes together -be it helping our husbands work or being a single mom and living in this fin for yourself world, somewhere we fell short and got side tracked. We allowed the devil to whisper into our ears and tell us "you deserve so much more," just like he convinced Eve. From listening to the enemy, we decided to get up off our knees and go get it ourselves. All in *the name of "Jesus wants me to have this."* In this matter, it's a lie that satan has given us in order to distract us, to get us caught up with no oil in our lamps. One thing the bible never spoke of, but I believe this like I believe my name is Melanie. The five foolish virgins may not have been able to go in with the bride groom, because they didn't have any oil but I'm of a surety that each had a Channel #5 bag, with branded pumps, fashion tailored designer clothing, hair laid to the side, pearls and earrings that sparkle for days and to top it off some Ed hardy perfume!! (*Can you smell me now*) These girls were "ready "for the king you hear me!!! They realized at the last minute that the King of kings had no regard for these things. (Yes the bible says for us to adorn ourselves, but not make ourselves our own idol, or anyone else's for that matter)

- *The smelling of the perfume is sweet like candy but do we smell like the Savior?*

- The ladies realized while they banged on the door that they had prepared for the wrong king, and they were swallowed up by the darkness of night. They had been fooled into being foolish.

- *And while they went to buy, the bridegroom came; and they that were ready went in with Him to the marriage; and the door was shut. (**Matthew 25:10**)*

- So many young and older ladies are preparing for the wrong king. The foolish went to the store (as they were accustomed to doing) and I'm sure they had their charge cards ready! Those cards were burning up with so much action, but the question is does all the spending really make us happy, or is it a temporary fix because we're looking for fulfillment in a second glance of someone who cares nothing for us. These women could not use their master, visa, or American express to get in to the bride groom. (they should have spent more time manicuring the heart)

- *Is it okay to shop?*

- "WHAT ARE YOU SERIOUS? OF COARSE IT'S OKAY TO SHOP. THAT'S WHAT WE GIRLS DO!" But their is a crossing the line though when it comes to overdoing it. Back in the day the ladies would every then and again buy a couple yards of fabric to make 6 beautiful items and this was usually around the holidays and birthdays when they splurged a little. These ladies were able to stay home and keep up the children, while husband worked and brought home enough to sustain the entire family. They didn't have to have the biggest anything! They lived within their means. The simple life! I realize times has made a drastic change and people are not who they used to be. Their are more single moms now and bills still have to be paid, and a way still must be made. I commend all mothers that are working through sweat and tears and lonely nights. You're still providing with the

Lord's help. Praise the living God! While doing this fantastic and tiresome job their is one small dilemma. We sometimes feel like if we had a mate then things would be so much more easy! Wheeew we would be able to do this and do that, but please take a minute to regroup. If we don't regroup even though these feelings are natural emotions, it can mess us up. Each year ending we get more determined and more desperate to find this mate. "The mate" at this point of waiting and waiting becomes "A mate" and at this point it's even more dangerous for us and our children, because we start trying to make this happen and how do we do this but to go shopping and max out our cards on apparel that men "must" take a second look at. We do this by adorning our outward appearance buying books on "how to make Him mine", playing games, and all these things- in our desperation this consumes us. (We turn into the five foolish) we eat, sleep and think of how to catch this man, how it will be when this man is caught, and how the lives of our children will change. Once we picture our children running, playing, and laughing with this gentleman from far away land, this makes us plot even more. Keeping up with the latest fashions and trends, spending money that should be saved and before we know it we are identifying perfectly with The five foolish virgins.

- How?

- Because our attentions can become so stuck on how to make this happen until this becomes 90% of what we are. God is calling for us to downsize this part of our minds that has nothing to do with Him and upsize thinking like Christ the Holy One! The devil always try to enter through our emotions, and so this is how he wins. He gets us going after what we want so hard until we miss the true King like the five foolish virgins. They did possess lamps though and we say we are daughters of God. Their lamps had no oil....do we, being daughters, have oil? Are we giving our oil seeking time to seeking a man? The bible says in

- *Whoso findeth a wife findeth a good thing, and obtaineth favor of the Lord. (**Proverbs 18:22**)*

- So we must allow our man of God to find us. But handmaidens, let's let him find us on the altar "getting oil" and not in the mall at Dillard's in the spandex section. A real Godly man wants his lady to cover her body parts and not show every dimple and varicose vein! We must downsize in order to upsize. The bible says whoso findeth a "wife" findeth a good thing. A wife is already married! This man who finds a lady who is already married finds a good thing? Yes, because she is already married to HIM!! A wife knows how to be just that. God has already taught her how to submit to higher authority. She's already married to Jesus and / crying out for more deliverance. She has a real relationship with God the creator and He in turn gives her what it takes to be that phenomenal wife, and the man that finds "this wife " gains favor with the Lord. So let's gain our territory back and stomp the devil's head in to the white meat! Let's pull out of getting the latest jeans and the latest perfumes even though we have a whole bottle we just bought a few weeks ago at home. Let's hault flesh from driving us to the place of beating on a door that has already closed. I decree right now that flesh no longer drives us to find someone that should find us, or going to get expensive things just to make someone who does not like us anyway, jealous! We must regroup as children of God. It's imperative that we rill it in and put flesh on a leash. It must die. The next time you are in a super market and a lady passes by that smells fabulous, yes give a compliment if you like, no don't ask where can you find that fragrance! The flesh is so greedy. It's okay for someone to actually have something that you don't. Let's down size the flesh and lift up our spirit man. Our spirits are crying out. We must surrender and be transformed. When being married to the Most High, we then turn our attention to what "He likes" and what "He wants" and when this is done God will willingly trust us with one of His sons, knowing that we wont love man more than we love the God of man.

- *Single ladies, are you married?*

- Only Jesus in the relationship will make it grow. If we continue on the path of the foolish virgins, yes a man may come and you may possibly even get married but happiness will be know where near it because the joy of the Lord is our strength.

- Nehemiah *8:10* says *Let's wait on God*, and you'll be so happy you did. He makes it worth your while every time. From this day forward we must think on our oil.

- *Seek ye first the Kingdom of God and His righteousness and all these other things "will be added".* (**Matthew** 6:33)

- The enemy never intends for us to believe this verse but we shall believe and error no longer. God is so proud of us for making such a courageous step! Downsizing in order to upsize! After Abraham found Sarah, she honored him by calling him lord. (*1 Peter 3:6*) but if you notice even in the bible that "l" is lower case. This means yes by all means honor and serve and forever be submissive to your husband but God is the Lord of lords! (Capital L always) Check it out Hand maidens! When we fall in line our lives will take shape and the Lord(capital L) will go above and beyond transforming us into Kingdom for His dwelling!

- **Behind The Veil**

- **_HELLO**

- We walk around day in and day out encountering people with super good attitudes!

- *Do you know any one who can have a bad day but still find time to brighten up someone else's day?*

- *Do you believe that a good attitude can take you further up than a nasty one?*

- **Note*** Our attitude determine our altitude in how high we go in God!

- We can never achieve a **G0OD** attitude without **G0D!** To try to actually achieve having a G O O D attitude without G O D we only have one letter left and that's "0"! (**G00d-G0d=0**)

- "0" I didn't know that my ways offended God.

- "0" I didn't know I had a serpent tongue tarring off the heads of true ones walking by faith and not by sight.

- "0" I didn't know I had the spirit of betrayal like Judas, and like Eve to betray the trust of God.

- "0" I didn't know God actually cared how I treat my neighbors!

- "0" becomes dangerous in this equation formula (*G00D -G0D=0*) because it's only one place meant and prepared just for the 0's of life. Those that will choose to be in the "0" line, has just one more formula to complete and it's concerning the destiny of the "0"s! (**HELL+0= Hell'0**) Hell is stretching it's belly for all the "0"s of the world! Hell and "0" just goes together!

- *Hell'0',* did you not believe that I would come back for a people without spot or wrinkle?

- *Hell'0',* because you chose not to take me seriously and all your life used the formula (**G00d-G0d**) You actually get to witness Hell is real.

- Don't be a "0" I didn't know! Take up your cross and follow Jesus!

- *That He might present it to Himself a glorious church, not having spot or wrinkle, or any such thing; but that it should be holy and without blemish!* **Ephesians 5:27**

- The "0"s will pay a dear price! (Hell+0) it just goes together! In hell all the 0's will be crying "0" Jesus but it will be long to late. Let's purpose in our hearts today that no longer will we be passive about striving for and achieving the attitude of God! He's waiting on us to set the "0" mentality aside and actually take accountability for our daily walk with Him!

CHAPTER 8

Organic Revelatory Mannah

Question:

How can a devil deceive many for generations with only three playing cards?

Answer:

Because the fleshly body is equipped to respond to these three cards at any given time, and it's only through Christ Jesus that we can respond a different way to these three cards that has made many generations fall.

The lust of the flesh, the lust of the eye, and the pride of life.

Have you ever seen something that you just knew you had to have?

Almost like even if you had to not eat for a week to get it you wanted it. Their was not only any second thinking about it you had your heart set and your mind comprehended and you had to have it no matter what. Most of us don't understand where we are because we don't understand where we came from. Let's start from the beginning shall we ladies:

Naturally: in the beginning we were a fetus in mommy's tummy.
Spiritually: *John 6:44; No man can come to me except the Father which has sent me draw him and I will raise him up at the last day* amen. (this is the beginning in God. We must first be drawn)

So let's talk about you as a fetus. Around week 15 naturally: your eye lids were still fused shut but if someone was to shine a light on mom's belly even through all that flesh and fluid you would respond in one way or another; by moving toward the light or away from it. Mostly fetuses choose to move away from the beam of light.

Spiritually: it doesn't matter how fleshed out a person is they should still be able to see the light of Christ in someone carrying it and respond either by moving away or drawing near. In week 19 you as a fetus started to develop your senses: smell, sight, touch, taste, and hearing. At this stage you were pretty much able to hear mom's voice and around week 23 your ears got better picking up sound. Even after birth as a newborn you still recognized specific sounds you remembered hearing inside the womb. Referring back to gestation, during week 28 your eye sight was developed so," we heard first."

Now let's glance back at our spiritual beginning again. **Gen 1:3** "God said". This is dealing with the ears also! Why would one say anything if nothing could listen and respond. God said, the earth heard, responded, and it was so! We, as earth, heard first. Here in **Gen 3:1** the "serpent said." He realized that earth responds to words and dealt with the ears also trying to follow the footsteps of God. Eve was the recipient of hearing the serpent's words. As a result Eve's ears opened her up to see and in *Gen 3:6*

> *"Eve saw that tree was good for food and pleasant to the eyes and the tree to be desired to make one wise she took of the fruit thereof and did eat and gave also unto her husband with her and he did eat."*

This shows satan's first recordings of using the three wild cards he has.(*1John 2:16*)In this very order did Eve sin. The lust of the flesh, the lust of the eye, the pride of life so the enemy attacked the ears first by spiritually touching Eve with his words and by him spiritually touching, she gained the courage to touched the forbidden fruit. (Like we do today) Before Adam and Eve's existence, it was a spoken word. "God said", and it came to pass. "Adam said"

> *"she's bone of my bone and flesh of my flesh. She shall*
> *be called woman. Therefore shall a man leave his father*
> *and mother and cleave to his wife becoming one flesh"*
> **Gen 2 vs 23:24**

So "Adam said "and it came to pass. They were walking in a spoken word ministry. Things happened and became law because it was spoken. The bible shows that ultimately Adam and Eve was fooled by the serpent and Adam by taking part of the forbidden fruit as the head made "motion into law not spoken ". Adam laid hands on this thing, and now we lay hands to reverse the curse off people whether it be sickness or evil spirits, torments, failing at prospering, poverty, or to impart. Adam made motion into law not spoken.

> **(Mark 16:18)** *They shall take up serpents; and if they*
> *drink any deadly thing it shall not hurt them: they shall*
> *lay hands on the sick, and they shall recover.*

Just because Adam sinned doesn't mean things he had done in the past changed. Every single animal was still named the same thing! Adam called Eve woman and women are still being called woman today. So Adam in perseness made motion into law not spoken (his action and not his spoken word became the new normal) and so instead of having faith to receive off spoken words only, many need the laying on of hands in order to believe, because now we believe we need that physical touch in order to believe. Some places in the bible, Jesus walked in this spoken word because that person's level of faith reached out to before the forbidden fall, and all Jesus had to say was "go, sin no more " or "go, your faith has made thee hold. **(Mark 5_28)** The woman with the issue of blood, needed that physical touch. That "motion" made into law without spoken word standing affirm. This doesn't make her in any way unbelieving. She did believe! One touch made her whole! She actually drew virtue from Jesus!! But Going back to the beginning in **Gen 3:7** *And they knew they were naked.* Think spiritually here: so they sewed fig leaves together to hide themselves. Notice Jesus cursed the fig tree later for having the appearance of fruit but not actually having any.

(False witness) Figs,... Yeah....not my favorite fruit! They hid because they knew they were naked.

Picture this. ...you're in the mall shopping for things you need and want. You used to be this super spiritual one on one with God type person doing what it takes and your leader loved you and much depended on you for different parts of ministry and all of a sudden you fall back, not going to church anymore, the world has swallowed you up. Now you're in the mall just having a little leisure time and you see this preacher, your preacher.

Do you hide?
Most often times yes.
Were you naked when you hid?
Of coarse not! (Not completely anyway)
But spiritually you felt uncovered right?
So you hid!! So Adam and Eve spiritually hid themselves as well.

> (**Hab 1:13**) *Thou art of purer eyes than to behold evil, and canst not look on iniquity.*

So God asked Adam where are you? God only looks upon Himself! This doesn't mean run wild because God is blind. NOT SO!(Our angels do report everything said and done by us every day!) (man look on the outward appearance, God looks at the heart) (God sees all and knows all. Know one can hide from him.) In this case God said where are you because Adam had broken the oneness he had with Father. These two had taken on the carnal mindset which brings us to the point of the "carnal scences " and *the deactivating of the devil*. Did you know that God gave us five spiritual scences that He wants so desperately for us to tap back into and by us taking this leap of faith, we can leap over the tactics of satan in our Lives! Wow, I know! Even from the very beginning satan tried to offset the plan and Destiny God had/has for us by trying to bring early perversion. Here we are today battling to take these layers of carnal clothes off to get back spiritually naked so God Himself, can walk with us and talk to us one on one again. Without the Lord and His wisdom we are meat for the slaughter. Often we try to perceive things that are spiritual naturally! This tend to cause us to error 100% of the time! One of the saddest things to me is when someone has made it up in their mind to do good and they still error for lack of wisdom and knowledge.

For example, the Lord has opened my eyes up to how vitally important it is to eat healthy! When God take control of an area in your life He does not half step. When He is done with you realize that even the way you thought was improved was very much so NOT! When God started bringing it to my attention how even the so called vegetable and fruit in the Market sold by producers are full of ingredients that over time cause toxic illnesses and ultimately lead to death or improper organ functioning of some sort. So when I visit the super market I can't help but notice those who seemed to have made up their mind to make healthier choices but not knowing that that fruit They are choosing over only has 1% of what it's supposed to have if that. Not knowing that the fruits or vegetables they are purchasing will never rot because they were made in a laboratory or cloned off other seeds etc. This stuff is real! I say all this to say that it takes the mind of Christ to understand God and not the mind of the carnal man. (Www.infowars.com Food: The ultimate Secret Exposed)(Eat organic as much as you can)

Take a look at this: Adam and Eve hid themselves behind fig leaves because they didn't want to be seen by God. They said they were naked. Today people take their clothes "off" because they DON'T WANT to be seen as naked. Go figure!

Today ladies expose the exterior body parts because they don't want the true exposure from the inside to be revealed. We've taken part of another knowledge that says it's okay! If you got it flaunt it. We expose our bodies in every way because this is what we want them to see when they look at us. Adam and Eve's insides were exposed while walking around naked. They hid nothing from God! They were open and honest, but as soon as they were disobedient they were shame-they took of another knowledge and knew they were naked therefore switching mindset that being spiritually naked is shameful and embarrassing. They chose to hide behind a curse which represents the fig leaves. They switched the joys of having spiritual fruit for heart ache and pain of having cursed fruit become their portion.

They tried to cover up, and with fig leaves which Jesus later cursed. This is spiritual. We to, walk around transparent until we feel grown and want to create a name for ourselves. Then we hide behind a curse as well. God can't help those hiding behind curses from Him.

So now we walk around naturally showing our body parts wearing revealing tight clothing because we are hiding behind fig leaves. We are fearful that if we put on clothing, people will look pass our appearance and see the real us(like God, who looks at the heart) .... our personality... who we really are inside, and that we are really hurting or depressed, It Exposes our insides then making us spiritually "naked" and vulnerable. You take these same people and minister a word of the Lord to them and tell them about their life and what they're going through and they just cry and cry and cry because deep down we really desire God's nakedness and not satan's. satan has all types of soul ties, diseases, and more demonic spirits tied to it designed to drag the person down while chasing a false love called lust. But God's nakedness promises freedom and the true experience of love! See the deception of the devil? The enemy has deceived many into believing a lie! YES God wants us to be naked! AT ALL TIMES!!! But they that worship God MUST worship in "Spirit" and truth. To walk around naturally naked today is to hide behind the curse of the fig tree. The curse being everything tied to satan's nakedness! Demon spirits! When we choose our nakedness then God chooses our name, Mine or not mine! In the garden it all boiled down to Adam and Eve being disobedient and choosing the wrong nakedness! "WHO TOLD YOU YOU WAS NAKED!?" God wants to know, because being naked before God is being fully clothed naturally! Worldly men can look upon a spiritually naked lady and not get distracted by our breast and butts because their not hanging out but they can actually be able to look at our insides where God is! We become transparent allowing God to manifest and minister to people even with a simple smile or a simple holding the door open for someone allowing them to leave wondering what that presence was that they felt from you and not I wonder was that butt or those breast real. See the difference?

* **Note:** "Nothing about us should pull people's attention away from God's Word and His manifestation in the service!" (I learned this from Apostle Darryl Glenn McCoy!)

This is when God start to trust us with His beauty!!!

Here's another example of how satan has many thinking naturally about spiritual things:

God sent Jesus to earth not as a grown man but as a baby (seed) form. Jesus was chosen before He was even born to die for our sins. We too, while in seed form was chosen by God to die so that others may live! Jesus died to Himself first *"never the less not my will but as thou wilt."* Then the shedding of blood took place. Jesus had to do things naturally because we were a people of natural mindset.

> *Jesus naturally carried that heavy cross!*
> *He was naturally beaten until you could not recognize who He was.*
> *People naturally wanted to throw literal stones to kill Him with.*
> *He naturally drunk from the well.*
> *Jesus naturally fed thousands with two fish 5 loaves of bread.*

Many other things Jesus did which had Spiritual meaning but the natural mindset could only perceive it literally which is why many of the multitude stayed confused and many walked away!

To begin being a daughter of the most high we must do what we were commissioned to do! Father has no respect of person. If Jesus had to under go these things. We have to do complete the mission as well.

Why are we shying back from responsibility?

We're comprehending that we'll die physically if we die out to our flesh. Flesh has fooled us to think this way.

Jesus carried the cross naturally, but God expects us to carry ours spiritually! We don't want to because it's heavy and it cost us friends and family members sometimes.

Jesus fed thousands with little food. Father expects us to do the same spiritually. We don't want to, because We feel like the little bit God has given us can't help nobody find life through Jesus Christ.

People wanted to literally stone Jesus. They throw stones at us with their words (words are spiritual) we run and hid or give in to be liked by people.

People beat Jesus until He was unrecognizable! Father has this same design for us. People beat us with their words and false accusations and false situations that didn't occur. Belittling and destroying our character along with the flesh being crucified my God!

This whole process is to remake, reshape, remold us into someone our enemies and even friends don't recognize anymore! But we don't want to take this journey. We have to step up to the plate and do what has been commissioned of us to do. This is when we stop being a puppet and chasing after words from other men because what or who can replace the words of God? Our five scenes have been so out of tune since after the beginning. Thank God for taking the passion of Christ to the extent that He did because the carnal mind sees blood, lashes, and stripes and we cry and weep and feel convicted about actions we know we can put under the blood and stop. The spiritual man sees the example before Jesus was naturally crucified the example of what we must become. Spiritually our flesh must become so brutally beaten, bruised and even until the point of not being recognized. Only then can the true spirit of God reign and rule in us. So yes people talk about us, lie on us, sew discord among the brethren, try to set up failure traps for us, work against us accomplishing "GG" God Goals, but these are all spiritual lashes on our flesh! We know this because they talked about Jesus also, but He still had to endure even as a good soldier. He had to be brutally beaten. Having our senses all off base and out of whack gives prefect placement for the carnal mind to take control! Because of this carnal mindset people saw and still see the crucifixion of Jesus to be the devil, and yes because of him we see it this way, but Jesus was sent for the remission of sins. So when the devil realized this, and that Jesus five senses was on point and (No carnal mindset) he then began to speak through others around Jesus. "If you be the son of God, free yourself and us too." All sort of things and people were laughing and gambling. But what satan didn't know was when God led Jesus to be tempted by the devil after fasting, that was Jesus's pop quiz then. The devil's carnal mind saw opportunity to make Jesus, the Great One, fall down and worship him, but being spiritually minded God made this test a great pop quiz because when the real test came which had "eternal life" stamped on it, Jesus had to pass. "If you be the son of God" they said. The devil didn't realize Jesus was carrying the finishers anointing. What ever we hang around is what we will become. Jesus didn't let carnal men impart into Him. He surrounded Himself with teachable men, and He began to impart into them, because everything He needed was in our Father. Being spirit led will lead you to the cross every time! You're either led to the cross or led to chains. Now don't think you're being led to the cross because you are ALLOWING your spirit man to be beaten by spirits of witch craft, sorcery and other demonic spirits from false prophets, teachers, preachers, evangelist and Apostolic belief systems, because when this happens the spirit of God does not come, the spirit of oppression, depressions, rebellion, and fowl play set up shop and before you know it you now have become spiritually pregnant with the demonic and officially have a new purpose and that's to see others bound as well. "In the name of Jesus of coarse". Many will say they came in my name, says God, but I will say turn from me ye that worked iniquity I never knew you. The will to rule and reign another person through their emotions is a witchcraft spirit that must be broke!

Why *am I writing this?*

Because God is calling for more from us. We are more carnally minded than we think. We even fast carnally. We feel pressed in our sanctified spirits to announce to certain ones that we are fasting when God said to do this in secret. You can look at the window or you can look through it. Look at a person or at the soul or spirit of that person. God Almighty wants to bring us to a point where we are not just looking at the surface of things. Your ears can hear words or hear spirits and motives. You can touch things, food, items, or you can touch the hearts of people with spoken word. You can smell that yummy cake in the oven and that's it, or you can smell victory in Jesus. We can taste good food, or we can taste and see that the Lord is good! *(Eph 5:2)* This scripture talks about Jesus being that sweet aroma.

They that worship must worship Jesus in spirit and in truth. Time to level up. We are spiritual beings in an earthly body. Knowing this we must choose to take care of what we don't see naturally. Our organs, heart, lungs, liver, etc. Why would God pour and invest such a new and refreshing oil in some thing that's about to break down or blow out? God is not wasteful.

> *"I wish above all that you prosper and be in good health even as your soul prosper".*
>
> *(3 John 1 vs 2)*

Regaining the proper use of our five spiritual instruments will make things so much easier and we will not continue to walk in error. God gave us examples and encouragement to return to that place. "Oh taste and see that the Lord is good". Ever been hungry for the word? We should be encouraged to use our taste, sight, scenes of smell, touch, and hearing more spiritually as our spiritual life takes its form. Being carnally minded we utilize our five spiritual senses God gave us carnally. How we choose to entertain our senses is what seeps to the mind the brain. Taste- we use this to feed our mouth, eyes, and stomach and we are becoming more and more uncomfortable. When we return spiritually minded we will put in our bodies what God delight for us to put into our vessels.

> **Hebrews 5:14** -*Even those who by reason of us have their scenes exercised to discern both <u>good and evil</u>.*

Where did we hear these words before? In the kingdom womb? Just like that little baby knows mom's voice once it has been born into the world, we should know God's voice being born again. Back in Gen..... good and evil.

> "Butter and honey shall he eat that he may know to refuse the evil, and choose the good." *(Isaiah 7:15)*

(Reflection) When do we start to eat for spiritual reasons and not just because it taste delightful? Eve looked on the tree and saw that it was good for food. It appeared pleasing to her so she took part. It indeed was not good for her and spiritually she was hiding from God, the very One who created her. .how silly. Paul says in (*Phil 1:9*) "and *this I pray, that your love may abound yet more and more in knowledge and in all judgment.*" If God's word is a two edge sword then we should be the manifestation of this and that double anointing should be upon us as well. Once the spirit of the Lord becomes the forefront of our lives, even when eating, drinking, and speaking it will become spiritual. When God fed people in the bible it was most always for spiritual purposes:

The two fish and five loaves of bread. (miracle)
Breaking bread of Him and drinking His blood. Do this in remembrance of me. (parable, symbolic)
Butter and honey shall he eat that he may know to refuse the evil. (spiritual reasoning)
God told Elijah to hide by the brook of Che'-rith God fed Elijah through ravens twice
(*1Kings 7vs 6*)a day and he had "water" not Kool aide for my cool aide lovers...not coke zero! :) God's plan for our bodies is for us to eat to live. The enemy's purpose for us is for us to live to eat! Go to bed thinking about what we'll eat tomorrow! Guilty as charged!

<u>*Are you aware that certain foods feed evil spirits in your life?*</u>

This is very true. Check out *Isaiah chapter 66 vs 17,18*.

> "*They that sanctify themselves, and purify themselves in the gardens behind one tree in the midst, eating swine's flesh, and the abomination, and the mouse, shall be consumed together, saith the Lord.*
>
> *18) For I know their works and their thoughts.*"

Astonishing right? Apparently certain foods encourage certain demonic spirits to grow stronger in our lives! God says for I know their ways. By what they put in their mouth, He knew them. Wow! Don't let demonic spirits stay alive in your life because of your menu. We can barley taste, see, smell, feel and hear God because we are constantly tasting, seeing, and Smelling the aroma of fast food chains. These things keep us spiritually and naturally bound and blind. If we are God's vessels then everything we put into it or on it must reflect Him. This is when the glory can show up!

What's going in your ears?

What do you hear?

Do you hear the Television and people in the next room or can we stop and hear the cries of those being persecuted many many miles and seas away?

On that Television show, can you really hear the cry of that actor that's so funny?

He's laughing on television and he appears insanely happy, but it's his/her job to "act" this way!

Can you hear the cry and tormented soul behind a plastic smile?

What's your sight like?

Still fooled by the enemy that everybody is doing stuff to you and you do nothing wrong?

Can we see Jesus in every thing that's being done and that it's all good?

How many motions are we making into law for our children, because they are watching us?

No matter how we may try to hide what we do, because our kids senses is still Kingdomly fresh they can hear the words that our mouths are not actually saying. Our clever flesh tries to fix up evil intent toward some one else and they know it, but the older they get the more they watch us, the more they learn the carnal way to utilize these precious Kingdom gifts naturally. So instead of touching with spoken words they relate touching to reaching out and physically touching something. We think that we are growing because we can see good and evil. But growth is in seeing _everything as good._ Walking in the spirit everything that happens "*has*" to be good because it's God!

Behind The Veil
_The skin I'm In

We all love the Lord right?

This is one of the most important things we can do in our lives! Besides God we love our families, friends, associates, and just people in general.

What about ourselves?

Do you love you?

Most people would say yes, I guess, sure. While others would start naming parts of the body they are displeased with and wish were more perfect! God made us all beautiful in our own unique way! Here's an idea.... embrace you! So what you've gained a little weight. To love you is to eat more healthy. Not eating healthy to loose weight but so your internal organs can take what they require in nutrition and function properly. In the meantime you're loosing weight because it's another benefit along with loads of energy and also because your metabolism is running the way it's supposed to now.

To be a vessel "fit" for the master's use we must seek God and ask Him what should we consume into our temple. A great number of Americans think on really looking perfect for the summer time! We tend to go overboard in the gym while trying every diet fad we hear about. America has made billions of dollars off people wishing to become fine as wine and a great many unsuccessful in doing so. This is the state America has been in for sometime! They do this by brain washing the weak minded. To be weak minded doesn't necessarily mean that you are slow or incompetent, just that in certain areas,. Say...food, money, or weight lots of people are weak minded and vulnerable and America capitalizes on people' s weak points. They continue to build an empire off of our insecurities. So being weak minded in these areas we do things and try things and spend money uncontrollably. Yes, we should love the skin we're in but not like unto an idol. Idol worship is of the world. Our form and the way we were built is made up to carry a load. The enemy knows this. Our body weight changes every few days either by ounces or by pounds. So we're used to fluctuating. Spiritually, we start to put extra things on to carry that God never intended like two and three jobs, unauthorized relationships, and ungodly addictions and we may feel a little sore at first because of the extra weight but then our back, feet, and muscles get used to the added pressure for a little while until we become worn down. We just carry and carry and then when about to break we consult God with the accusation finger and say you said you would not put more on me than I could bear so we ourselves start to strip things off of us that we spiritually need like prayer times to a lot time for the fleshly things we've picked up! God wants to relieve us of the pressure. We think we can handle it because we've gotten used to the weight but God sees you won't be able to cross the finish line with that substantial amount of weight invited. Straight is the gate and narrow is the way. We have to strip off what makes us feel like a woman...needing every man's Eyes to be plastered on our chest! We must strip off the desire to be fantasized about which is why we shop spandex, come on somebody! Strip it off, it's weighty and it's heavy! We won't make the journey stripping off Godliness so we can bare to stand carrying junk. Who told you you were naked? Who told you you had to be a sex symbol and keep up with the latest trends and fashions? Take that weight OFF your mind and ask God how it is the "He" wants you to dress! You would be surprised what types of fabrics and material God would love to see you in! The chains are breaking off right now. God will have you to become lighter. We can't allow the skin we're in to destroy our birth right.

We must be set apart. To be set apart does not mean for all "church folks " to go buy an Island together and live on it. Do you know how easy it would be for Jesus hating people to come and drop a bomb blowing everyone to shreds all at one time? Not wise! To be set apart simply means to think differently!

> *Let this mind be in you which was also in Christ Jesus!*
> (**Philippians 2;5**)

The world love themselves! They spend big money on themselves: to get bigger breast, bigger buttocks, big hips, smaller noses, fat reductions, and make ups and creams flown in from Italy. God spoke to me one day and said these word

> "*Don't let the skin you're in cause you to sell your birth right.*"

This caught me by surprise. I never thought myself to be anything more than I was, but I wrote these words down anyway! When Father says a thing you don't always have to understand it right then, but you must obey. Sometimes God gives us a word for us in the future or to warn us that when He puts His beauty on us ..don't get caught slipping. God had purpose for these words! He never ever waste words. Neither should we. Let's not let the skin we're in cause us to sell our birth right. Our birth right is to be that light! God's offspring. The salt of the earth! Salt is flavor. Our purpose is to be the evidence that God is alive and living in us! Our purpose is to live a life of faith showing people the evidence of things not seen! Showing people the evidence that God lives! Let's regroup. Shall we become kingdom? After all it's never been about us. We made it that way! Let's not sell our birthright for popularity, fame, fortune! Is it really worth it in the end? I am a friend of God, He calls me friend! We hang out in the secret place where He whispers things to me and I whisper back and tell Him how totally cool He is, and that I'm so glad to be close to Him. I call Him my refuge and my fortress! He shows me I'm correct by protecting Me everyday. Yes we are to love ourselves/ our bodies but only to glorify God and to please our husbands. We were not made for ourselves. We must come to grips with who we are! Ladies, we give our last names away in marriage, we give birth, we give ourselves to our jobs and to our children, we give ourselves to God and to our ministry, we give ourselves and our bodies to our mates. We are givers so to not be replenished by the replinisher is to walk around feeling spent. This is many women today. It's not the first thirty minutes that go by in the work place you don't hear a lady complain about how tired she is! Some don't even have children and are not married! Wow, I think to myself. I'm not tired at all, but hanging around tired people listening to tired talk what do you think will happen? You become tired by excepting that demonic spirit in through your ear gates! I disassociate myself quickly. I'm a lively stone! I'm full of energy and ready to complete this day while giving God thanks and kicking the devil's tired butt! I love me, but only because God lives here! As He is my refuge and fortress protecting me, I must protect my ear gates and eye gates because the Glory doesn't want to see and hear just any old nasty thing. I can't allow others or myself to offend my King of kings! I've worked to hard and gave up to much to get to this secret place! I bid you come. Let's see everything as good again!

CHAPTER 9

The Fruits

We know and have seen from history that objectives will always be. Things happen that we have absolutely no control over. Although this will happen weather you are saint or sinner, the best solution is going into problematic areas with the problem solver. Along with Jesus comes nine wonderful things called *the Fruits of the Spirit!* Another word I also like to implement for fruit is personality. The *personality of the Spirit* of God is what we are so drawn to and drawn to become like! With these nine weapons the enemy is sure to leave your situation dizzy.

In *Galatians 5:22* it tells us *that the fruits of the spirit is Love, Joy, Peace, Long suffering, Gentleness, Goodness, Faith, Meekness, and Temperance.* The bible also states that in *verse 25, "If we live in the spirit, let us also walk in the spirit"*. Have you ever tried to handle a spiritual situation naturally? This method is what the typical woman does. Emotions start to flare up and words are being said. Handling a spiritual situation naturally is no good and nothing good can come of it. Handling a natural situation spirituality is a great way to over come the wicked one and his devices. Can you imagine going through your trial with love and Joy and even understanding for the person who's acting a complete donkey toward you? Everything would go over so much more smoothly, allowing your faith and goodness to manifest. You wouldn't have to leave feeling condemned later on by something you said and then wondering how on earth will you open the door to ask for forgiveness. In the meantime the devil is whispering, *"I thought you were saved, I thought you was supposed to be a good person, they will never forgive you*". Do me a huge favor and bypass all his tricks and scheming ways! By exercising the fruits of the spirit in your life the Lord God Almighty will grant you with larger doses. Have you ever thought about what kind of life you might be able to live with extra love to give people? What about a double dose of joy, peace, long suffering, gentleness, goodness, faith, or meekness! I can tell you upfront that you'll become a people magnet. Both good people and bad will flock to you. Good folks in order to experience what you have to offer and bad folks to potentially kill what you have to offer. Children, young adults, adults and the elderly as well will gravitate to you because the truth is, they want to experience being in the company of a person who has the personality/fruits of God. Someone actually loving on them with real pure love and not anterior motives are rare! No matter what situation we face, it's nothing that the fruits can't handle. Throw a little love on any fire and that fire will eventually just die, no matter how hard the opposing individual tries to keep it going! God is so much into you that He gave you nine of these fruitage weapons! These should be exercised in our lives everyday because in using them we strive toward perfection. We strive towards being like Jesus, we become pleasing to God, and prompt Him to want to answer our prayers quickly! Even those silent prayers that you've never spoken of, He will answer. Try expressing joy and peace. How many of your family members, friends, coworkers, and strangers alike would hunt you down to just be in your presence because their life is in turmoil while going through despair, currents, waves, and the storms of life. How many would search for you because they know with assurance that God's joy and peace remains with you and they can actually find the relief they need with just a few minutes of you talking and praying with them. Do you know that one of the best times to plant the seed of salvation to someone is while they are in some type of despair? This is how Jesus got some of the names He has now from people and generations of people who needed Him desperately in one way or another. One of the many beautiful names of God is Savior! Does the term "Jesus saves" ring a bell? Jesus saved us from our sins and from ourselves, but even in Him having saved us, we are still being saved in different areas of our lives every day. The Areas we feel like we are drowning in- Jesus is still holding out His hands and still being that great Savior that He is! We should be eternally grateful for every situation the Lord delivers us out of However the "level up" is necessary says Father God. Pay close attention to these passage of words as they are critical to your divine walk with the Lord. Is Jesus asleep in the bottom of your boat? (*Matthew 8:24*)(*Mark 4:38*)

> And behold there arose a great tempest in the sea insomuch that the ship was covered with the waves: but He (meaning Jesus)was asleep. And His disciples came to Him, and awoke Him saying Lord, save us: we perish. And He said unto them, why are ye fearful, o ye of little faith? Then He arose, and rebuked the winds and the sea; and there was a great calm. (**Matthew 8:24-26**)

<u>When the storms rage and the billows roar, are we calling the Messiah to rescue us out of every little trial and test?</u>

*Note- Their is a major difference in "being pulled out of the fire" and "going through the fire."

Why did Jesus seem like He was aggravated that these men called on Him as a *Savior* to save them from this terrible storm?

When I was a babe in Christ Jesus I always called Him to rescue me out of every little test and trial instead of help me to endure as a good solider. It had become my daily prayer. Then God of coarse would extend that *"peace be still "*in my life, but I realized after some years that I wasn't really elevating. My confidence in God had sky rocketed though because I knew that He cared enough for me to come quick and help me! Now I was yarning for that elevation in Him though. God started to show me little by little what I needed to do "for myself" and I started to war with the weapons God had given me. (The Holy scripture and the pulling down of strong holds) This is how we become strong in the Word. Strong enough to walk, then strong enough to run! At some point in our lives, God expects us to exercise the gifts, talents, and weapons against the foes of Hell and stop crying out save me from this, save me from that! It's okay to call on Jesus as savior, that's who He is, but doing this all the time shows the Lord that we're still in "*babe*" mode. The level up is necessary for those sons and daughters of God more mature in the faith.

The dilemma with this method of crying "save me" all the time when you've been saved for years upon years is that eventually you'll have to go through this trial again until you come out right. So then we start to experience the cycle of circles that seem to be never ending. When we can take the test with the Master watching us while being silent and pass because we have utilized the study tools He gave us to pass it with -we can then accelerate beyond where we are! "*Elevation is necessary* ", says God! Jesus said "*oh yeah of little faith*".

Why would He say that when they needed Him?

Because faith is substance. His attitude is saying, have you no substance in your belly to sustain yourselves? Did you really have to call me for this with everything you have been taught by me concerning our Father? Jesus wanted them to put the teachings they took part in into action. War with the scriptures the word of God!

> "*Now faith is the substance of things hoped for, the evidence of things not seen.*" (**Hebrew11**)

Let's break down the word substance and the word evidence because we can't become Kingdom without these two words!

Substance means_ the real physical matter of which a person or thing consists and which has a tangible solid presence.
Ex) *proteins make up a great amount of* **substance** *in the body.*
Ex2)*Ghostly figures with no* **substance**.

Evidence *means to be or show evidence of the available body of facts or information indicating whether a belief or proposition is true or valid. Proof, confirmation, verification. "The evidence of things not seen".*
Evidence, by Merriam Webster dictionary means_ *something which shows that something else exist or is true: a visible sign of something.*
Now let's examine these few scriptures and then we will tie it all together to make a beautiful bow to fit our spiritual attire as the bride

of Christ because the bridegroom is coming *6:13_But yet in it shall be a tenth, and it shall return and shall be eaten: as a tree, and as an oak, whose "substance "is in them, when they cast their leaves: so then Holy seed shall be the "substance" thereof!*

(**Luke 15:3**)states_ *And not many days after the younger son gathered all together, and took his journey into a far country, and there wasted his "substance" with riotous living.*

"**Riotous**" meaning_ *disorderly, loud characterized by wild and uncontrolled behavior!*

While **Hebrews 11** says_ *Faith is the substance of things hoped for.*

<u>*Does the things we hope for have substance? Could they perish?*</u>

That substance is supposed to be the evidence of things not seen and material things are seen. Many times we call ourselves exercising our faith in things we desire in the natural realm and when it doesn't happen we feel very heavily disappointed inwardly. Fact is...faith is supposed to be used in a certain way and this way is concerning the things of the spirit. The things that shows evidence the God is very real and present in our lives, swelling in His Kingdom/in us_ in the earth realm. The enemy's job is to beat us down and cause unbelief every time we use faith the wrong way and things don't happen for us.

Ex) That substance *hoped for* is supposed to show people around you that God (not seen) does in fact exist and is very much so real! This substance should be fruits of the spirit that we hope for on a day to day basis. It points to the evidence that **God** is alive and well! Material things are nice but they have no substance and so for years we have put our hopes in things that have no substance and when we don't receive it our faith is shot. We must use the Word of God correctly. It wont work outside of it's divine purpose and neither should we!

> (**Matthew 6:33**) *seek ye first the kingdom of God and all these other things will be added.* (**Phil 2:5**) says *Let this mind be in you which was also in Christ Jesus:*

(stay with me and lets paint this picture) God calls those of His choice, friend.

> *No greater love hath any man shown that would lay down his life for his friend. (**John 15:15**)*
>
> *Henceforth I call you not servants; for the servant knoweth not what his lord doeth: but I have called you friend; for all things that I have heard of my Father I have made known unto you. Ye have not chosen me, but I have chosen you, and ordained you that ye should go and bring forth fruit and that your fruit (substance) should remain: that whatsoever ye shall ask of the Father in my name He may give it you. (Fruit) (spiritual)*
>
> ***John 15:13*** *says Greater love hath no man than this, that a man lay down his life for his friends. 14)ye are my friends, if ye do whatsoever I command you.*

How can we be real friends of God if we choose not to lay down things consisting of our lives? You know, flesh stuff!

(Things we want or desire in this natural life.) Truth is, the more we develop an appetite for natural things in this life, the more we stop looking forward to actually meeting Jesus face to face. We settle for Him being a fad or just something we do for a thrill and chill or just to feel good about ourselves, but when you truly love someone you'll want to meet them face to face. Telephone conversation only works for so long! The bible said *do unto others as you have them to do unto you.* Jesus the Christ died for us!

Who's in line willing to die for Him?

Know ye not that your body is the temple of the Lord?

If you don't want to stay in a filthy house then don't put Him in one.

By faith (substance) Abel offered unto God a more excellent sacrifice than Cain, by which he obtained witness that he was righteous, God testifying of his gifts: and spiritual by it he being dead yet speaketh. **Hebrews 11** offers full examples of what faith is and how it is properly used.

(**Hebrews 11:26**)*Moses; esteeming the reproach of Christ greater richest than the treasures in Egypt: for he had respect unto the recompense of the reward. 27)By faith (substance) he forsook Egypt not fearing the wrath of the king: for he "endured "as seeing Him who is invisible.* (The level up is necessary)

Hebrews 12:2 *looking unto Jesus the author and finisher of our faith (substance)* Amen.

Babies cry for Dad when they fall. It's totally okay to be a babe, if you are a babe indeed. Mature sons and daughters get up, dust off, and admit their sins. We Then renounce and turn away. (We cry and pray, we rise, we turn remember) Simple.

Always crying to be rescued is a set back in the long run for the mature saints, because we spend our entire life not gaining muscle. We go through the same trial over and over again. We can't continue being rescued from being tried as pure gold is tried.

<u>*Why is God revealing this to us?*</u>

Because He wants us to arrive to the next level finally, not wanting us to perish for the lack of knowledge. (Eating steak and drinking wine but still pooping in diapers) level one was the babe stage!

Level two is being *refined*! Once we have been refined, our bodies shall be changed. (***Phil 3:21***) (**1 Cor 6 15-20**) when Jesus stretch up and stretches out in us we will begin to take on the form of Him! Forget the "brick house " song! We'll begin to look like mansions and our insides as refiners gold, because we'll have been tried by fire and not compromised. This gold will be transparent gold and God will allow it to show through us so brightly and to others lost and needing direction!

The transparent vessel will be transparent when witnessing for God and transparent enough so people can see straight though them and see God. (*Spiritually naked*) (evidence of *things not seen*) After being refined in the fire like Gold and God see's that you can be trusted and you can be used, (*going through your trials the correct way*) then level three is the *Glorified bodies*! For those praying God's kingdom come and His will be done "IN" earth as it is in heaven, we will experience this on earth! *The glorified body!* How are you seventy five years old and still jumping rope, 40 years old still appearing 20. When pain in the body becomes no more that's a blessing. When your body begin to look like it's been chiseled by an artist, watch out! Glorified bodies will be given to those who has leveled up spiritually because God knows you'll point people who praise you because of your build, back to Him. All the glory to Him! Bodies that the gym or personal trainers will not be able to take credit for! These people will be trusted by God not to use His glory to make others fall into a lustful state of mind.

So now does this inspire us even more to level up?

God wants to make you a mansion! A lot of times we as believers get comfortable in the babe stage, not that we love being first saved so much, but that we think we are allotted more room to make mistakes(*things we desire to do that's wrong*) so we choose to stay in the babe phase and do things we know are wrong, and because we stay in this stage illegally now we do the crime and then cry for God to save and deliver us out and we eventually start the method of *crying wolf*! Many Christians cry wolf to the Lord and because of sin going on in our lives, sin brings us to this raging river with sharp cutting edge rocks and drop offs, and raging winds and now when it's time to cross and we holler "Savior Savior" hear my call. Jesus comes with His compassionate heart and the keys to our hell at the moment and He rescues us! Just for us to get on the other side of this huge storm and continue the same sin. Yes, we do well for a few weeks. Attending Sunday or Sabbath school and feeding the poor in the soup kitchen twice a week we may even tell our testimony to a few people how God just really showed Himself faithful and mighty, but all to soon we go right back to practicing the same sin that got us in trouble in the first place. Crying wolf defiantly has an expiration date. Sometimes we follow the instructions of the Lord and we do well for a few months, but that door to sin was left cracked open and sin creeps right back in even after we were doing so well at one point. Take Je-h'u for an example in **2 Kings 9.** The prophet Eli'-sha sent a man to Ra'-moth-gil'-e-ad with oil to anoint Je'-hu to be king over Israel. Now this young prophet gave specific instructions to Je'-hu while anointing him king on what the Lord had desired him to achieve toward Ahab, which was to smite the house of Ahab so he could avenge the blood of the servants of the Lord.

After hearing this would your decision have been to obey the instructions of the Almighty or to go celebrate your being a king first and start to flex your authority in certain areas in the Kingdom?

Je'hu's decision was to obey the command of the Lord. (*Which God knew this the reason he was chosen in the first place*) After Je'-hu notified his brothers of the huge change that had just taken place in his life, he immediately went and began to destroy the house of Ahab and Jez'-e-bel with them. This really meant a huge deal to God! In *vs29* it says *after this great act of courage and strength and even wisdom of tactics on Je'-hu's part, he departed not from the sins of Jer-o-bo'-am.*

But God in all His mercy and grace gives us another chance and a word of encouragement to keep doing good because His will is that we prosper! Even after seeing Je-'hu continue in his sin He spoke the word in *vs 30* saying *and the Lord said unto Je'-hu, because thou hast done well in executing that which is right in mine eyes, and hast done unto the house of Ahab according to all that was in mine heart thy children of the fourth generation shall sit on the throne of Israel.*

Pause: Do you think maybe if Je'-hu would have released his sin that God's ultimate reward to him would have fell on him as well as the fourth generation?

Play: vs 31 But Je'-hu took no heed to walk in the way of the law of the Lord God of Israel with all his heart: for he departed not from the sins of Jer-o-bo-'am which made Israel to sin. Thinking back over your life, how many great works have you done to where you know the Holy Ghost was proud of you and that the unconquerable King Jesus smiled on you?

You knew your fruits of the spirit was in tact that day or that month/ year, But somewhere we get caught up, we get distracted and therefore we loose focus of the promise. Once loosing focus of the promise we forget why we bare the fruits of the spirit and because the fruits of the spirit are so *"heavy"* we will tend to put them down therefore automatically picking up the works of the enemy, which is the works of the flesh. But the cold and deadly thing about picking up just one work of the flesh is that it silently and over time kills all the rest of your fruits of the spirit. One...by....one. Remember, in one fruit of the spirit getting destroyed the works of the flesh immediately takes it's place. And of coarse we don't choose, like at a buffet line, which work of the flesh we will take, in fact most often times we are so distracted until we don't even notice this detrimental change has taken place, until an opportunity or situation present itself and satan throws that flesh fruit up to the surface and you become stunned at your self as to where that even came from.

"I've never said anything like that".

"I've never done anything like that".

It's because satan picks which work of the flesh will replace that spiritual fruit just destroyed. He makes sure that he picks one of his that will spread in your body rapidly and that will choke out any anointing, truth, Joy, peace, temperance, and anything else reminding Him of God. Beware! Keep your spiritual fruits sharp by fasting and prayer. If you feel one growing weak, ask the Lord to renew the strength because the enemy would love to wipe us out with the slip of one fruit. This is satan's plan for your life. He wants to burden you down leading to the ultimate Hell destination.

Doesn't God's will seem more sufficient for you?

Allowing ourselves to posses any type of flesh that the enemy operates in is very dangerous. Maybe you've renounced and gotten delivered from bitterness, lust, envies, being jealous of others and their success, just maybe and this is great news! Hallelujah!! The Angeles are singing and some are even playing tambourines and the trumpet.

Now what?

What about those friends you hang with?

    After all, the reason you hang is because you have so much in common. Yes, spirits and all! This is amazing! We never see or seem to think that our friends have the same demonic spirits lodging in them as we do! What we will admit when being asked by one " why do you hang so close together "? Our reply is, she just gets me. She understand me. Sometimes even when I don't say anything she already knows what I'm thinking or how I'm feeling. We even finish each other's sentences sometimes. We love the same music, clothing, lipstick brand, cars, and the best thing about it is that we are both saved". (*Take a pause break*) you both saved huh. We never stop to think that demonic forces could be our soul reason for being connected to another person.

Have you ever heard of *"Birds of a feather flock together "*?

    Do you know that demonic spirits love to feed off of each other to stay alive and stay strong? They also feed off certain television shows, certain foods, and certain places! Mostly demonic spirits connect with other spirits to keep the individuals locked down to where they think they are normal, saved' and nothing is visibly wrong! But when "real" deliverance has taken place things seem to change all of a sudden. Yes, you still desire to get together this Thursday night for movie night and have a great time, I mean what's the harm in it right? But you can't seem to get over something that was said by way of telephone when you talked to your bestie the other day...your ace...your best friend forever. You ponder the thought over and over in your head until you finally talk yourself out of what that really meant, so to make conversation feel better to your conscious you pretty it up with a few added words to the end like *"but I know God is able so I'm going to trust him.* So you all get together and your friend is venting to you about something that has transpired and instead of you listening attentively like You usually do you are trying to keep strife from getting into your spirit because it's thick in the car. Even though they (*your friend*) are talking about what someone did to them, you already know how your friend is. Bitter, vindictive, and likes to play "*victim*" to name a few character traits. You know she/he likes to play with these spirits and you know in your mind by being around this person that they blow things way out of proportion! Not just friends, this could mothers, fathers, sons, daughters, aunts, uncles, and cousins alike. But the thing is, the old you used to buy in to these things. Some how now the more your friend (or relative) talked and the more demonic forces operating through the works of the flesh manifested, the more in tuned you got and the spirit of divination that would use to arise in you and you would start giving your saved but ungodly council that, to you, sounded like so much wisdom, does not arise anymore. See how demons compliment each other. So now that God has actually come into your life and you have a brand new start, now the same thing that's been happening for years is now starting to bother you and make you feel down right yucky!

<u>Side bar</u>:/ Notice I said " the same thing that's been going on for years "Their is no elevation in God when we allow flesh realms to dominate. God does not elevate flesh. So satan takes it upon himself to do what he does best. (He has a Grammy for it) satan makes it appear to the individual that they "have" in fact elevated over the years. <u>How </u>does he do this?

Tell me does conversations like this sound a little familiar. ...

"Wow, I remember the last time you were crying over (insert a name) and I was giving you counsel and telling you it would be okay. Man that was in high school, now we are grown, my how time has passed! Now you have a career at the firm and I'm the best selling author of forty two books. Just look at us!"

Yes just look at you. Maybe your jobs has elevated giving you a pacify big enough for you to ignore that you as a person are still going around in circles because obviously things are still the same in your life when you look deeply. Oh and your friend. ... Still crying over the same matters she did years ago it's just more grown up now. So besides the jobs and their age, where have they grown? Elevation in God takes God. Just because one get's a six figure career or is working right under the president of the united states, if God has not elevated you in Him then you'll take your same demonic forces with you from poor street to penthouse boulevard, but now guess what, you can afford different things to ease your mind when the demonic adultery starts to manifest itself in you. Well you know boyfriend has to go back home to his wife leaving you miserable and feeling unfit like dried up goods. (Nonperishable items just sit and sit in the pantry) so you take that money and now make purchases like alcohol. You know, to help sooth you. Before you know it you're drunk in two states. His state and your state. So now the works of the flesh drunkenness has taken place and in two forms. Drunk physically and drunk spiritually because you attend church every now and again to fill an empty void. So with these two boys playing ball murder rears his head up and says let me play! Now thoughts of killing his wife comes to mind because he's giving you ignorant reasons why he can't leave. Now with murder in play full and strong you start trying to coach him on evil things to do to get her to walk right out that door, how to manipulate and under hand and now you've just allowed yourself to become the teacher of witchcraft! Congratulations! Another work of the flesh, of coarse hatred rides with witchcraft, and with all these works of the flesh manifesting out of you, the others just come and join the party and now you're taken over by satan but congratulations on your new career at the firm! Wow, such an accomplishment. Round and round you go! I've actually seen things and people allow satan to control them just like this! It's happening everyday.

(*Back to scene one*) So now that you're actually free from this demonic curse of thinking the way you used to, you are literally trying to stay free but your friend needs your help and all you can think about is getting out of that car and away from that spirit of strife that you never noticed was their So strong in your friend. Meanwhile She's noticing that you usually chime in with your advice that she never takes anyway And that you usually give your spill about what you would do but you are sitting in silence with only a few head nods and a silent prayer of deliver me from this evil. While you're trying to make up your mind to maybe give true Godly advice and wisdom on her situation the demonic spirits are regrouping in her. Those demonic forces in her immediately notices that they have nothing to connect to within you and by the time you reach the movies the both of you feel very uncomfortable and are kicking yourself because you didn't come up with an excuse to cancel girls night. BEWARE OF SATAN AND HIS DEVICES! Now that he knows something is different in you and that you have actually taken a real elevation in God, because your friends demonic forces told him (Demons report back to satan like angels report back to God),"Now he has switched there assignment from just running ramped in your friend to making them, through your friend or relative, find a way to assassinate you! It just got deep. *(life jackets please)* So kind Christian hearted you, have switched to the mode of be a hero and save my friend from demonic attack and influence of the works of the flesh, and the demons in her have switched gears to assassinate at all cost!

Just take a minute to think about how you believe this will play out with the two individuals. ....

See the thing about the enemy is, he knows if you're not in the works of the flesh that you're obviously in the fruits of the spirit so he begins to attack with God's permission. How does he have God's permission you may ask. *2 Corinthians 6;14* explained it best when it states

¹⁴ Be ye not unequally yoked together with unbelievers: for what fellowship hath righteousness with unrighteousness? and what communion hath light with darkness?

Anytime we step out of the word it gives the devil permission! (satan can't do anything to a true son or daughter of God without God's say so as long as we are walking in the light) How does he attack, you may ask?

He'll use your friend to play on your sympathy like they really desperately want to change.

"I really do! I look at you and I marvel, like wow I mean I hold you on top regard because I know where you came from and to look at you now. ...wow! I want this change for me too."

Now she's using the works of the flesh demon spirit Idolatry. Putting one high up where God should be is not good. News flash *change is as simple as stop, turn around, go in the opposite direction.* It just takes a willing mindset to do it. This is to make you lower your guard, which is Jesus (*because He's not going to share His seat with you. Either you are on it or He is*) only so the demonic spirits in her can attack you spiritually. Before you know it, you have accepted this cunning like spirit and accepted what it had to say, and how it made you feel and accepted responsibility to actually take on being someone's golden image, those spirits assassinate you spiritually and cause your old demons to penetrate you faster than you can say

"wait... What"?

Now you wonder why you were walking on sunshine for two months straight, but today you're wondering what your ex boyfriend, married to somebody else, is up too. Because the demonic forces from your friend has also penetrated you and is now operating inside you with the rest of the demons God delivered you from and you wonder why now you're more worst than you ever was before! Stay clear of soul ties! It's very important for a child of God to watch who you fellowship with.

> **Ephesians 5vs11** says *and have no fellowship with the unfruitful works of darkness, but rather reprove them. 12) for it is a shame even to speak of things which are done of them in secret!*

How did this happen? Now you're trying to hide the fact that you're more worst off than your friend!

(**Matthew 12 vs 43-45**) " *when the unclean spirit is gone out of a man, he walketh through dry places, seeking rest, and findeth none. 44) Then he saith, I will return into my house from whence I came out; and when he is come, he findeth it empty, swept, and garnished. 45)Then goeth he, and taketh with himself seven other spirits more wicked than himself, and they enter in and dwell there: and the last state of that man is worse than the first. Even so shall it be also unto this wicked generation.* It's because you have allowed your liver to be clogged with deadly toxins and now the sinking has begun. (*We must have the Holy Ghost to be kept*) The liver is completely contaminated! The liver is what cleanses the body. *"De" liver* produces proteins that are important in blood clotting. It is also one of the organs that break down old or damaged blood cells. *"De" liver* plays a central role in all metabolic processes in the body, in fact in metabolism *"De" liver* cells break down fats and produce energy! (*Www.ncb.nlm.nih. gov*) Give "De" liver credit for being one of the hardest working organs in your body as it performs hundreds of functions! "De" liver processes anything you eat or drink, and either repackages it for your body to use or eliminate it. If you get the analogy I am trying to make, now do you understand why satan is after your *"de" liver- ance?* He wants to clog up your spiritual man. He wants to contaminant it so bad until it can't expel bad spirits out of the body that may try to attempt to come and stay. Where *"De" liver acne* will say "get the behind me satan you have no place here"! If "De" liver is clogged up and not functioning properly all types of spirits would be able to live in you and breed more. We must cry out for deliverance daily! It's a day by day thing and we must keep the maintenance up on our daily devotion to God to stay cleansed and pure. Another good way to protect your deliverance is by not trying to be a hero to everyone proclaiming they need help! The Holy GHOST will give you a green light on who it's okay to help and who not so much! Know that God is the only one who can fix your friend and that change is up to them. Also you must make a 100% stand. Let your friend know that you have allowed the Lord to come in and "de"liver you! Now that this has taken place you must change your surroundings. Let your friend know that you would be happy if they went all the way into Jesus and allowed the Lord to deliver them also. If they refuse to understand what you are saying, let them go quickly! More than likely this is to frustrate your decision and ultimately make you feel stupid!

Are they worth your elevation?

Are they really worth demonic forces running in and out of your life like a revolving door?

Are they worth you never actually experiencing healing?

Are they worth your destination being hell? Take a long look in the mirror and ask yourself. ....

Is my friend worth a miserable life and then a miserable death?

The answer is no. Leave no room for the devil. Either they get *right* or they get *left* because this train is moving! ALL ABOARD!!! Plain and simple. You MUST preserve your fruit!

Behind The Veil
_Chart It

I can't express to you enough the importance of writing things down! When you get to a certain level of commitment in God the enemy will begin to fight your mind and actually make you think God is sleeping on you. As we get closer to God, He sometimes start to speak to you in code, numbers, or symbols and not always in voice. Sometimes it is in picture form that He will speak or through bill board or sign. Other times He'll allow you to keep seeing the same word is various places! The chart is very necessary! With daily life going on the enemy tends to cloud the mind and we then think at the end of the day that God hasn't spoke. This day turns into months and you'll begin to think you're out of line and out of tune with God. So because of the subtle Demonic you'll stop doing the things you used to do because of feeling like God is not listening or speaking to you the way He used to. But God is speaking all the time! It's our job to chart it. If God doesn't exercise different ways to speak to us then it would be just that easy for the demonic to shut down our line of communication with God by clouding that area of our lives with something we deem "so important," and we actually do come into the place of not hearing God. God speaks all the time! The question is do we take time to *notice, listen, and chart?* Chart it! Out smart the demonic by using a pen and pad or a notebook on your cell phone device! Simple and easy! If we choose not to out smart the enemy, he'll out smart us every time! Even though God is still speaking to us the enemy will throw convictions, bills, work, children, church, stress and because it's so much it makes the word God spoke to us like :

"F*orgive*"

seem like it never happened. So the demonic will start to choke out the word of the Lord in your life, and then we stop seeking God with an attitude of what's the use? God is not wasteful so He then turns us over to the millions that depend on a word from Him through other men and women. This is one of many ways the enemy wins over us! Write down what God gives you. He takes time to lead us every day! He 's a g00d g00d Shepard! It's up to us to Chart it chart it chart it!

CHAPTER 10

Only A Father's Love

Have you ever known a girl or young lady who has not experienced ever having a father figure in her life?

Even though no little girl or boy deserves to be absent of a father, these things do happen.

Maybe dad was scared and left when the mention of her being conceived was made. Maybe her dad really did love her but mom wasn't seeing eye to eye with him and he just figured it would be easier to just leave all and start a new life. Whatever the case may have been, we know that the Decision of not being in her life has affected her in some way or another. Now some of the young ladies are nice, but maybe a little "*to*" nice. Especially with some of the fellas pretending to care. This young lady might have a hard time saying no, only because she doesn't really know fully who she is. She never had the opportunity to know who she was, so now this empty hole that seems like it could possibly be filled by someone special, only comes to show her that the reality remains that this man was the very same as the last- he just had different packaging! He saw the empty hole from afar, He came close, took everything he wanted, and left, never filling the void or even pretending to care like he would. Now along with this empty hole she has created many many soul ties. Every time she opened herself up to a young man hoping he would lead her to herself, she created another soul tie. A soul tie is usually a spiritual/ emotional connection you have to someone after being intimate with them, usually engaging in sexual intercourse. All soul ties are not sexual. Soul ties can also be attachments to things and people like mentors, best friends etc. to the point that when you want to be rid of them from your mind and your life, even when you are far away from them and out of their presence you still feel as if they are apart of you. You feel like apart of you is still with them to causing you to feel incomplete, as if you've given up some of yourself intangible that cannot be easily possessed again. (Www.urban dictionary.com) This is one of the saddest things when it comes to the female. A lot of times we simply have no clue who we are, so we go into "*fix it*" mode and grab the nearest guy that seems promising. We then make a even bigger mess by creating many soul ties and by these men actually becoming a part of us we have all these emotions and feelings to deal with! We end up trying to rebuild ourselves with pieces of others that simply doesn't fit our mold. Sadly we continue this vicious cycle until we simply over heat, feeling burnt out, depleted, spent, yes we become spent, or settle for Larry down the street who stays at home all day playing video games while you go out and bust your butt for security. Either way you've taking care of your man and whether you can afford to or not, it still doesn't make it right. <u>One thing that's even sadder than this</u>?

When our little girls grow up thinking this is how it is supposed to be.

One day I was in prayer talking to Elohim and He said these words to me in such a settled voice, He says,

"*Many of my daughters are Fatherless.*"

I paused in mid sentence with reverence. I'm talking to God about one thing and He completely interrupts the conversation with something off topic! Naturally, when this happens, you're like what tha what...... But when God does this it is so special because it shows you what He's burdened about at that very moment! When God starts to reveal His heart to you....My my my!!! One day I was seeking the Lord in prayer and just telling Him how great He is and He says,

*"When I open a door I open it wide enough for the whole
family to go through it and not just one person."*

At this point I knew He was telling me this to relay the message to a certain individual and I had to be obedient and tell her no matter how mad she may have gotten. Thankfully she received the message with understanding. God is about family!

Often God does speak His heart to me! Some things I can never share and others He has permitted me to. His daughters being Fatherless is something He wants us to know.

Many are fatherless because they have not taken advantage of spending true time to have a genuine relationship with "The Father!" God is waiting every day and every hour to have a Father daughter relationship with His girls. Let's get even more personal, those whom have a dad, yes you benefit from Him, but being absent from our one true Father has nothing but cons in store. Even though we may think we know who we are and what we want, we still have no idea what God's will for us is. I'm blessed to still be able to have my dad who's raised me, along with my mom, my whole life! I'll always be grateful to Pastor John L Cook Jr and Lady Elect Darlene Cook for raising me to fear the one true God! It is them that taught me that they are my earthly parents but I have someone bigger to answer to! It is dad who always told me,

"Never love past the truth!"
(Meaning never love a lie)

I say all this to say that natural parents are very very important so how much more important our Spiritual Father?

*"And call no man your father upon the earth: For one is
your Father which is in heaven."*
(Matthew 23:9)

Many people has stretched this verse out to different measures, but it's self explanatory what this verse means! No reason for deep philosophy here. With this knowledge being known, do you notice that Americans take a whole entire day to intentionally disobey what Jesus plainly said? (including the most holiest Bishop and the holy prophetess) Yes that's correct! *"Happy fathers day!"* Sound familiar? We go along with it because it is the normal thing to do. How does this make our Lord feel though? You know how the bible talks about when demon forces leave and are cast out of an individual how they come back and when they see that your temple is clean, then the demons go get seven more demons more wicked than himself and the last "state" of that man is worst than the first?

Well we somehow proudly go around claiming the United State of America.

When *united* means:

"Made *into or caused to act as a single entity or formed or produced by the uniting of things or persons.*"

State singular means:

"The *condition of a person or thing, as with respect to circumstances or attributes*". *(A state of health)*

So when we claim the United States of America, we are actually saying I am one with the state America is in today! I'm united with the political views that condone same sex marriage, abortions, the morning after pill allowing women to destroy the sperm cell of what would have been a beautiful baby boy or girl_ united with the health laws allowing food chains to actually use embalming fluid in ice cream, and cleaning products in different foods that kill people over time, United with the
. viewing of people according to how much they make, united with the greater than less than factor concerning race, united with drug Lords, pimps and cartoons that send out demonic messages to children every chance they get, united with teachers raping students and schools setting the pedestal so high In education until the average child think they are incompetent and spends life discouraged and settling for any old thing, United with the White house actually using God's symbol of promise, the rainbow, and flashing it as a demonic sign that the homosexuals are out, let's have a party, United with America who claims *"In God we trust*

" but has never specified which God she is talking about because not all of her ways edify Jesus and that's just to name a few!

All of these revelations Father took His time to teach and share with me. "Liberty, *in God we trust*", is stamped on every coin used as American money! We say this nation was founded on Christianity and grant it children of God do live here and hold and has held the standard but the nation is evil. Deception runs through it like water in a river. *Painting white roses red* America has done for centuries!

<u>Did you know that the statue of liberty is a pagan goddess given to America by the French?</u>

We say America loves God but America for centuries now has spoken of the god she loves. ***Liberty, in god we trust***! This is what has had the children of God's mind baffled for so long about why America is the way she is. They are not referring to these scriptures:

But whoso looketh into the perfect law of *liberty*, and continueth therein, he being not a forgetful hearer, but a doer of the work, this man shall be blessed in his deed. **(James 1:25.)**

> *So speak ye, and so do, as they that shall be judged by the law of liberty.* **(James 2:12 12)**

<u>How can Most laws made in America go against the teachings of Jesus Christ but America was so called founded on the bible?</u>

<u>Who's bible?</u>

<u>Why has America tried to shut the mouth of the Children of the one true God?</u>

Further more, these school systems make our children pledge to this pagan goddess every day!

> "I pledge allegiance to the Flag of the United States of America, and to the Republic for which it stands, one <u>N</u>ation **under God, indivisible, with liberty** and justice for all."

Do you know what indivisible means?

"Unable to divide or separate."

Your child with a pagan god, they make to confess this every single day at school indivisible with **liberty the pagan goddess**! They have to say that they pledge allegiance to what the "republic" stand for! Daughters of Zion stand for what Jesus Christ stand for and so do our children!

Check this song out;
My country,' tis of thee,
sweet land of" *liberty*", **of thee I sing**;
land where my fathers died,
land of the pilgrims' pride,
from every mountainside let freedom ring!

Remember this song?

I do too. They made us sing this at school! They made us learn it and one by one quote it to make sure we had it right! *Harmless right?*

It's harmless for those who could care less about God, the ten commandments, and what Father says in His word! This land is not God's land. "Sweet land of Liberty". The same pagan goddess found on our money. The same pagan goddess this land has an idol statue of in New York Harbor in New York City.

Remember this patriotic song?

"This land was made for you and me." Check out some of these verses

"I roamed and rambled and followed my footsteps."
God said "His Word" would be a lamp unto our feet and a light unto our path. (*Psalms 119vs105*) *To follow* ones own foot steps is to walk or proceed backwards, which is what America is doing the reason judgment is in the land. To follow your own footsteps means to backslide.

Another verse of this song;

"There was a big high wall there that tried to stop me
A sign was painted said: Private Property
But on the back side it didn't say nothing
This land was made for you and me"

This verse teaches to go beyond when you are told to stop. This teaches to forsake the laws and commandments of grace concerning us which disqualifies us for the unlimited grace and power God wants to pour out on His.

> "Having the glory of God: and her light was like unto a stone most precious, even like a jasper stone, clear as crystal; And had a wall great and high, and had twelve gates, and at the gates twelve angels, and names written Theron, which are the twelve tribes of Israel : **Revelation 21:11-12**

<u>What does this pagan goddess named Liberty mean anyway</u>? *the state of being free within society from oppressive restrictions imposed by authority on one's way of life, behavior, or political views.*

This means liberty from the one true God only to enslave us with their unholy unrighteous satanic belief system. Father says to remove their demonic yoke off our necks and to take His for it's light!

America, you are NOT a Godly country and I call you out you demonic spirit of deception! This same America that the saints of God claim to love has set out war against our daughters and sons!

<u>Are you aware that when America tries to send movie films to other countries they are made to force the actresses to cover their bodies in a respectable manner throughout the whole film?</u>

Where as we may get a movie with the lady half naked playing in the film, the same lady is made to put on wholesome clothing to record the film again for other countries. This teaches our young girls to go around half exposed and unladylike.

Even tinker bell, the princess and the frog, and other cartoon films have to dress the characters in appropriate attire with NO NAKEDNESS showing. Tinker bells has a long shirt and shirt on in other countries but America wants to teach our daughters to become sluts and hoers because that's what she is. She wants to teach our sons to lust after ungodly naked women instead of wholesome descent ones! I wage war against you America. Link (you tube video "Hijab as weapon in Islamic Iran" starting at 6:41minutes to 11:14)

Even America's symbol was placed and designed to degrade Jesus. They placed the flag for the representation of this country and they nick named it "old glory." (en.m.Wikipedia.org)

> *Old* meaning *belonging only or chiefly to the past; former or previous.*

Interesting enough they chose as a mockery to put seven red stripes on this "old glory". Seven because it's one of God's divine numbers.

> But He was wounded for our transgressions, He was bruised for our iniquities: the chastisement of our peace was upon him; and with His "stripes "we are healed. *(Isaiah 53:5)*

To further broadcast the meaning of this flag concerning this is the blue behind the stars. Blue is the third primary color. It spiritually signifies the Healing Power of God.(by His stripes we are healed) It is the most sublime subject and color which represents, biblically, the Word of God. The*15ᵗʰChapter* of Numbers, verses *38-41*denote this biblical meaning of Blue (fringe of the borders a rib band of blue). The very fact that the Sky is blue stands for the presence of Yahweh. God's chosen nation Israel is also denoted as blue from the time of David. In *Matt 9: 21*, the woman who had an issue of blood for 12 years says "I shall be whole again, if I touch the hem of His garment)- the garment hem is also Blue. (Www.color-meanings.com) on this "old glory" we carefully observe six white stripes. White meaning Bride of Christ, surrender, light, purity, completion, triumph, and peace.

The **number 6** is significant in the **Bible** because it is the **number** of Man, and the **number** of imperfection in man's work. It is a human **number**. The **number 6** is concerned and related only to man.(The Bible numerology code number 6 -AstroVera.com)

And now the stars.... what does the stars mean? Their were 50 stars and relating back to the bible – 50 Represents power and celebration. The Jubilee came after the 49th year, and Pentecost occurred 50 days after Christ's resurrection. (***Acts 2***) (***Leviticus 25:10***), (http://www. bibleprophecytruth.com/topics/bible-numbers#sthash.yzx9xd0P.dpuf.

Numbers vs 7:64(7 red stripes) and(64 subliminal messages on the flag all together) says that,

"A prince offered one kid of the goats for a sin offering."

Only Jesus wasn't a goat. He was the sacrificial lamb for our sins! This same flag was hung to mock Jesus as old and retired "the old thing." They made us in school age gather around the flag pole and pray around this flag. Little did we know. The system made us sing songs to "liberty". They made us put our hands on our heart and swear being indivisible with the pagan goddess liberty. America have not begun to pay for her deceitful ways!

The devil is a lie. Go in your pocket, piggy bank, purse or savings and try to find the oldest coin that you can! If it has "Liberty, in god we trust" on it then observe the date on that coin and you'll see just how long America has been painting white roses red. To claim we are apart of the united state of America is to unknowingly invite those seven demons in and our state will be worst than the first! Well what was our first state you may ask. Our first state was kingdom! We knew without a shadow of a doubt that we were not from here. We knew we had a purpose on this earth and that was to be used by God in whatever way He saw fit! We as daughters knew that God sees us and everything we say and do! We knew that "He" keeps records and He rewards us for our faithfulness that "He" blesses us when we sew good seed and do good deeds to/for others and be obedient and submissive to Him! But because we have now chosen the state America is in we, like America, have become united in taking God's character and giving it to another pagan idol called santa clause. We, like America, teach our children at a young age that santa clause, not Jesus, knows when you are sleeping, knows when you're awake, knows when you've been bad or good. Santa watches you all year, you be good and do good to others and be obedient, "he" will reward you!

The bible says:

> "Train up a child in the way he should go and when he's older he wont depart!"
> (***Proverbs 22:6***)

In The state of America we teach our children young how to not fear God, but santa is watching so be good! It's not cute, it's demonic and God does not think high of this at all. We are spiritual beings in earth bodies. Jesus never sent us here to conform to the state this country is in, you have no clue of the Evil America is doing and has done concerning God. The state of America has had generations of people for decades who celebrate independence day because they think the declaration of independence was adopted by the Continental Congress. (Https:// en.m.Wikipedia. org) When in fact all that took place on July the second not the fourth! (Www.archives.gov) I quote:

"Independence Day Should Have Been July 2"

–July 2, 1776 is the day that the Continental Congress actually voted for independence. John Adams, in his writings, even noted that July 2 would be remembered in the annals of American history and would be marked with fireworks and celebrations. The written Declaration of Independence was dated July 4 but wasn't actually signed until August 2. Fifty-six delegates eventually signed the document, although all were not present on that day in August.

So what did happen on ***July the fourth***? You ready for this? Alice goes to wonder land. (Lewis Carroll written) Dodgson Carol uses the garden of Eden situations making Alice his representation of Eve who is led to temptation by the characters and situations she encounters. Alice starts out as a child but through acquisition of knowledge, she becomes fully prepared for the adult reality outside the garden. (God told us to come unto Him as little children) The white rabbit with the pocket watch constantly reminds Alice of the brevity of her childhood and that she must sooner or later give into adulthood. In one episode the Cheshire cat sits in a tree and gives Alice knowledge, and Alice sees her whole world differently. The cat stands as an embodiment of satan who talks to a female while sitting in a tree and leads her to new understanding. Alice consumes a liquid because it is not marked poison, but it makes her shrink, and after that she is no longer distrustful of any wonderland food. Eve ate of the forbidden fruit. Even though not poisoned, it robbed her of that oneness with God, and now she/women don't question what they eat much anymore. (Some do) To fall and to grow in the same moment Alice and Eve both experienced. The food not only cause them to fall but to grow to big to be in the company of where they were. Alice physically and Eve spiritually. Alice awakes, shaking off wonderland and leaving it forever. By Alice taking control of her own Journey she arrives into her own garden of deception.

(Freedom: What do July 4th and Alice in Wonderland have in common M.Huffpost.com) (Independence day)(Author: Lewis Carroll 1865 novel written by English author Charles Lutwidge Dodgson under the pseudonym Lewis Carroll)

The reality is this: America celebrates on the fourth of July for Eve's independence from God. ALL the gatherings and barbeque, drinks and games are deception. It's to make everyone unknowingly celebrate and make mockery of God. It's to fill the skies with pollution from fire works which makes us look up towards heaven grinning and laughing at God that we have become independent now. We only think we are grinning at how beautiful the fire works are but God sees a whole different thing! He sees His people looking up and making a mockery of Him. Independence is what is keeping us from entering back in into the secret place. Independence day! The earth actually celebrates Eve's departure from God. God sent us here to transform and to make a difference so that people may see your good works and glorify the Father "which is in heaven" not santa in the north pole. Do you see how deceptive the devil is.

> "My people are destroyed for lack of knowledge. Because thou hast rejected knowledge, I will also reject thee, that thou shalt be no priest to me: seeing thou hast forgotten the law of thy God, I will also forget thy children. (**Hosea 4:6**)

They believe in Santa anyway. Wow, And looking at the state America is in and claiming to be united with her views is poisonous! Americans actually take a whole day, Fathers day, to rebel against what Jesus has said and they take the time to call every single man they come in contact with "father". Rebellious generations! Mostly even men we don't even know We take the time to do the civil rebellious duty, being united one nation under they pagan god "happy fathers day"! Satan's tactics!

How does that make God feel?

Does it make Him want to pour blessings out on you when He said call no man Father?

Does it make Him want to Heal your body or put more jewels in your crown?

How does it make God feel when you stand during testimony service saying giving praises to God the head of my life and giving honor to my father in the gospel and then proceeding to call your father's name?

I have heard this all my life and I choose to take a stand and become united with the state of Jesus, *our Father which art in heaven, Hallowed be thy name! Matthew 6:9 God* is the Father of the gospels. Many spiritual leaders go hard for Jesus and has been through many many things and have not taken down the standard! They say for God I live and for God I die and they mean just that! I honestly commend these men of God! Have we ever stop to think that some of the things they go through is because "WE" have tried to fill an empty void and put them in the place Santa Claus used to be? ***"The gospel of Jesus Christ"*** keeps ringing in ear.

146

Should He be the Father of it since it's His gospel?

Connected to the state and views of America now we choose to call man father and we call Father a "man" When He plainly *said "I'm NOT A MAN THAT I SHOULD LIE "*,and because we're confused we believe we must do right because some way some how pastor will find out and He'll know if I have been naughty or nice. So we try to conform to another man creating yet another soul tie and once we find out the void hasn't been filled now instead of wondering naturally and sexually, the wondering spiritually begins from church to church calling this one father, that one father never really giving thought that soul ties are being created and we wonder why we don't know who we are and what's our purpose.

Why do we constantly get upset and persecute the five fold?

Because we have thrust them in the place of God! Then We get ungodly and real messy when we find them to make mistakes. We call everybody and then actually think it's okay to talk about them and to treat them like a junk yard dog when we see a short coming in their lives!

How evil and confused is that?

Father sent us a perfect example Jesus Christ who walked without sin. Because we choose our way we throw men's of God in deadly positions. They cannot live up to being God to you. Those who have no fellowship with God as Father but claim salvation are the modern day Pharacies... They are proud and they are arrogant ! These only Worship Him in a public place where they can be seen and where they can be heard by people. They don't practice His ways. They want a platform but have nothing beneficial to say.

God is using false Christians as a diversion while the real soldiers are suiting up and getting ready for battle. Then false Christians will be used as human shields to block the attack of the enemy. Why human shields? Because it appears they are in the fore front of everything right now! When the missiles take off...it hits the front liners first! To many ladies have never understood why they are here in this place today. It's because the state of America has marred Jesus teachings and we just conformed instead of transformed and now God is calling His daughters and sons to WAKE UP! God is the Father of the Gospels, that has been passed down from generation to generation. Alfa and Omega! The beginning and the end! One Father.

> *"And He gave some apostles; and some, prophets; and some, evangelists; and some, pastors and teachers."(**Ephesians 4 11-27**)*

He never gave some Fathers because those not united with the state of America and her ways, have only one Father God, *Hallowed be Thy Name. Matthew 12:46-50* gives an example of how to become united with Jesus views and strip yourself of being united with the demonic state this country is in.

While He yet talked to the people, behold His mother and His brethren stood without, desiring to speak with Him. Then one said unto Him, behold, thy mother and thy brethren stand without, desiring to speak with thee. But He answered and said unto Him that told Him, who is my mother? And who are my brethren? And He stretched forth His hand towards His disciples, and said behold my mother and brethren! For whosoever shall do the will of my Father "which is in heaven ",the same is my brother, sister, and mother.

Jesus never said the same is my Father, sister, mother, and brother because Jesus knew and always specified He had but one Father and that Father is in heaven! Jesus didn't come to conform to the state of the places He went, but He transformed people to the state of His mind!" *Let this mind be in you which was also in Christ Jesus!"* When you know who your Father really is, then you know who You are!

> *For the perfecting of the saints, for the work of the ministry for the edifying of the body of Christ: Till we all come in the unity of the faith, and of the knowledge of the son of God unto a perfect man unto the measure of the stature of the fullness of Christ: That we henceforth be no more children, tossed to and fro and carried about with*

every wind of doctrine by the sleight of men, and cunning craftiness whereby they lie in wait to deceive: but speaking the truth in love, may grow up into Him in all things which is the head, even Christ: From whom the whole body fitly joined together and compacted by that which every joint supplieth, according to the effectual working in the measure of every part, maketh increase of the body unto the edifying of itself in love. This I say therefor, and testify in the Lord that ye henceforth walk not as other Gentiles walk, in vanity of their mind, Having the understanding darkened, being alienated from the life of God through the ignorance that is in them, because of the blindness of their heart: who being past feeling have given themselves over unto lasciviousness. To work all uncleanness with greediness. but ye have not so learned Christ: If so be that ye have heard Him and have been taught by Him as the truth is in Jesus: That ye put off concerning the former conversation the old man, which is corrupt according to the deceitful lusts; And be renewed in the spirit of your mind; And that ye put on the new man, which after God is created in righteousness and true holiness. wherefore putting away lying, speak every man truth with His neighbor :for we are members one of another. Be ye angry and sin not: let not the sun go down upon your wrath: Neither give place to the devil. Amen!

(Ephesians 4 vs 12-27)

<u>So why are women so confused these days?</u>

<u>Why are women fighting to be treated like equals to men?</u>

<u>Why are women trying to be actual men?</u>

Because we are Fatherless! A father implements and instills values in his children. They look at him and immediately they know the potential that lie within them! They begin to see his ways afar off and close up and they pattern their lives after the values and morals given from him to them! "Our Father which art in heaven Hallowed be thy name". When we actually take time to see our Father, observe Him, that even His name means "*honor as holy*", "*make holy; consecrate*". "Greatly revered or respected!" This is who our Father is! We must stop the madness and come to the realization that our Father has been here all the time just waiting for us to pull off the old man and put His ways on, His values, love what He loves and hate what He hates! Hallowed be thy name. Out of all the names this name was instructed by Jesus for us to call to differentiate God from all other pagan gods. The enemy, who uses America to get what he wants has worked through sore evil people to get them to dishonor our Father's name by dedicating a whole day of demonic activity! *Hallow-ed* be thy name. *Hallow-ween*. A day of the dead and day of people walking around like zombies, murderers, victums, sexual perversions. This is all to dishonor our Father! But because we presume Fatherless, we think it's cute and fun, and hey, let us give and get candy! America, united in thinking abominable against God! United state of chaotic behavior! The clean shall separate from the unclean or go down as unclean. God is life and love! Hallow is life, love, and peace! Halloween created for devil worshippers and blasphemed people. Its about death and destruction!

Trick or treat?

Throwing eggs at people?

We teach our children satan's way! We teach them how to rebel and disrespect our Father! Trick or treat! We may think that it is cute right now and yes satan allows us to get the treat for years while tricking us all along. His trick is to get God against you for participation in this blasphemous day. His trick is to get God against our children for our actions and or children's children! The cold part is that his trick is embedded in the name itself! Halloween! His trick is to wean us away from our Father *Hallow*!! He has this whole creative activity going on this day that has no attributes of God in it. His trick is to train us and our children and grand children what demons look like! To get our ears used to the screams of hell! To get you and your family to a place to think subliminally that hell isn't so bad! I mean we spend a whole day pretending and dressing up like the demonic and hearing screams and being scared and its actually fun! Wow! And satan Is just counting down the days to show you that you were tricked and that the fowl smell of hell has opened arms waiting for you! He's waiting to show our daughters that nope, tricked you, theirs no little people dressed up like princesses here, just demons ready to rip off your flesh! He's ready to show our sons that he is real! Why do we participate in a day called hallow-een? Because we are fatherless. This same America takes a whole day and call it a day full of love!

<u>*We all know God is love right?*</u>

<u>*So America, why do you stick an arrow straight through the heart?*</u>

<u>*Are you implying that you wish you could kill God?*</u>

We all know to puncture the heart in such hatred makes it stop beating and it is no more. Of coarse you have cupid and the wings..blah blah blah....but look at what it really is. America wishes to kill love. She'll never tell you that. She wants millions of Americans to keep fornicating on Valentine's having sexual intercourse without marriage and this helps push the arrow through the heart as well.

Hallow says it's time to come in and get our birth right! No more ignorance! No more claiming the demonic state America is united in. We shall not participate on April fools day any longer. No more teaching our kids to be fools of satan because we participate in a whole day full of lying and laughing. Who are we really laughing at? Is it the joke or the prank or is our flesh unknowingly to us laughing in disobedience at God? You'll find church people who have turned to the world and the worlds ways say that it doesn't take all that, it's not that serious! Tell that same stupidity to the only eight people who made it out alive in the days of Noah! Don't let people's worldly lust around you cost you to be accountable for taking down the standard! We are not from here. No more conforming to her ways! Our mind is being renewed! I no longer fight for equal pay of a man! This is deception! In the older times men had whole families to support. We have our focus on what America tells us to put our focus on so my question is:

Is America, being a woman, your Father?

Can You see how demonic?

How same sex marriages are every where is so sad. Our Father says pull off the old man. Take on his mindset and live! Daughters take after the nature of their father! Our Father's name is Hallowed meaning "honor as Holy, make Holy consecrate", greatly revered or respected." These characteristics should be in us also.

Why are women fighting so hard to equal men ?

Why are women choosing their own way?

> John14:6 Jesus said unto him, *I am the way, the truth, and the life: no man cometh unto the Father but by me.*

Instead of seeking our Father and allowing Him to tell us who we are and what He has placed inside of us to bless the world with and to win people to Christ, we go our own way. To live a for filling and blessed life is God's will for us. We choose everyday to omit having a Father daughter relationship with God and we choose the empty hole that we fill with soul ties that make the empty black hole deeper. We choose to go around in this vicious cycle and we are not happy enough that we are ruining our lives by pushing our Father back. We pass this to our children and we pass our hazardous advice to our friends and family! Anyone who is willing to be silly enough to listen. All the Fatherless need to feel whole is love. God is love and two plus two equals four. A person who is Fatherless spiritually has chosen this way of living. Only our God make up for those who may not have had a dad growing up, because God is fulfillment! Time For God's daughters and sons to come back home. We have been in the wilderness long enough. Those that will, let's go home. What since does it make for us to stay outside in the rain and storms when God, our only Father, has set aside a place for us to dwell with Him in the secret place!

"He that dwelleth in the secret place of the most high shall abide under the shadow of the Almighty."

We have a secret place with our Father! No more standing out in the rain. God desires for us to claim Him and to desire wisdom! The beginning of wisdom is the fear of the Lord.

Do we fear going against God's word?

Do we fear Him when we choose our own way?

> *But whosoever shall deny me before men, him will I also deny before men, him will I also deny before my Father which is in heaven.* **Matthew 10:33**

In other words take my love, support, wisdom, understanding, joy and everything that comes with me or I'll disclaim you before my Kingly Father! Please remember that it's not with our mouth only, that a person can deny Jesus! It's more so with our actions!

What are we doing that proves Jesus walks with Us?

What proves we are friends of God?

The bible says after this manner pray ye. " Our Father which art in heaven, Hallowed be thy name."

Our Father is indeed in heaven! We know longer have to be those Fatherless kids that the Lord spoke of. Let's make Him proud! Surrender and come home! Our Father wishes to have super with us!!!

Behind The Veil

_Freedom From Influence

Dearly Beloved,

On the day of judgement when we stand before our King we will be free! Free from influence and from pressures of strongholds! Free from familiar spirits like witchcraft, Jezebel and Ahab, talking about people and killing them to others with our mouth just to name a few. We will be totally free!

No demonic influence will be there to strong hold us any longer!

It will be us standing before God with every knowledge that we ever learned of Him. We will be faced with everything we've ever heard in peoples passing conversations in the market place about what God can do and who He is. We will be held accountable for hearing the preacher preach at our local church, by hearing television evangelist, by reading the bible at different times, and even by little things our children may have said to us like "God can do it mama He loves you!" We will be judged by our knowledge and what we chose to do with it.

This sounds beautiful. ...this *freedom of influence.* The kicker is this is when God pulls the book of remembrance out and shows us the things we did in our lives even with the knowledge of Him and who He is. The choices we made contrary to God instead of obeying His word, the people we destroyed with our tounge because we let jealousy and strife influence us, and what about the days He sent us into dark places to be His light in the earth and show people through faith the evidence of things not seen. (which is Him) We chose popularity, or we chose to fight back against those talking deceitfully about us just to fit in with the crowd -because actually being a light means we have to be hott! A light in a room does not follow the in-crowd, but the light stands alone so much until everyone in the room begins to need it without being aware that it's a necessity until the light is removed. This is when you notice the light is gone and you miss it. God will show different ones how they rejected the purpose of their earth life which was to be that light. Because nobody pats the light on the back and says good job for lighting the room, because nobody wants to come close and hang out/ hold conversation with you, because know one chooses you to call you up and have girl chat with ! The light is to hot, it's also blinding and to bright, and because the light is to sharp it exposes the enemy and where he is hiding. We unconsciously and consciously made the choice to reject the light. We allowed influence of demonic forces and people with their flattery lips to lead us to this point of standing before Jesus and looking at the disappointment on His face with words you know He's thinking.

> *"I spent all that time investing prayer for you, praying that*
> *your faith failed you not, praying that you would listen*
> *to me and take heed resisting influence of the demonic."*

The influence of the demonic wouldn't be standing here now to face our Father with us. The look of a broken hearted King is hell in itself, but knowing that you're the reason for this sadness is to much to bare. The look of a broken hearted King that has done everything for you is a look one NEVER EVER forgets. A taunted memory to keep just before getting handed over to the enemy for eternity of suffering, pain, weeping, and clinching teeth together so much until they break -but the look on His face. .. the one time you get to see His face and it has that look of total disappointment, because you chose the fallen angel.

"Because ye thought less of the light I gave and made ye to be, the light in your generation I instructed ye to become but ye told me no. For this cause ye won't spend eternity with me because I Am that I Am. I Am that light! Ye were simply the offspring of me. But ye chose to be ashamed of what people might think and hid your light under a bushel until it went out.

Did ye not believe that ye came from me?

If this is true then ye commit one of the biggest sin against me of all time. The sin of Unbelief.

Do I still love you?

Yes, but ye have made the choice that I was to hot for you, to blinding, and because you had to be alone like me, (I dwell in the secret place) you chose the influence of popularity! You rejected me and now ye go to a place where you'll feel my presence no more."

Self righteousness wont be their standing with you before God influencing you that you're right. Lying wont be their with a good excuse as to why these choices were made. It'll just be you, taking the things you chose to do like the adult that you are.

"My presence no more shall ye feel. That sweet smell of fragrance you always chased after for your home, car, and office will never be indulged in again.

Did not you know that you received those sweet smells from me?

Now you go to a place where you're not reminded of me. .. You'll smell nothing sweet ever again. No sweet smells of cookies baking in the oven or beautiful smelling fragrances will you be able to enjoy. Only the smell of betrayal, sour distrust and worry. Also the smell of sickness, boils, and the fowl smell of deadly diseases. The smell of billions of people burning but never being all consumed.

Did you not know that the sweet sound you chased in time past from the waters of my ocean was from me?

You loved it so much until you bought recordings and sound tracks with nothing but my beautiful nature sounds. The birds chirping and the way my animals communicate with each other and my weather patterns. You delighted your ears in my craftiness and creativity but you rejected my light. You were ashamed of me before your friends and family so now I'm ashamed of you. Now you go to a place where you are reminded of me no more. Your ears shall witness screaming of old and young in every language at the same time. The screams of torture pain and regret, because I was nothing but a tour to you and my house a tourist attraction. You never had plans of being intimate with me. You only wanted things from me that would build your status quoe. You'll experience The screams of every influence you chose over me as they rip your flesh from the bones. You'll hear the flames of Hell as they crackle and pop when they for fill destiny to antagonize with fatality. Instead of being the light you chose to be consumed by fire. You chose not to see me because I exposed secret sins and darkness, in your life, and those friends that were no good for you, you chose to beautify yourself and to attract men that were not your husband, You rejected my light but *did you not know beauty is of me?*

I made the spirit of a person beautiful. I made the physical body beautiful also.

The form of the body that you so loved to admire, did you not know this was my creation?

All the beautiful vibrant colors of earth tone fall, delightful daisy spring, electrifying summer, and deep sea winter. I put that together quite nicely right? Now you go to a place where you know longer be reminded of my goodness. Never ever to see beauty again. When your eyes flash away from a hideous sight they wont be able to rest on my beauty only more pain and anguish. You'll see death on the undead and destruction on those who can never be destroyed, over and over you'll see turmoil of children and adults alike. You'll feast your eyes on famine and pestilence. You get to see your influential demons face to face and they will become your daily bread. You'll eat and sleep them! No more will you be able to look at the ocean and see me or enjoy my handiwork. You have made the choice not to be my light because it was costly for you. I sent my son so that you might live and that was costly for me but I chose love beloved. Why have you chosen to reject me and now you go to a place where you wont feel me anymore.

Did you not know that something as simple as someone holding the door open for you was an act of my kindness?

Something as simple as someone saying good morning to you. That's my kindness things that made you feel warm inside...my sunset, my feel and comfort of having a family and intimate time with your spouse, feeling me in prayer holding you close, or in church service at the altar, seeing me in those special ones choosing not to reject me but carry the cross like Jesus and gaining hope you'll experience these things no longer. You wont taste of me anymore because you chose influences over me you wont taste and see that I am good. You'll not even taste your tears!

Did you not know that tears were of me?

That's my handiwork! I gave you tears as weapon for those who sought me in how they should use them. Not those that took my tears and used them for manipulations and gain of fleshly things. No, my tears wont go with you because they are apart of me. You'll cry and weep for eternity without having the luxury of tears to lubricate your eyes. You shall inherit blistered dry eyes from the heat and the crying that will produce none of my tears. These things you have chosen when you rejected being my light. When you rejected it you rejected me and you chose satan. Go! Turn away from me. I know you not!

Some has already faced this. But to you, I send mercy like I sent to them. They chose me not! You choose me this day and live. Choose me through all the influences of the devil, and your life will never be the same. You'll experience me in such a mighty way. Choose me this day and live!

CHAPTER 11

The Unpaid Debt

"Greater love hath no man than this, that a man lay down his life for his friends. Ye are my friends, "if" ye do whatsoever I command you." Amen.

(John 15: 13-14)

<u>Did you know that many many people are walking around with a debt so big that it would break their entire credit report?</u>

We walk around thinking mainly of bills, family, what's for super, and how can I achieve the goals I have set in my mind and believe me, this is enough to keep the mind busy! Don't mention having kids, a husband and a ministry. It's enough to blow your top! Satan knows this and enjoys this very much. This makes it easy for him to slide unforgiveness, envying, and strife in, making it where we're to busy to even deal with these issues. We may think of it once church is in motion and the word is going forth. Our hearts get pricked a little and we may shed about five tears to the lap and then back to our regular mind sets we go...

"What's for dinner, I wonder what Paula them will have, they always BBQ on Sunday."

Satan has a huge tactic in motion that is a sure way to get people into Hell's gates faster than they can say "O I didn't know". One, because Satan has in his back pocket a wild card that will catch a host of pastors, apostles, teachers, evangelists, prophets, prophetesses, elect ladies, ushers, choir members, mothers in the church, deacons and deaconesses, and just plain old pew warmers who sit and observe. Satan hopes know one will expose the wild card he holds close to him so secretly and on the day of judgment he will use this card and many will have no choice but to go with him. The Lord wants you, who has taken time to read these passages he has instructed me to write, to know about this trick and dart of the enemy so you wont get caught in the snare. No matter how good "you thought " you were, satan will use this card if you're found guilty.

When Moses died, the devil was fighting over his body. The actual devil showed up to claim Moses! Out of all the wonderful works God did through Moses! This means the devil had rights to be warring over Moses. The main wild card satan will try to use on many of us is this:

"And forgive us our debts as we forgive our debtors!"
Matthew 6vs12

Now you may think this is not major, oh but it is!! For those who do not keep or have not kept this part of our Father's prayer along with all sinners of the world must be notified in such an urgency because Jesus paid the greatest ultimate price when He gave His life so that we may live. Jesus paid our debts with His blood. We who are obedient walk in a part of the law that protects us. (Yay) Those who choose not to forgive their debtors has the blood of Jesus on their hands. God's sons and daughters are covered "by" the blood of Jesus! Praise God! But those soldiers who actually beat Jesus and crucified Him was covered "in" the blood if Jesus.

What do you think God would do to a person with Jesus blood on their hands?

In our day and time a person with another persons blood on their hands, to the death of that individual, would be prosecuted by the law! *"Forgive us our debts as we forgive our debtors."* If we don't forgive others "WE ARE NOT FORGIVEN FOR THE DEBT JESUS PAID FOR US!

*"But he was wounded for our transgressions, he was
bruised for our iniquities :the chastisement of our peace
was upon him."*

Isaiah 53 5-6

Your debt to Jesus is defiantly "Not" forgiven if you have not forgiven
others for their trespasses! "Wild card." Most often people like to slack around
when it comes to truly and honestly from the heart forgiving someone.

Be ye angry, and sin not: let not the sun go down upon
your wrath: Neither give place to the devil. let all
bitterness, and wrath, and anger, and clamor, and evil
speaking be put away from you, with all malice. And be
ye kind one to another, tender hearted, forgiving one
another, even as God for Christ's sake hath forgiven you!
(Ephesians 4 26-27;31:32)

Lot's of people feel it's okay to go along with bitterness, unforgiveness,
and petty differences that they choose to take to heart making the body
sick, not knowing satan has appointed them a demon that whispers to them;

"It's okay, you're right to feel this way, God understands."

Little do they know he can't wait to pull that wild card out at the right
time and claim they soul, because it's no way God is going to let someone
with Jesus blood on their hands into the kingdom of heaven! Murderers
they are. God is coming back for a people without spot or wrinkle.

Are you forgiven of the biggest debt of all times?

Forget your credit report to this natural world. Have you been
cleared of the amazing supernatural debt that has traveled through
every generation and every blood line. This outstanding debt is massive
! If you harbor unforgiveness this same debt is big enough to get you cast
into hell! This major debt that has traveled through time and through
everyone's bloodline can cause life to many and cause death to many!
This debt can not be worked off by your perfect attendance at church,

or by going door to door saying Jesus saves! It all depends on you and what you choose to do with your heart.

> "For this is my blood of the new testimony, which is shed for "many" for the remission of sins!" (**Matthew 26:28**)

He didn't say ALL!

Have you made your final choice?

Satan has made his and many people will stand before God bloody from head to toe because of "the unforgiven debt". Choose life today! Forgive and be forgiven, because the "wild card" is waiting on you!

Behind The Veil
_Lust, the Demonic love

Everyone was built to love because it's super natural! However we must be in God to utilize love because it's simply what He is and when not in God we are trapped by a form of love called lust! Take the horseshoe for instance, it's original purpose is to be a shoe for the horse so that different particles wouldn't get stuck in the horse's foot. This shoe is designed to allow the horse to go at a further distance with healthy hoods. (It's not mandatory that all horse's have shoes but it can help prevent excess or abnormal hoof wear and injury to the foot. This is just an illustration.) (Horse shoe-Wikipedia) Many people use this same horseshoe as sport to play games and entertain superstitions of good luck or bad luck.

What if you had a horse but chose to take the shoes off it for entertainment?

It's all fun and games for a minute until we realize we can't get far when needing to travel by horse because it has no shoes. Therefore all types of things get connected to the horse's feet causing him to slow down then stop. Love is the horseshoe which can take us further in God because God is love, but often times because we feel it's to expensive to follow God we use lust the form of love that barely even get's us up the road! To this lust is attached all types of demonic activity that slows us way down to an eventual stop.

America eats and eats and eats some more! However the eating is not the problem, it's the underlying love (lust) for food! The lust of consumption is what many Americans deal with and it's demonic.

God is paying close attention to our judgment call in this hour.

What's your judgement and why do you feel this way?

Do you call all men dogs in your mind?

Are all women gold collectors?

Do you think children are the devil?

What's your judgement on life?

In every way we must make sure our secret judgments line up with the word of God, because the spirit of lust is already and has already been in the land. We somehow mistake it for love so it has a deeper deception. Now surfacing we see lust for same sex marriage or marriage in general, but at the root of lust is under lying

Lust for *power*

Lust for being *prejudice*

Lust for *hatred* (you have to find somebody to hate or be offended with)

Lust for *retaliation*(the love of getting somebody back at the right time)

Lust for *rebellion* (liking to get up close to authority so you can rebel)

Lust for finding *dirt* on people so our mouths can curse us by talking about it,

Lust for *war,*

Lust for the *old way* (an eye for an eye)

Lust is a choice. We must examine ourselves closely because the body loves to find reasons to lust! Lust will cause us to finish and with nothing to show for it. It all depends on you(U). Will you go back to Pharaoh or will you stay free?

CHAPTER 12

The Ace In Spades of lucifer

A host of people ask themselves at least once a week, why do I feel like I'm in prison?

I wake up, shower, eat, use the restroom, work, come back before dark, shower, read a book, bed time and wake up again to do the same exact thing! We tend to call this " *having no life* ", meaning no fun, and no adventure.

I'm here to tell you that their is hope at the end of the tunnel! The Lord has given me bread and war strategy to share with you! Often times we as people try to get rid of the problems without finding the root of the issue ! Doing it this way, as we have lived and learned, causes the problem to come back up later like weeds in a garden. In the previous chapter we talked about Satan's wild card of the unpaid debt. In this chapter we will discuss another major card satan dwells on to make sure we and our children never see the promise land. It's yet another way lucifer keeps an individual bound with no way out, but first let me say this;

Have you ever tried to defeat a foe but you didn't know anything about them, their weak points, or tactics?

This is a very hard enemy to beat because you could be attacking them where they are strong at which simplifies this equation to you getting tired and quitting as a whole loosing the battle! So God gives us scripture and strategy to war against the enemy with! He's exposing the devil to those who will take heed and victory is yours for the taking. We look around and have no earthly idea how we got bound, but knowing that freedom is nowhere around. You're right you have no earthly idea because this is very spiritual.

How can we fight a spiritual battle using natural things to do so?

"For we wrestle not against flesh and blood, but against principalities, against powers, against the rulers of the darkness of this world, against spiritual wickedness in high places". (**Ephesians 6:12**)

We go through this life getting hurt, mistreated, talked about, abused, and plain done wrong by people. Those of us that are saved, we take and take some more of the devil's foolishness through people until we feel we are at our wits end and we start to retaliate only to keep a same mindset. So we do little things and set little traps for people to teach them you better not mess with me! We sew a little discord and make sure our friends hate this individual when the harm hasn't been done to them at all. We add more lies on top to make it really seem that this person is a ugly hearted monster, fake in being genuine, and claiming Jesus! Of coarse nobody likes to be bound alone, so sewing discord to friends is the next best thing to the carnal human mind to do. They need to be bound with me. Once they are bound by my web of lies, they will start to see through my eyes! They'll see what I tell them to see! They'll think about this person how I tell them to think and feel how I want them to feel and I become lord in their lives since they obey me now! Wow! Be very careful who you call friend! Two words I get out of friend is fired and end. Natural friends will fire you and end a good name you once had. Ok so now the friends are bound to so you feel better that you're not going to hell by yourself. Moving on.... so we come up with a whole team of ways how to get a person back and we retaliate and we invite the vindictive spirit to come right in and get comfortable in us. With us being saved and all, Mr. Vindictive never wants you to realize that you've invited him in so he'll bring along a few friends, maybe jealousy and theft. Mr. Vindictive will go way down in you to make sure you never suspect a thing. That you never call his name out in prayer. If you ever come to the point of wanting deliverance, you'll just bring up jealousy's name because theft is pretty slick as well! You May be pondering why theft is slick. It is because theft has two sides. He has a side for sinners and he has a side for pretenders. Let's call it side A and side B for "Alarming" and "Break neck". Now side A and B typically deals with sinners! Thief has to make sure he keeps them bound so side A (alarming) makes sure that when they go to steal things that the sound goes off, they get caught, face in the paper, they go to jail and they are physically bound! Side B, which is break neck, deals with sinners as well but it mostly specialize in the "pretenders". Those claiming unconquerable King Jesus but not choosing to totally surrender to His lifestyle all the way! Break neck is slicker than oil grease because this part of Thief deals strictly with the spirit. How else can you capture those claiming to be in the spirit? So break neck deals with the tongue He tells the person he's living inside of to fight against those who are really striving to be righteous and take a end time stand. Now literally fighting them could end them up in jail, so this is not the action break neck is going for. He leads them to fight by sewing discord in some form or fashion against some and stealing their Godly influence away from people who would have been able to gain strength from that person by watching their lifestyle with pure untainted eyes. They would have been able to gain from the way that person may handle war fare, the way they respect authority figures, how they treat God, and that God Himself has been placed in that person! Break neck, through individuals, steal chances of that person ever being able to witness or testify to those you have now spoiled their name too. Break neck is way more lethal than alarming because with break neck, the cops that you see will not throw you in prison and you do not have to serve a natural sentence taking time away from life as you know it! Why did God choose the term "break neck" for this particular passage of writing? Because when the neck is broken all chance of us being evidence that God is real is dead when It comes to that individual!

> *Now faith is the substance of things hoped for "the evidence of things not seen".*
>
> **Hebrews 11:1**

Have you ever thought that maybe it takes real genuine faith for a person to walk the way they are walking when it come to living like the word says to live and Doing what the bible says to do?

It is know way around it, it takes faith to walk the Jesus walk! Walking our faith walk shows evidence that God *"who is not seen "indeed"* exist and is very much alive and Kingly! It's break neck's job appointed by lucifer to break the neck of those who actually stand in the evidence and influence line! The line of people that by faith they walk the walk and do less talking. Those people that become the word that people that are not of the faith and that are of the faith can read and be inspired and they influence change! These are the people breakneck wish to assassinate. He wishes and works to assassinate their influence and the evidence that God actually lives! The cold part is, God sees the individuals who allows Satan to use them, and God does punish them, but we become so Fed up with the way these people have treated us until we exercise being vindictive and by spiritual law get throw into prison!

Here's how: Now that vindictive has come in and brought thief in, you not only steal from individuals and be deceptive about who they really are, but then You become bitter all over again. God had your enemies numbered and was fighting in your behalf until you started tampering with what didn't belong to you in the first place.

> *Dearly beloved, avenge not yourself, but rather give place unto wrath :for it is written vengeance is mine; I will repay saith the Lord.* **Romans 12:19**

So breakneck has us spiritually stealing from individuals and crossing boundary lines stealing from God! God said *"vengeance is mine."* This means if you take matters into your own hands you're thieving and nothing comes to a thief but prison.

When were the times you felt like you were in prison?

Check to make sure it's not because you've allowed vindictive to come in and bring jealousy and thief. Many "pretenders" are bound in spiritual prison while walking around scot free as a bird. Never looking at themselves twice noticing something is wrong and unless they cry out for deliverance and get free, satan has their cell marked with death penalty! Break neck is cold blooded!

Did you know that unforgivness toward any person is vengeance?

Sure is so please be very careful and search your heart today! Vengeance means *punishment inflicted or retribution exacted for an injury or wrong.* Countless people take on unforgivness when someone has hurt them for no reason, but unforgivness is another form of vengeance. I urge you, if you're being done wrong, let that be enough. Don't add to your being done wrong by making God cast you into prison as well because you retaliated with unforgivness! It's so much easier to cry out to God using your tears as a weapon, forgive that individual and move on letting unconquerable King Jesus deal with them. God is the best at vengeance! He goes down even to the third and fourth generations! I took my hand off situations long time ago! It's not worth getting God all mighty offended with you.

> "Then *Jesus was led up of the spirit into the wilderness to be tempted of the devil. And when he had fasted for forty days and forty night he was afterward an hungered.* **Matthew 4; (1,2)**

Why would God send Jesus to be tempted right after a forty day and night fast?

Answer

Because this is the prove it ground. You either will or you wont. You'll either go forward or backwards. Also usually on a long fast, flesh has totally surrendered to spirit because it has gotten really weak. Jesus took the enemy back to the scriptures.

"It is written."

Are we taking the enemy back to scripture when it comes to unforgivness?

Are we writing our own script day by day action by action?

Blessed *are the merciful for they shall obtain mercy.* **Matthew 5:7**

Ye are the salt of the earth: but if the salt have lost his savor, where with shall it be salted? **Matthew 5:13**

How can we be salt if we bare not forgiveness?

Jesus came for the very remission of sins. He came so that we could be forgiven. Hundreds of thousands of believers say don't ever denounce Jesus. Not even to save your own life, but people have already done just that by harboring unforgivness in their hearts! Nobody can see it but them so they feel safe, but God knows that heart is not pure. This spits on the very reason Jesus came in the first place. So we could be forgiven.

"But forgive us our debts as we forgive our debtors!"

"But I say unto you, that whosoever is angry with his brother without a cause shall be in danger of the judgment"

(Matthew 5:22)

If you are going through any type of unforgivness, search yourself. Let us discrete this thing.

Is this offense actually an offense, if so let's move on to number two: if not let's tarry a little longer beside number one.

1) *Has this person really committed an horrible offense toward me or am I in my feelings?(emotional)*
2) *Is this offense really necessary?*

If this is a person that I just don't like, just don't know what it is, and this person has never done anything to me personally, then sometimes we can be in the wrong line when it comes to asking God to purge us of unforgivness when we should be asking Him to root up all envy's, jealousy, malice, division and strife.

<u>Division? Why division?</u>

Well, its just another word and example for sewing discord!

"Again, *if two lie together, then they have heat: but how can one be warm alone? 12)And if one prevail against him, two shall withstand him; and "a three fold cord is not quickly broken."* **(Ecclesiastics 4 vs11-12)**

Why do people intentionally sew discord? Because they desire to unbraid unity between two people causing division, causing a lack of harmony between two people. A three fold cord is not easily broken. Any relationship with true harmony has two people and Jesus. A *three fold cord* is not quickly broken. So Satan uses people to sew and *dis-cord* this three fold cord by causing division and disagreement/disharmony.

You ever known a person who whispers to another,

"I don't like her/him. It's something about them."

Before you know it your friend can't stand them either. Division, strife.... why strife? Its not common to walk in a place and just not like somebody you don't even know personally. It's not natural to just start rolling your eyes and having a messed up spirit towards someone you have not taken the time to get to know. Secretly you despise this person. You wish harm would come to them or they would just leave. That's a strife spirit.

<u>So is forgiveness important?</u>

"Agree with thine adversary quickly, whiles thou art in the way with him. Lest at any time the adversary deliver thee to the Judge, and the Judge deliver thee to the officer, and thou be cast into prison. Verily I say unto thee, thou shalt by no means come out thence till thou hast paid the utter most farthing."

Matthew 5:25

This is Satan's ace card. To get you cast into prison through your unforgivness! How many people do you know in this position right now where hurtful things has happened so bad that it could have taken their very breath, and will to live and instead of crying out to God and telling Him about it letting Him feel like the King that He is and applying His vengeance on behalf where He sees fit- they take matters into their own hands and become vindictive or we let unforgivness set up and grow in us like a tree with the branches of theft and jealousy and every time we run the memories through our mind that unforgivness gets watered more and before we know it, we are prisoned because the adversary which is devil, don't play fair so prison is where we end up!

Yes, big hat wearing sister Louis who always has an amen in her belly is sitting in her seat fanning but in prison. So prison where brother shoe shine is, but he always down to feed the hungry, prison. Let's look at prison for a minute. (the devil's ace) Prison is made mostly for thrives and robbers that's it ! To name a few things people tend to be jailed for is; stealing, killing, not paying the IRS, abuse in the home, and selling illegal drugs. All of these have some form of theft involved whether stealing someone's life or money owed or stealing someone's peace or innocence .

So now we find ourselves in a spiritual prison and the Lord says by no means will you come out till you have paid the cost to be a thief.

Why does God sound mad ?

Here I am going through what has happened to me, and the pain is so great I can't let go, I can't forgive. (You can) The devil is happy because he knows you're about to be cast away to prison bound and knows he's about to prove us to be disobedient and an " ignorant thief."

"To *obey is better than sacrifice.*"

1 Samuel 15:22

This is the very reason why God ask us to leave our gift(our sacrifice) at the altar and go obey me by practicing forgiveness to your neighbor. You ever seen a thief on the show cops and how silly some of them really are? They violate someone else's property, while engaging in robbery they may see some real nice shoes, so instead of grabbing everything up and getting out they sit down right then and take their shoes off and put the nice ones on almost like they are shopping. (so funny)This is how satan looks at us when we steal from God. When we can't forgive we throw ourselves in the prison of prisons because we have just then stolen the very thing we are expected of in heaven and that's to give God glory. That's to give Him praise. So we become a glory stealer when we choose not to forgive. Why/How? Because we think this is about me and what I'm going through. "No!" This is bigger than us.

> *"Dearly beloved, avenge not yourselves, but rather give place unto wrath: for it is written, vengeance is mine, I will repay saith the Lord."* (**Romans 12:19**)

Again vengeance is His, not for our hands to be placed on. Feed and give drink to your enemies God said. Vengeance means. Revenge, retaliations, payback, satisfaction. But in this case "satisfaction not guaranteed." The Lord is exposing the enemies wild cards and is showing strategically what weapons He is using to stop God's elect! Thank you Jesus for caring for us!

How does lucifer use his card unforgivness to make us disobedient to God?

> *After this manner therefore pray :our Father which art in heaven.*
>
> *(Matthew 6:9)*

If God is truly our Father then we should obey what He says! Not just what we agree with but everything He says! If we don't forgive, prayers are hindered and we are thrown into prison with others who have disobeyed the law of God and debt has to be paid because we have stolen what is His and His alone.

"Hallowed be thy name," He said.

Why did God with all His wisdom and glory specify His name?

He did this because the evil one rules the airways and some be their that call him father. So lets take a run down of lucifer's sneaky unforgiving plot.

Unforgivness would label me as a thief and robber and I would be thrown into spiritual prison never to come out until I paid my debt in full. Not only that but my prayers would be hindered which mean I would be pursuing a father but it wouldn't be our "Hallowed" Father because disobedience to God means our obedience would be to the devil which causes self righteousness/now the Lords prayer becomes :

"**Our father which art in heaven, disobedience, thief, and robber be your name. Thy Kingdom Come** (*which is destruction*) **Thy will be done in me, as it is in heaven. Give us this day our daily bread.** (*Thinking on past hurts, and what he\ she did, what she said keeping that thing alive not giving it to God become that daily thing you deal with. Tears and complaining become that daily bread of bitterness strife envy's jealousy has become that daily bread.*) **And forgive us our debts as we forgive our debtors.** (*the evil one ate that verse twelve up and swallowed it, because he knows that's the very key to you getting out of prison, to you being set free, to you moving forward and not looking back, to you feeling so light until you can fly with the eagles now and leave the chickens clucking on ground! If you repent right tell God you'll do things right then God will de-liver you!*) **And lead us not into temptation but deliver us from evil.** (*The devil laughs at this one when you're praying to him through disobedience to God! He says sure I won't lead you to temptation. I'll make you temptation!! When you go you'll be tempted to steal a woman's job even though you have a job. You'll be tempted to steal a woman's husband even through you have a husband. Youll be tempted to be a person's God even though they have a God. And I shall give you a new name and it shall be envy. You will never ever be happy with what God has given you. Because just like you have corrupted this prayer through your disobedience, your mind will be corrupted. You'll believe a lie rather than the truth and you'll never see your wrong again. You'll say*

*its everybody else. Evil will breed in your nature.) (***2 Thessalonians 2:11)***
For thine is the kingdom and the power and the glory forever amen.

(And the devil says "yes, yes I know power and glory is mine, and to that I say "LIFE WITHOUT PAROLE!!")

Sad stuff but true stuff. We can by pass all of this if we just submit and be obedient to God and forgive.

Did you know even when you don't forgive yourself this happens also?

Yes indeed it does. So how do we move forward? We move back to forgiveness. Back to obedience! Ask that person for forgiveness, don't wait do it right now!! Then we ask God for forgiveness, and we forgive ourselves and mean it from the heart. When slew foot tries to bring bad events back up to our minds or through our friends or family reply "next!" Next. I'm waiting for my next blessing, next breakthrough, next assignment because this simply doesn't work anymore. Next means I can't wait for my next time of prayer and fasting! Glory! When the enemy come to your mind tell him he's a lying dog and that nothing but God's word shall stand. The blood of Jesus be against you satan, I'm free! Check mate!!

> "*The wicked shall be ransom for the righteous, and the transgressor for the upright!*" **Proverbs 21:18**

By following God's plan we get to cash our enemies in for a reward! We forgive those who wronged us. We get extra points by treating it like it has never happened. Its time to cash in. Cash those enemies in to God and experience your rewards that you won't have room enough to store!

Behind The Veil
_Evidence Or Just Existing

When thinking of the word woman, what comes to mind?
Midol, emotional roller-coaster, high heels, tight clothing, perfume trails, hair styles, jewelry, flowers, shopping, laughing and giggling, attitude, or work of art?

Maybe a cooker, cleaner, someone desiring marriage, someone desiring to be equal with men, possibly desiring to make a man fall in some shape form or fashion, or someone that can never have enough material things?

Sadly these things mean we're simply "existing" as ladies and not being or have become that "evidence" God sent us down here to be.

The name Jesus never came to mind when thinking of the average woman because Jesus explained it best when He spoke to me last year and told me that many of His daughters are fatherless!

A fatherless daughter doesn't really know who she is so she begin to take on all these different identities and forms and looking for love in all the extremely wrong places developing soul ties to things and people and creating a whole new out look on life Calling herself a woman. This is why the name Jesus does not come to mind when the woman is spoke of. Since Eve, it seems like the woman just fell from grace. We allow any and everything to pass through our sacred gates.

Gates of a woman are:
Her eyes
Ears
Mouth
Her hidden parts

When this is done, signals are sent to the mind, which then turn to seeds and seeds to trees and trees to manifestation of what we do and where we go!

The woman....stripped of all her glory because she allow all to access her gates and so we minimize ourselves to just being needed for one thing. We thrive on being wanted for sexual pleasure and once this is given to the individual and no love is received from him it reminds us how empty we feel. The vicious cycle continues because we reject our Father, having no identity. We have gone from being rightfully named Adam, but then woman, then Eve and while being confused becoming wife and then mother and we wonder why we don't know right from left.

One fact that will be hated by American women's mindset is that their is no room for "woman" in the Kingdom of God! The woman has to much stuff attached to her. One day she's this the next day she's that and God can't trust a double minded split personality person!

We must become daughters! Jesus said,

"Verily I say unto you, Whosoever shall not receive the Kingdom of God as a little child, he shall not enter therein." (Mark 10:15)

"Enter ye in at the strait gate: for wide is the gate, and broad is the way, that leadeth to destruction, and many there be which go in thereat: 14)Because strait is the gate, and narrow is the way, which leadeth unto life, and few there be that find it."

Matthew 7 13-14

The woman comes with to many things to enter into the straight gate. She's to big and to wide spiritually. Her ways are forever in error. She stands toe to toe with her husband and with her apostle, teacher, pastor, prophet over her. She has her own mind her own way.

"Let this mind be in you which was also in Christ."

(Philippians 2:5)

With Christ being the head of the man then we as ladies should fall into place and harmony has an occasion to manifest because of one mind. Once we come to know who we are by actually spending quality time with our Father then we start to become evidence that our Father exist and is real. We start to take in His characteristics! This is our ticket into the pearly gates ladies! This is the way. To become a daughter we become evidence.

Daughters obey their Fathers, and seek to please them. Before they marry they want their Father's blessing and wisdom on it. Daughters are always taught to fall short of a man. Why? Because her Father teaches this. You can never ever be equal to or be a man.

Transition:

If you look at the word woman it's just two letters more of being Man. Ironically we find ourselves trying to be more than man at times.

I'm smarter, I'm better, I make wiser decisions, I'm the brains of this operation and this is not right. To be a daughter means to be evidence of our Father. God loves us, but He doesn't need us if we choose not to become evidence of His existence.

> *Faith is the substance of things hoped for, the evidence of things "not seen."*
>
> **Hebrew 11-1**

> *Substance* means: *the real physical matter of which a person or thing consists and which has a tangible, solid presence.*

God! Faith is the God of things hoped for. The God of joy, the God of peace, the God of strength, the God of long suffering, temperance, love, and meekness. All these things are evidence that God is very real and His ways are real. (Things not seen)

When this mindset is taken on that we are spiritual beings in earthly bodies and we are to see spiritually we begin to use faith the correct way and by using faith the correct way it causes natural things to come to us as well as a result of our hearts being in the right format. A lot of times we go against scripture without awareness because we try using faith for materials when the bible says seek ye first the Kingdom of God and all His righteousness and other thing will be added (*Matthew 33*)

A lady don't have a baby and then travail. She travail and then bring forth. ..it's the law. So is the law of faith.

"And without faith it's impossible to please God." Meaning without being evidence that God exist I'm useless. Because faith is the only way God can be seen in the earth realm. Through our being daughters and yielding fruits of the spirit.

CHAPTER 13

God's Enemy

Their are those elected by God to five fold ministry that actually do have the mind of Christ. Then on the other side we have the popular club, which is preachers, teachers, prophets, and the others in " high rank " who influence while not actually having the heart and mindset of Christ. These are the ones who use the term " *bridge the gap."* Many gospel rap artist use this term as well. Bridge the gap simply means let's make a bridge across the valley so the world can walk right into the church, experience the thrill, and feel this Holy Ghost fire. They may get warmed by the fire, experience the chill, and be influenced to change. They will hear the word and be convinced that this is where I need to bring my money on the weekend. These posers has actually made this happen! They took their time allowing satan's guidance and made settle movements, not to alarm the church, and they did things naturally but spiritually it was laying the bridge plank by plank. We heard of one *Bishop* getting his ears pierced for a wedding. ..plank. *Preachers wives reality TV* show. ..plank. Plank. *Preachers daughters reality* plank plank. *Gospel artists hanging out with secular artist.* .plank plank plank.... *Prophetess wearing spandex and see through clothing plank plank plank .. ladies wearing jeans in the pulpit. Plank plank!* How can anybody grab God looking at your fat fanny? Plank plank plank. This veiw is not religious but it is wisdom. *Preachers getting caught up in scanda*ls plank plank. *..preachers scamming people for money* ...plank plank and now this big bridge with beautiful lights on it has been built over the valley to the church house and many are flooding in! Where we once had the world, then this big valley gap-then the church is not this way any longer. This demonic act is getting dealt with by God Almighty and people have not seen the calamity this world has yet to face. People of God do you see that these posers influenced by the devil has created this dreadful demonic act all in the name of Jesus to keep us silent and thinking everything is okay. Well, I'm crying loud as instructed by my Master, my Lord, my Savior, my King of kings and ever lasting Father.

> "Cry *aloud, spare not, life up thy voice like a trumpet.*"
> (**Isaiah 58**)

God put the valley between the church and the world for a reason. To build a bridge in disobedience is evil in the worst way. *Just think about the towel of babel. (Gen 11:1)*

> "Wherefore *come out from among them and be ye separate, saith the Lord, and touch not the unclean thing; and I will receive you!*"
> (**2 Corinthians 6 vs 17**)

Now in S*ong of Solomon chp 2 vs 1* we plainly see why the church is seeking no deliverance today!

What is the use of "bridging the gap " when none of the world is making any change, but they are all flooding the church house on Sunday coming as they are across a demonic bridge that was built on deception, disobedience, lies, Idolatry, envying's, and greed?

I'll tell you why this works for those who built this bridge in error. It all points back to greed and money. They could care less that nobody is changing. The pimp is still the pimp, he just pay tithes now. The whore is still the whore, she just pays tithes now. The adulterers is still fornicating they just pay tithes now and have more options of married men or women to pursue. By building this bridge in the first place shows people whom do not fear God. The satanic con artist holding illegal titles that they paid 50.00 to receive from the web, has done the ultimate of the demonic! I wouldn't let them even lead me on what type of fabric softener to use!

These down low satan worshipers has put their heads together and figured out a way to bypass people having to go through the valley before entering to the Holy sanctuary of God. Theirs a "Lily" in the valley and its bright as a morning star. That Lily is Jesus! They came up with a way to get people into the house of God without going through an encounter with JESUS. *"THE LILY IN THE VALLEY."*

"Verily *verily I say unto you, He that entereth not by the door into the sheep fold, but climbeth up some other way, the same is a thief and a robber."*
(John 10:1)

"Jesus said I am the door: by me if any man enter in he shall be saved, and shall go in and out, and find pasture."
(John 10:9)

You simply cannot find pasture on a bridge. I have heard not one complaint from a "bridge traveler" yet about not having any pasture to dwell in, which proves to me that you can't be a real sheep without Jesus!! Did you understand what I said? You simply cannot find pasture on a bridge. A bridge is for going and coming. The world is coming and going back the same way they came in. A pasture is for dwelling and for being taught how, when, and what to do to grow. So the Satanist claiming Jesus name has done this evil act and caused the church to think in terms of progression and how many people can enter into the church. "If" any man enter in he shall be saved, and shall go in and out and find pasture. The key word being "if"! The satanic heads have taken the if and "bridged the gap" and now you rarely see change in people. Now the church world is stuck on this *"come as you are "* crap which when checked in the strong concordance this is mentioned no where! The bible does in fact state

"Come unto me, all ye that labor and are heavy laden, and I will give you rest."
(Matthew 11:28)

"Come now, and let us reason together, saith the LORD: though your sins be as scarlet, they shall be as white as snow; though they be red like crimson, they shall be as wool."

Isaiah 1:18 -

The key word is *"reason!" Nobody is reasoning with God. People want it their way!*

"Then said Jesus unto his disciples, If any [man] will come after me, let him deny himself, and take up his cross, and follow me."

Matthew 16:24

I'm not understanding where come as you are is implemented. Jesus always let people know in order to follow Him, this must be done that must be done. Yes you have sin but pull it off! Lay down the weight! People still stuck in the rut of "come as you are" for 5 and 6 years. God is a God of restoration and redemption so who are people actually serving because you barely see restoring.

"Incline your ear, and come unto me. Hear and your soul shall live."

(Isaiah 55:3)

God wants people to come to Him that will *"hear!"* Incline means *to have a tendency to do something;* Willing, ready. Those that are coming across this illegal bridge does not have and do not desire the gift to hear, and so they continue in error. They are in the house but lost! The cruel sick demonic part is -now they continue in sin without the reality of the curse to let them know they are in error because of their tithes and offering paying. Now we have people that are "Blessed to be cursed forever!" The demonic forces of darkness knows how to cover itself in sheep clothing and look okay enough to blend in with people who are actually trying to do right. They will eventually think it's okay to keep dressing whore like and coming into God's presence. These are people who bypass the *Lily* in the valley. Most people of authority wont send them back and tell them to come correct, but they draw them in close while overly expressing that God loves them the way they are and continue allowing them to spread ungodly influence sending the church into a backward spiral with little morals and before you know it these people fifteen years down the road is still whoring around, stealing, killing with the tounge, committing fornication, and lawlessness! All because we refuse to bring them face to face with sin and tell them you must repent and ask God to clean you! People have chosen an easier path.

"Enter ye in at the strait gate"

(Matthew 7 13/14)

Strait meaning:

1) *a narrow passage of water connecting two seas or two large areas of water*
2) *used in reference to a situation characterized by a specified degree of trouble or difficulty.*
3) *(of a place) of limited spatial capa city, narrow or cramped.*

"For wide is the gate and broad is the way that leadeth to destruction and many there be which go in there at: Because strait is the gate and narrow is the way, which leadeth unto life, and few there be that find it."

These satanic wolves in sheep clothing has offered the church world a wide gate, and the church has embraced this wide gate because of a few thrills and chills. God spoke to me and said these words concerning the church that we know today:

"Tourist attraction"

I sat up in the bed focusing on what I heard Him tell me. It wasn't until I looked up the word that I knew exactly what God meant and how He was feeling. (Wikipedia tourist attraction) *Tourist attraction is a place of interest where tourist visit typically for its inherent or exhibited natural or cultural value, historical significance, natural or built beauty, offering leisure, adventure and amusement.* Father said it best!

Does this not describe the church today?

They are interested in what will happen in the service. Some go because it's family history to do so. This was great grandma's church. Some go to make role call while others are admiring how fine the preacher or elect Lady is. Believe it or not some go because of how beautiful the building is! But all these are tourist because they come to visit the house of God but they never take Jesus home with them. They never allow Jesus to be apart of their daily life. They never become the church. Let's dissect the word "strait" definition. Yes, we mostly know that definition three is mainly what we think of when reading this passage but let's extend our minds a little more. Definition one talks of a narrow passage of water.

> "But *whosoever drinketh of the water that I shall give him shall never thirst: but the water that I shall give him shall be in him a well of water springing up into everlasting life.*
> ### John 4:14

Seems like being in God does not give a lot of wiggle room. It's narrow and strait, but once the decision is made and commitment is the proof the you are serious, then God begins to take you and let you experience those two large bodies of water that's connected to that narrow strait! Then you get to swim and spread your wings, grow, and become spiritually mature while also experiencing the "no limit " in God! It seems narrow at first and it is, but once in, the possibilities in Jesus are endless. You'll see that what flesh made you think was bondage was actually freedom! That narrow strait is Jesus in the valley, the main thing the satanist in sheep's clothing built a bridge over. Definition two: yes, we all must go through hard times, but this is to show you personally that:

> "God is our refuge and strength, a very present help in trouble."
> ### (Psalms 41:1)

These trials are His introduction of who He is and who He will remain to be! Our Savior! The enemy will come up against us, but now knowing who God is we should be confident that He will show up and show out! God says come from among them and be separate. The choice is ours ultimately but disobedience in this will quickly cause God to see you as an enemy.

> "*The Lord said unto my Lord, sit thou at my right hand until I make thine enemies thy foot stool.*"
>
> **Psalms 110:1**

Pharaoh placed his feet upon his enemies. In this case his enemies were Semites, who were caught in a snare. The subjugated persons literally had their arms tied behind their backs and had been made his foot stool. (Www.bible-history.com)(a menhotep11 1448-1420Bc)

The footstool is mentioned in scripture as a part of the throne of the king and symbolizes God's throne.

> "*Exalt the Lord our God, and worship at His footstool-He is Holy.*"
>
> **(Psalms99:5)**

So it was when they brought out those kings to Joshua that Joshua called for all the men of Israel, and said to the Captains of the men of war who was with him,

> "Come *near, put your feet on the necks of these kings.*"

And they drew near and put their feet on their necks. If we choose not to work in obedience to God, we immediately start walking in disobedience and the devil rules and reigns in this realm called the carnal realm!

> "And Joshua said Unto them, fear not, nor be dismayed, be strong and of good courage: for thus shall the Lord do to all your enemies against whom ye fight."
>
> **(Joshua 10 24/25)**

But disobedience pushes us into the carnal realm. The *"Do what thou wilt"* realm meaning if it feels good to your flesh then do it. How many of us are in this realm day in and day out, not seeking the desires of God but releasing in every area the desires of our flesh. We see people on television stations, co hosts, and Disney movies and we want to become just like them. Get the same hair style, the same tote and shoes, The same nose, HELLO! You see how the enemy has no boundary lines? Before you know it you want the same man, the same mind. ..now what would she or he do in this case? See how the world quickly takes the place of God when we are supposed to consult Him about everything and become more like Jesus Christ? We sit up and think on lyrics of what type of woman this trap rapper said he wanted and then actually go out in the world and try to be that. We make it back to church on Sunday and cry and snot and blow out snot long enough to reach Kansas telling God why is it no man of God wants me, and I keep attracting thugs that only want one thing and goes upside my head. They not interested in my mind or my dreams only what I can do for them. God sits while giving us that *reassurance of silence.*

Why should the King keep repeating Himself to us when we constantly choose ignorance over wisdom?

Why should God Almighty keep spending time on our case when we exercise not being willing to comprehend two little words that even a two year old can comprehend?

Those two words are *COME OUT*!!! God told us to come out and be separate from the enemy and because of choices we sometimes make, we reap tears that are bitter and produce no oil. So we do this for years with hope that these tears will allow some oil to be in our lamps when the bride groom comes, but sadly tears produced by the world comes out as vanity tears! These bare no oil. Only what we do for God will last and with quality. We could take what God said and run for our lives but we choose the way of the world and if we don't come out, the expected end is us being God's enemy.

"Ye adulterers and adulteresses, know ye not that the friendship of the world is enmity with God? Whosoever therefore will be a friend of the world is the enemy of God!"

(James 4vs 4)

The earth is the Lord's footstool so we must make sure we are not the ones with our hands tied behind our backs with God's feet on our necks! Surrender and obey! COME OUT SAYS GOD!

Behind The Veil
_Book Your Flight

Question:

If you had a chance to take one out of two trips of a lifetime, would you search out both places to see which one you prefer to go to?

Would you find witnesses or references to see who has been and how was their experience?

Would you just be excited and set on one place because you heard so many great things about it and you believe some of your family members and friends actually moved to this place?

It's good to answer these questions truthfully! Picking only one place to research at the beginning is pretty good.....I guess.

What about along the way when paying the cost for this trip overtime gets a little expensive?

If starting to cost too much would you still keep paying?

Would you still pay if family and friends made light of you and told you that the things you're doing are not necessarily needed and that the trip doesn't cost as much as you are storing up?

What if in the end the pilot demand you take first class with no exceptions?

This means you either fly first class or you'll have no seat on the plane. Everyone doesn't have the same journey. God chooses our seat and how much we will pay.

Would you stop storing up so much because of influence?

Would you somewhere along the lines stop moving forward and start thinking in the back of your mind that maybe the other destination isn't so bad?

I mean At least the other destination allow you to fly coach. Others say they are going and they seem pretty happy about it. It's way cheaper and I can work less and play more and still go. So we start to work less and play more all while still some kind of silly way thinking we will still by some miracle land the trip we originally set out for and everything will turn out great!

But when we step to the gate and the attendant says we haven't paid enough. ....then what?

What, happens when you find out that everyone else planning for the opposite destination is in line behind you begging also to get on flight 777-66?

When we research both destinations we realize that no matter how costly trip 777-66 to heaven may be we still must count up the cost and pay our share because there are no other alternatives for us. If you ever take a minute to research Hell, you'll never almost follow a pop star, television host, husband, wife, friends, associates, demonic forces, or false preachers and teachers there again. We'll realize that paying the cost for flight 777-66 is a necessity!

John 9:4 *I must work the works of him that sent me while it is day: the night cometh when no man can work!*
Book your flight today!

CHAPTER 14

The Intimacy of Jesus

Have you ever just needed that one thing and once you got it you were satisfied and could now go to sleep in peace and Harmony?

It might be chocolate, or your favorite dish or a book and maybe intimacy with your hubby or knowing all the kids made it home safely. With some people it may not be a daily thing, it may be an over all feeling of being accepted loved and cared for. All these things matter to the human mind and works toward someone topping off their day with that sensual pleasure or emotion most desired at the time. With Saul, he was restless and wanted a word from the prophet Samuel so bad!

"Saul disguised himself and put on other raiment and he went, and two men with him and they came to the woman by night: and he said, I pray thee divine unto me by the familiar spirit, and bring him up, whom I shall name unto thee. And the woman said unto him, behold, thou knowest what Saul hath done, how he hath cut off those that have familiar spirits and the wizards, out of the land: wherefore then layest thou a snare for my life to curse me to die? And Saul swore to her by the Lord, saying As the Lord liveth, there shall no punishment happen to thee for this thing. Then said the woman whom shall I bring up unto thee? And he said, Bring me up Samuel."

(1Samuel 28)

Let's take a quick look at verse five and six.

Vs 5 says *and when Saul saw the host of Phi-lis-'tines he was afraid, and his heart greatly trembled.*

Vs 6 says *and Saul enquired of the Lord, the Lord answered him not, neither by dreams, nor by U-rim, nor by prophets.*

So we observe in verse five and six that Saul was afraid and what he so desired more than anything was a word from the Lord. At this time Saul didn't desire a great feast with friends or to conquer someone's field of cattle, or not even to achieve or capture another concubine, but when it came down to life and death Saul desired a word from He who knows our beginning from our end, He who is known as our rock of ages, and He who has the very power to curse or bless! I speak of my Master Jesus Christ. Saul, when it came to life and death, needed and desired that one most important thing that out weighs every situation and every dilima. Saul desired that one word from God. Often times we see this in ourselves today. This same desperation, that one word from the Lord, one direction, one peace of mind to go forward and then we can sleep peacefully. That one word. Many times we, through ignorance, become an enemy to God like Saul did. We become disobedient and take part in the world when God gave simple instructions to come out. And when we so desperately need that word from God, He's not in a place to be found because with our sins we force God to hide His face from us. His desire is not to look upon sin and disobedience, but to destroy it. Yes, the Lion of Judah will roar His great and terrible roar on sin and anyone connected to it. We force God in many areas of our lives to use the rod. We even teach our children to be the enemies of God by allowing and teaching them to do what we do. (Inside scoop)

"For I know the thoughts that I think towards you, said the Lord, the thoughts of peace, and not of evil, to give you an expected end. Then shall ye call upon me, and ye shall go and pray unto me, and I will hearken unto you. And

ye shall seek me, and find me, when ye shall search for me with all your heart. And I will be found of you saith the Lord: and I will turn away your captivity and I will gather you from all the nations, and from all the places whither I have driven you, saith the Lord: and I will bring you again into the place where I caused you to be carried away captive.

Jeremiah 29:11/14

See God's natural thoughts toward us are good and not evil. He wants to see us prosper and be in good health even as our souls prosper. We sometimes choose the error road many times to please friends, family members, our fans and at the same time we place a no vacancy sign on our foreheads when it comes to God so we force ourselves to be a Saul simply because we choose not to search for God with all our hearts! Now that Saul needed God, that one word from God in this life and death matter- God was know where to be found.

Recap: *"And when Saul enquired of the Lord, the Lord answered him not, neither by dreams, nor bt U-rim, nor by prophets."*

1Samuel 28:5

No answer! No answer for your mom who is fighting for her life. No answer for your son who just would not listen to you and now he's greatly facing time in prison going through detrimental things. No answer for your daughter who can't see past her nose and she's convinced that this man really loves her even though he beats on her and treat her like a stick in the mud and is always accepted back with a simple unfelt apology without flowers. No answer for the grand children who are rootless with no respect for nobody not even themselves. No answer for the amount of bills which is way more than the money that you bring in? No answer, because we have torn ourselves away from God like Saul. Now we as humans do the next best thing! Let's take a look at what Saul did in desperation:

> *"Then Saul said unto his servants, seek me a woman that hath a familiar spirit, that I may go to her, and enquire of her, and his servants said to him, behold, there is a woman that hath a familiar spirit at Eri-dor."*

1 Samuel 28:7

Wow!wow!wow!

Should we take a pause break?

Just going back into my life alone there were times I dabbled in sin following weekly horoscopes and things like this and hit a huge brick wall, like we normally do, and I needed a word from God like Saul. I needed direction, but because I was in sin and sin in me I wanted help, but my heart did not desire change so a quick fix to get me out of my current situation became the goal. Sin abided and I couldn't get an answer from God (not praying whole heartedly and desiring complete change at all) I sought out people who had a form of truth, but not those who would tell me like it was, you know the uncensored tone, *"Get right because hell is hott"*. So we tend to seek out passive people with a form of Godliness but deny the truth!

The truth of what?

That God really do deliver people from burdens! That He's a strong tower, a fortress, a great strong hold that holds down every demonic strong hold. Yes, He is a deliverer that can deliver you from you. Now this next part is interesting.

> *Vs 8 and Saul disguised himself, and put on other raiment, and he went, and two men with him, and they came to the woman by night: and he said, I pray thee, divine unto me by the familiar spirit, and bring Me him up whom I shall name unto thee, and the woman says she fears her life.*

Saul tells her nothing will happen to her. Saul disguised himself. These passage of words just hit home. Numeral times when going to seek out wisdom from people ready to give it, but not ready to live it like friends, employers, internet sources and like mega preachers who write inspirational blogs who obviously think life is about swelling words with no righteous living to back it up. (Not all of them) but even when seeking out these so called spiritual but dead people, with the ones that will listen we disguise ourselves anyway in and through the whole situation. We paint our hellish selves as the one always being done wrong. We may tell them "my husband stays upset with me all the time and I cook dinner, I clean, I make sure pajamas are laid out when they get home from a hard days work and I just don't understand what I'm doing wrong. Then we start to shed tears, in that moment actually being manipulative and believing our own lies, and we top it off with, I know I'm a good woman I just don't know what to do. And Barbra sympathizes with you and gives you non biblical wisdom and yet in all these emotions spilling out all over the place you forget to tell Barbra that you always spending the bill money! Yes, Saul put on a natural disguise but we all the time wear spiritual ones! In order to seek God whole heartedly we must strip off the aprons of Adam and Eve and come back before God confessing all sins and asking forgiveness from our creator. Purpose in our minds and our hearts that we'll wear NO MORE APRONS before God! If we don't make this declaration, we will become like Saul in 1 Samuel. Our last meal will be that of a familiar spirit. God came that we may have life and have it more abundantly. More than anything else this generation need a word from God, and it starts with you and I. We must seek God whole heartedly with no more aprons, no more disguises, no more blaming others for our own short comings and failures. Once we reach proper intimacy with King Jesus, we then will maintain proper daily intimacy by praying, fasting, reading the word of God and loving. We will see that proper intimacy with Jesus will impregnate us with His mindset. Praise the living God! With God and His mindset working through us, watch out world because nothing you have to offer entice me anymore! Your demons are not just no longer wanted in me but now I have the authority and power in God to cast them out of me and then other people. I am now certified through Jesus Christ, to even win others from their own destruction mindset and encourage them to put on Jesus! Just one word from God is all I need. COME! And I'm running with all I have, not looking back for a moment like Lot's wife. I'm pressing toward the mark of a high calling in Christ Jesus!

Behind The Veil
_The Insubordinate\Defiant

Today, right now, how do we see our selves?

In this beautiful life we have been granted, we are constantly known as being and encouraged to be rebellious by the world. While we blame Eve often times it's time to look in the mirror and approach the situation! If we must continue to be known as being disobedient we might as well go down in history for it right ladies!!

Take a quick look at these to ladies; Queen Vashtie and Queen Esther again.

• Both:

Strong ladies
Beautiful
Broke a rule in the palace
Chose to face a near death experience
Both had not been called by the king in A while

Esther was beautiful! She was told never to go before the king without being called or she could face death. There came a time when she was in bad position and her people were about to be killed! Either she was going to face being what we have been labeled for years and go before the king without being called in order to,by God, save her people or to stay hid away in her humble place and let the people fend for themselves. What do I do Lord? My people will be no more if I sit passively like a duck. I'm going before the king without being called."

Here we have Queen Vashtie who was beautiful! She was told when the king sends for you, to never Not come. You go when you are sent for. A situation arose with Queen Vashtie one day. Her husband the king had been drinking at his many parties and was drunk. It was no telling how long it had been since he sent for her and now today he wants to send for me and flash me around like I'm a piece of meat for all his friends to drool over. I've had enough..

"No I'm not going to be made sport of in front of drunken men!!"

Both of these ladies could have been labeled rebellious but why was one exalted and praised above the other? Because one's actions was out of selflessness and the other out of selfishness. One thought about the needs of others, the lives and well being of others; while one was thinking on self pity, self emotions, self worth.

One took authority for granted.

The other took authority and used it for God's glory.

Queen Vashtie used her looks to withhold from the king.

Queen Esther came into the Kings presence with God's Spirit on her making her look even more radiant to the king.

If we feel being hard headed is our strick 9 then why not go down in history for it?

Let's stand up and tell society No we will not go before other men showing our bodies in these revealing clothing you put on the sales rack for us. No I won't stop believing that Jesus is coming back for me. Yes, I am in fact the bride of Christ. No, I don't need your approval of who God already told me I am. No I actually DON'T think sex before marriage is cool. No, I will not lie on my tax returns! Yes, I am a vessel fit for the master's use. No, I will not take down to peer pressure. No I don't care what you think about me.

When we stop thinking like the world has programmed us to think, the beauty from our vessel will shine brighter than stars because Jesus will have taken habitation in those who stand up against the world!

CHAPTER 15

The Cunning Way Of lucifer

God has always been our present help in the time of need! Wonderful Savior, Counselor, Friend, and Master, our Lord God is! Life is so worth living with Jesus guiding us through the catastrophes of life. It's like going on a roll coaster. Down hill, up hill, through valleys, quick right, sharp left, but you come out without a bump or scratch because of God's Holy protection! His Holy Ghost seat belt is used everyday! Those who have never experienced Jesus before takes this same joyous ride of learning wisdom and growing, but to them it's like a bad dream, a night mare even. A storm that tosses and tares up the body, mind, soul and spirit! They have no spiritual seat belt. We can naturally understand how an individual, who has no protection would look at those of us who are actually covered in the fullness of God's grace as if we are crazy for having a phenomenal time with Jesus on this coaster of life. People that are not fully surrendered would look at a person who actually does glory during tribulations like this person can't be genuinely happy, secure, and without worry, stress, or fear! They wont comprehend how you're not getting banged up, bruised up and with the wrong attitude about what's going on. So confusion, anger, resentment, envy, jealousy, and divinations set into the mind! It's only one way to our Father, that is through Jesus, but now that all these spirits set into this individual whether it be coworkers, church leaders, members, family, or friends, pride comes in also and takes a seat in that person's life. Pride goes down deep so it can't be spotted or detected by the person it is using.

In this chapter I would like to focus on the mate. (Your husband)

(However; these things can happen with others as well) So now this person, who *choose* no spiritual seat belt, has allowed all these things spiritually to enter them and is now spiritually blind and deaf. (Going through trials the wrong way with the wrong attitude can cause this to happen in an individual as well) They are confused by all the storms, trials, and life blows that come to your life, while you take it all in stride because you trust Jesus. People of Unbelief won't understand this. The more you buckle down and still give God praises, honor, and glory reading your word and being joyous in spite of everything that looks to be in shambles the more this person will stop wondering why adversity doesn't affect you and if they have opened themselves up to the spirits previously named they will begin to yield their members over to divination and allow satan to use every part of them to "become" the adversity in your life! Their unspoken unthought-unthought- through goal will become to see you crumble up. Unthought through; meaning if you crumble -being a married couple, they crumble as well because in God's eyes yall are one. At this point satan is looking for that surprised, startled, deer in the head lights look in your eyes- When you realize the adversity is not on your job, or at the market, it's now actually coming from the place where you go to get away from the world and from life pressures. The place you think about when you're away taking care of business and you see different acts of lucifer. People cussing, fussing, stealing, car wrecks, spirits of adultery, fornication, fakeness, and tight nasty clothes, and you just want to get home and unwind your mind and embrace family, embrace security! But now adversity is coming from this place! If you are currently in this place I urge you pray and tell God to take your emotions away. This may be the first time you have heard this, but God lead me to pray this about a year ago and my life has never been the same!

Can you imagine how confused people and satan would be if you showed no emotions to the things they did or said to you?

Do you really comprehend that giving God your emotions actually brings you closer to walking like Him, talking like Him, thinking like Him without a care in the world what people say or how people feel about it? Why?

Because you entrusted your emotions to God! When we as ladies do this phenomenal unheard of thing and God sees that we actually trust Him to this point that we choose to only feel what He wants us to feel we will start to experience a new life. Only react to what He wants us to react too, then God takes Kingship in our lives! We have heard millions of times that women are made up of emotions. If I in fact give all these emotions to God then I become made up of Him not being able to be manipulated anymore by tears, sad words, flowers and candy, a car, or a bonus on my job because I've chosen to give my most vulnerable self to God! I trust Him with me. When this is done, get ready to be looked at strangely by people around you! They looked at Jesus the same way! Get ready for people to whisper about you!

> "I don't understand why she just walked off that job. She know she has bills and kids to see about. Her boss was good to her. She's crazy."

These type things are talked about among people whom are still controlled by deceitful emotions and they can't understand you for the life of them. It's none of their business that the boss tried to sleep with you or make you go against what you stand for in the faith. Etc. Talkers will talk. Giving God your emotions makes these things seem very small and non-existent! Once you hear the voice that says "I got you," no other voice contrary to His matters anymore!

So if satan sees this emotion on you, this gaze of terror that adversity has made it to your den of safety he then goes on for the kill over the next coarse of days or weeks hoping that bitterness and depression will take you out. Scriptures to remember on your journey:

> *"He that is slow to anger is better than the mighty; and he*
> *that ruleth his spirit than he that taketh a city."*
> **(Proverbs 16:32)**

> *"And the peace of God, which passeth all understanding,*
> *shall keep your hearts and minds through Christ Jesus."*
> ***Philippians 4:7***

How can you have peace if emotions always have you worried about stuff?

People think Jesus was cold hearted when He told the man let the dead burry the dead, but Jesus gave/ trusted God with His emotions! Jesus walked in compassion and love! Many will detest, and say compassion is emotion and the two may seem similar so I provided the definition:

> *Emotion is a natural instinctive state of mind deriving from one's (your) circumstances, mood, or relationship with others.*

> *Compassion is sympathetic pity and concern for the suffering or misfortunes of others!*

One deals with yourself and how "you" feel and the other deals with wanting to see "others" well! To go even further so we wont be confused, giving God our emotions allows Him even to tell us "when" to have compassion! With emotions we go give out compassion also. ...to every body. ..and they mommas! That's not God's will!

> "For He saith to Moses, I will have mercy on whom I will have mercy, and I will have compassion on whom I will have compassion."
> **Romans 9:15**

It's in the book. Not face book but the life book, our daily bread. Philippians 4:7 talked about that peace that passes understanding.

I remember when I had first gotten married, my husband and I were maybe going into our 9th month of matrimony and I forget what it was that "He "did (smile) but I know it hurt my feelings so so bad and I got very upset so to the point where I started to literally feel hot. We were staying in Gulf Port, Mississippi at the time that I grabbed the keys and left the house in a rage of anger and sadness mixed together! I remember driving with tears running down my face not knowing where I was going. I ended up pulling in at this shopping center. I sat in the car about thirty minutes and then proceeded to go into this department store. To make a long story short I came out with a bag full of very "very" nice night wear! The kinds you never want the kids to see. So while walking to the car I felt confused. I was thinking, Lord he just crushed my feelings, why would I come to this store and buy these things that he can enjoy with me? I drove back home and walked through the door.

"What's in the bag"? He says.

At this point I'm to embarrassed to tell him. Here I am just married, I'm supposed to be teaching this man how to treat me. You don't just hurt my feelings and get away with it!! But here I was having spent my money on a bag full of good times for him.

I said "just a few nick knacks," and high tailed it upstairs.

I hid the bag for a few days still trying to figure out what had happened. I finally confessed to him what had transpired that night and he enjoyed seeing my picks, but I could tell what he was thinking while I proceeded to show him the different pieces. ....

"I HIT THE JACKPOT WITH THIS GIRL"!

I said all this to say that God was working on me even then gradually taking my emotions because it wasn't me who chose to go get something nice for someone who had just crushed my feelings. That peace I felt while shopping for him passed my understanding of why am I not buying things for just me like a tote, or shoes or things like that. When God takes control of our emotions the devil has no wiggle room!

More power up scriptures:

> *"Set your affection on things, above, not on things on the earth. For ye are dead, and your life is hid in Christ, in God."*
> **Colossians 3:2and 3**

> *"For we walk by faith not by sight."*
> **2 Corinthians 5:7**

> *Trust in the Lord with all thine heart: and lean not unto thine own understanding. In thy way acknowledge him, and he direct thy paths.* Amen! (**Proverbs 3 5-6**)

This is one of the most important things a daughter of Zion must do! Give those emotions back to God! He knows exactly what to do with them. If satan sees that you have taken a shift in your spirit concerning this and instead of fussing and dancing around with your hubby in a state of confusion and saying words that do not line up with scripture that also releases more demons and attacks, you immediately go into a praise attack and worship fit know matter how crazy it may make you look. A Hallelujah fit giving God praise and thanking Him for your mate! Thank God for allowing them to walk in their correct role with authority speaking nothing but blessings on them and serving them. This is when the devil knows he's only a breath away from loosing the battle because the best card he has to play is *the spouse card.* (for married couples) That one whom you become one with. Look at Adam and Eve! The spouse card got Adam and Eve in trouble. Naturally Adam wanted to relate to Eve and Eve wanted Adam to share some down time. Pay close attention and understand. Yes!

Ever been in a situation where maybe you or your spouse wanted down time?

A little more watching television shows with popcorn, or whatever down time is to them, might have been desired but the other spouse was seeking God reading and studying the word or pushing Kingdom assignments. But your spouse comes in and says "come on baby, enough with that, you've been at it every day. Come spend some QT with me. (Quality time) Let's engage in a movie or playing games, and let's just hold each other. (All good things) You can finish that later. You always doing something spiritual. Don't be so heavenly minded until you're no earthly good", he says. So now you feel bad and wrap up the revelation God was just giving you.

Or you reply back spiritually to a natural situation by saying we watched movies last night and the night before that, so I really need this time set aside for the Lord so I can in fact be a better spouse for you as well as a better daughter for God, could we reschedule?"

Now that's a Jesus answer!

Why?

Because of coarse God is all about family and family time! God wants you and your spouse to experience great things together and enjoy one another so being in God and being led by Him, you'll be able to give a God answer like this because God would never ever require you to give all of your time to just reading the bible or just staying at church. God is about balance, and when you live a balanced life, God answers make since and become spiritually strategic weapons! This answer wouldn't make since if quality time with your spouse never happens. (So lets say quality time does happen) Yes, your spouse may be startled with this answer and stager back a few steps because they were just hit with a moment of truth! Truth is, it's not your spouse who said that in the first place but a demon of distraction! You bet! So regroup, realize, and know that you can't do anything in this moment to appease this demonic force. The only thing this demon force is looking for is to complete the mission they were sent for and that's for you to stop, and hault what you are <u>doing</u> and come enter into distraction. So if the reschedule speech doesn't work, you know exactly what you are dealing with and this demonic spirit will go back into his handy bag and pull out "operation abandonment "I may find another to for fill! (An operation explode emotions plan 1a) Being connected to word and on the outside looking in we know that Satan's plan is to cause this distraction one way or another!

Being in this situation you have to ask God to show you the test before it comes and while you're in it so you can handle it the correct way. The devil would rather complete this operation in a more settled way as this is his nature to be subtle.

You never hear about a snake standing up out of the grass and screaming and crying have you?

The enemy knows if he stay settle then he can use this or other things like this to throw you way off when time comes to seek the Lord and get a break through, and you wont even notice the trend. Your spouse, well surprise, they wont notice the trend either because it will be satanic powers working through them! So "operation abandonment I may find another to for fill " works like this:

"I don't understand you sometimes. Why do you have to be so serious all the time? That's what's wrong with church marriages today. Not enough time spent together but always trying to be spiritually minded. This is why marriages end up in divorce, or how little miss sweet thang stick her head in the door and is willing to do whatever! Why you opening the door for the devil?"

Wow! Demonic forces are clever when talking about the devil like they are not associated in order to get you to do what Satan wants you to do! Beware of this. And now this operation is to get your emotions pumping, your juices flowing and your mind off of the assignment at hand. This operation is here to plant seeds of doubt (satan's crafty) distrust, and religiousness so even if you decided to stay and seek God, now the mind is wondering or you're eventually up screaming (operation abandonment in action) who is *little miss sweet thang*? Has somebody said something to you? Oh you leaning another way now? So you thinking of divorce? How long you been thinking about stepping outside our marriage? All I'm trying to do is get a little reading/ praying in, my God! What you mean I'm always trying to be spiritual? That's a lie and you know it. Meanwhile in the future, you try to be less spiritual by not reading praying as much and unknowingly actually gives the devil plenty room to come in. This argument goes on until the words run out. Followed by silence. .. then apologies. .then what? Well, for a person not aware of Satan's devices, followed by, *"baby you right, let's watch that movie and I'll get the popcorn."* and satan sits back and grins that evil sly good looking grin and says to his fellow demons, "operation abandonment I may find another to for fill. ..check mate!"

Has this or something like this ever happened to you?

How did you handle it?

Were you aware that it was a trick of the enemy, but felt yourself going along with it uncontrollably?

This is why it's very important for us all to give our emotions back to God, because without emotions, operation abandonment would never prevail because you're confident in nothing but God's word that says *"all things work together for the good to them that love God, to them who are the called according to his purpose. "***Romans 8:28** Knowing and believing is two different things. When methods such as abandonment operation and things like this stop working it's because of maturity In this area and wisdom of the game but Sometimes it takes years all according to your determination to defeat. once it has no affect on you anymore *(usually at this point the two has decided to go separate ways never even detecting the devil;) He thinks she's the anti- Christ, and she thinks he's vindictive and misleading)* this is when satan is huffing and puffing mad! His eyes are red and his veins are popping out of his temple. He now realizes that a very dreadful thing has occurred. ..you've matured! You've been elevated by God from his little sly games and the kicker is through Jesus, and going through trials the right way, you've elevated without bitterness, strife, hatred, and the works of the flesh. She respects him and he treats her like the weaker vessel that she is and actually loves her with know hidden sexual motives! Satan is pissed! He hates with a passion to be pulled out of his character, or comfort zone. After passing these cunning test with the Holy Ghost to guide us we begin to see satan for who he is. We will actually have pulled Satan back to the garden. Now he is naked, just a snake you can see, and It's you and him and because he's naked with no demons covering him as clothes, you'll actually see his weak areas! The areas that are black and blue bruised from your prayer life. The places that's all but torn open from your consecrating and the cast around his foot from where you commanded him to fall in his own snares and traps and from when you fasted. You see his earlobe hanging on by a thread and one of his eyes swollen shut, because God gave you what you needed to weather the storm. Praise God! Being a child of the King, you know how we were programmed to do and be. So do it! Be it! Do like David! Go in for the kill and slay that giant! Beware though because now satan has been stripped. He's always been able to see your weak parts and capitalize, but now you'll be able to see his! CAPITALIZE! The enemy wants to destroy you before you go down in history for others coming along that we, like Jesus, also mastered the devil with Christ living in us! Satan can't have this testimony floating around and people actually witnessing this by looking at you and looking at the unity in your marriage and relating, having hope and faith, so what does he do? He gets wild like a crazy man afraid to die. He gets reckless and just starts swinging wild like someone throwing jabs in the air hoping to at least hit the target desired one time.

By this point you should have made it to the secret place of the Most High, but if not yet then this is how satan counter punches in his hazardous rage of discontentment. He calls all demons he has had to study you and study your spouse. They get together and figure out every area of your life not covered under the blood because he, himself, wants to come in and do the job at point blank range! When/ if he finds an entrance way he will come with a vengeance. A hazardous vengeance. The spouse he's found access to will then begin to color way outside of your covenant lines. (If not found in the secret place) This is another attempt to get you in frustration mode so that you can begin speaking death and not life on your marriage.

Proverbs 18:21 says *death and life are in the power of the tounge: and they that love it shall eat the fruit thereof.* (Always enjoy the fruits of the spirit) so naturally the enemy may come to aggravate your spirit by spouse allowing trash to run over for two weeks, but he hates when you take it out, or being disrespectful again to you, maybe catching late night phone calls, speaking things against the bible, calling you names to make you feel stupid, or maybe going a step beyond and sewing discord against you to others to make sure and try to put your light out. You may find them more on edge with lots of excuses why and find flip on flip off emotions taking place. One minute happy the next minute throwing acquisitions and spiritual knives because the goal is to drain you of all the oil that you have so that you become depleted! And because this person wasn't found in the secret place or chose not to stay in this place, the enemy now use them again on every hand to cause frustration to your intellect and common sense. This is where the devil knows he's about to loose the battle so he doesn't mind being obvious. He may even try to throw a car wreck your way, or cause you to get fired from a work place, or cause your named to be scandalized by lies and disseat. All these things are to get you to a point where you have had enough and the only other thing to do is to exit your vows and put a divorce into motion, because all you're seeing is a major hindrance. Someone who simply doesn't care for the kids or you anymore. But if you could just stop for a minute and focus in truly on what the problem is and what's going on You will see enemy and not your spouse who may undoubtable love you! You will see that it's not your husband at all but the devil himself. The one who has had demons study your likes and dislikes. He's Had demons to actually study your thought process and how you operate this is why we are to pray without ceasing and meditate on scripture and when he see that the things which used to get you down don't get you down anymore; now he has become ratcheted and at all cost. So we have come to the point where the Holy Ghost within us has pulled satan out of character and has exposed his where about (in the secret place) not being able to hide anymore. Lucifer does not want your light to rub off on your spouse. He can't have you influencing them to become a better man and surrender to God. The bible says

Romans 8:28 *And we know that all things work together for good* so all of these events come to make you strong. This is how we war a good warfare. By taking the things the enemies does and finding ways to glorify God with it! Believe! Paris, John, and Asia our three children are taught this! Always find a reason to glorify God! Believe it or not your spouse is still watching to see if you demonstrate the love of Jesus like you talk the love of Jesus. They have a front row seat in seeing how God has actually matured you from where you used to be, from how you used to get upset, from how you used to curse them out but now you only speak blessings on them! You have nothing but kind words to say to them. You still serve them and God is blessing! The more you "demonstrate" the more you set those demons straight! The more we demonstrate love, the more love God gives us to demonstrate! He creates circumstances for you to be able to demonstrate love so don't be discouraged! (The light shines brightest in the darkness) So now by grace and wisdom of God you have taken satan's devices and used them for a weapon against him by demonstrating the light of Jesus before him and before your children, and friends who are defiantly watching and have a front row seat which in turn makes lucifer just loose his mind! He looses his mind when we take on the mind of Christ! In case where the enemy is loosing grip you may see a natural disaster like someone breaking into your home destroying your things or maybe your house burning down, car getting stolen and things to this nature. Just know that satan is ratchet like and God through you have literally pulled smooth talking alley cat satan out of his comfort zone! (This is when we walk in the word)

> *2 Corinthians 11:14 says and no marvel; for satan himself is transformed into an angel of light.*

So by God's grace and through much much praying fasting and studying the word of God we have caused this angel of light to transformed back into his state of darkness, of rage, and with foaming at the mouth like a dog. *Ratchetness!* Now that he knows God has brought you to a place where you can see, now he has two alternatives, to *fight* or *flight*. If he choose *fight* then you know what to expect! If he chooses *flight* beware because he's planning to give you smoke in mirrors! You May get your dream job, dream house, dream car, dream man and all these things! He'll plan to take you high but this is only to drop you! The bible said

> "*seek ye first the kingdom of God, and his righteousness; and all these things shall be added unto you!* **Matthew 6:33**

so wait on God and get what "He" has for us, the blessings "He" want to pour out on us! It wont be smoke in mirrors either! So in all aspects of satans devices we fold under God (the shadow of the Almighty) and watch missiles dissipate because God's word is a two edged sword! It reeks havoc on the devils head! Glory!

If we Never pray for God's Kingdom to come, then why would God let us come into His kingdom?

Coming to the point of actually making satan show himself in the true form that he is and being able to see him miles and miles away takes God. Period. You'll know when it's the devil in flight mode because whatever he offers wont line up with your spirit man, more so your flesh and what "you want". It could be to go and preach and Satan will accommodate you, but what does "God' want for you at that time? To see Satan coming from a ways a way we must cast away how we see things and put on God's eyes! I don't mean just going to church a few days a week because the devil could be the very one preaching to you. The enemy lives at the church house as well. This is why the church has to be in us! God is looking for a church inside the church!

Will you be that church inside the church of God?

Meaning allowing him to dwell in your body and you then take your body to gather together with other believers. This is the only way you will keep protection against church hurts, and the only way you'll keep the church fleas of unforgivness off of you! You must become the temple of Christ for God to live in! God is the only one who can defeat the devil, so to get to this point of making satan show his real self you must allow God to poses your temple! Allow God to saturate you with His sweet smell that repeals the enemy back! Have much intimacy with God and He will impregnate your mind with His mind and your thoughts with His thoughts and your ways with His ways! The only way to take your life back and the things that the enemy stole from you is to get fully engulfed in God! Don't look to the left or to the right but keep your eyes on Jesus.

Proverbs 3:6 says *In all thy ways acknowledge him and he shall direct thy paths.*

We must acknowledge God in everything we do. This is how we reach the climax in God! You don't want to be on the same level of warfare all your life. Going through the motions over and over again but allow God, through your obedience to Him, to show you how He sees you and to see the enemy how He sees the enemy because time is short and the hour is at hand! Take that no vacancy sign off and let the Lord all the way in. He has many many things He wants to teach, show, and explain to you! He wants to impart into you! The way forward is back! Back to God! Back to prayer! Back to forgiveness! Thy Kingdom come oh Lord! Thy Kingdom come, Thy will be done in Earth(me) as it is in heaven. Amen.

Behind The Veil
_I Don't Care If You Black Or White

When speaking of race people normally get real real touchy! This subject has left a sore spot over the generations and so it hurts when being picked with. The truth is that none of us can change the past no matter how hurtful and belittling it is for both sides of the coin! Another truth is that no matter the color, every lady that is born again is your sister if you are born again as well! All Of God's children share the same blood! Isn't that amazing! That's beautiful. Early one morning I retired to my study closet and the Lord began to speak with me. I could tell by the way He was communicating that this was information He wanted me to share.

God is displeased with the way our sisterhood has become. The Lord said where their is unity their is strength. Ladies are the driving force of the country. We may not sit in leadership positions but we do sit close to the man's ear gates and we plant seeds whether good Or bad and those seeds grow into trees! What have we been telling our men concerning race against a different color female? Even if that old man is stubborn WE are the ones who nurture and raise our children. Why are they turning up the same way? I honestly believe it's because of ladies that the men have not gotten it right. With me being a lady of color it's not right to talk to my husband against any other race of women because it doesn't mean he will hate the women, it means he will hate the men of that race. Whites alike. If you talk to your men against women of color they won't hate the women of color but will continue the hatred for men of color! Grant it they will put up a front of hating women of other nationality but underlying it's simply not true. I know that may be shocking. Maybe not.

Father love deeply EVERY female He ever made! We all must put petty differences aside and see that we must fight as a unit. One body in Christ! If we choose not to fight as a unit the enemy will continue to win and we will fall into hell by the droves because Father simply wont allow anyone of a prejudice nature in His Holy Place that is sacred. It's not going to happen and the enemy has deceived us into making all of us think that God will let underlying hatred slide! He wont do it for me, you, or our children! Yes, the women of color had to bare heavy burdens but so did the Caucasian women! Many people look at how nasty some Caucasian women can so call be, but do you really know her story? Father shared her story with me and He wants me to share it with you as well! I've heard many times how the women of color were treated but rarely to none did I hear how the Caucasian ladies went through hell as well!

Have we ever taken the time to look at it through other eyes?

How does it feel when you try to be all you can be for a man?

Forget race, let's look at this through the eyes of being a female. Let's all put ourselves in the Caucasian lady's shoes.

It's wedding night now that the big day is over and You dress up for this man you can now call husband. You are so excited to share your life with him although nana already schooled you that he deals with the slave girls. Even though feeling a little distraught you still have faith that YOU can make him change because he's never experienced your love before or having children with you! You spray perfumes on the pillows and bedding trying to make the bedroom inviting to the man you wish to please and true enough that night was pretty special, now still most nights he tells you he's tired and for you to just go to sleep and then later you here him get up and see him put his big brim hat on with his thick leather boots and so you secretly followed him only to see him go into the hen house with the slave girl who probably was kicking and screaming and maybe loathing going in to do with him just what it was you desired with him. For these same women to get pregnant by your husband and bare children that sometimes he made YOU raise. Now you realize that you are for show and tell in his mind and for child baring to carry the family name. You hear him moaning in sequence to another lady's screams of horror and disgust or of passion. Yes, WE ARE EXPOSING EVERY BIT OF THE EVILNESS IN THE DEMON OF HATRED!

Can you see how hate passes from generation to generation?

(Caucasian women didn't feel whole just like the women of color didn't!)

Can you see how we are all alike?

Can you see how hurt,pain,and tears flow though all of us?

Can you see that we all alike have those deep wounds, covered up by make up and a plastic smile,of feeling like we're not enough?

That's your sister who was taught to hate you! That's your sister who never feels like she's enough so now all this work must be done and money must be spent for....bigger lips, hips, behind. She feels like she's not enough so now she want's it all. We hate each other more and more and the devil for centuries has played sisters hurt against hurt. We tend to think...at least she got the house the fine cars the clothes but can you imagine having all that but not the most important part of the man.... his desires, his mind and his anticipation, his soul being intertwined with another. Let's all pray for each other because generations of hurt, anger, misuse, abusiveness, competitions, strife, envy's, and even feelings of murder we have all been through! Satan has pit us against each other and through hurt and anger we let him. Even after being treated this way we all had to keep thriving! We all had to survive! ALL OF US! How would we feel to know our husbands were off snatching women from their husbands and raping them? How would we feel if these same men chose to rape men as well? NONE OF US WAS ACTUALLY THERE TO ENDURE THIS SO WHY DO WE ALLOW THE MEMORIES TO MAKE US HATE EACHOTHER? Why do we continue to allow satan to cause us to hate the women of color? She is YOUR SISTER! Why must we allow old demonic history to cause us to hate the Caucasian? SHE IS YOUR SISTER! I'm choosing not to pull back on this subject in fact let's get down and dirty with it! Do you know that The Almighty God sees how you smile and treat men of color ever so nice and respectfully but you have such a nasty demonic evil spirit towards the women of color behind their back? You headed to hell sis! Do you know that The Almighty God sees how you smile and treat the Caucasian male ever so nice and respectfully but you have such a nasty demonic evil spirit towards the Caucasian lady? You headed to hell sis. God isn't playing with you! You choose to keep playing this game then you choose to loose! God is not petting this spirit any more in us! I pray that God expose every snake because it's time for the sisterhood to stand strong and fight the real enemy! PLEASE LET IT GO! Cry, pray, rise, and turn from the way you may see it please please please! No body wins when hate is involved. I stated all of this just to say the Lord wants us to know that both sides are deeply hurting even though the plastic smile is plastered to our faces. Many have not gotten over deep rooted issues even though we claim salvation! If this is you and you are still hurting deep down inside Father wants you to give it to Him because He was their and He knows what to do with it! He desires all of us to join hands and fight as a unit and kick the devil's monkey butt because for all these years he has stolen something so important from us....a real chance at sisterhood and unity! Please join forces with me and Jesus to say NO MORE! It all starts with one decision. I'm not black, I'm not white, I'm Kingdom!

CHAPTER 16

The Person of God

We always think of God our Father as someone who protects us! When you say the name God,

what's the first word that pops into your mind?

In mine is the word, *"everything"*. We as people hold God to such great responsibility and standard. I know this may sound odd but it is very true. We hold God to such high standard. We even call Him the *Most High*! When things go wrong in our homes or on our jobs we go to God in much prayer for Him to fix the problem! When we fall, we fleece God to pick us up. When we're sick we ask God for a healing. No money in the bank? No problem, just petition God for a way being made! Desire the finer things in life? Awesome! Just quote a few scriptures to God for the purpose of actually trying to jolt Him into the mindset of believing He must give you this car you want or house because He promised you this. So each week we church and pay tithes and offering and participate in little church duties and in return we expect God to be God and do these things noted above when we need them done and it almost feels like a business! Lord do the things we need done and we'll pay you.

Ever thought of the president as a machine? We expect him to go into the white house and get it done. Very seldom do we think of the president as a real person. Once they hit office, we almost never think that they need or deserve a vacation, family time, or to hang out with friends and just go shopping or shooting!

215

Why?

Because he is the president of the united states and his job is to protect the states and keep us moving forward. Point blank.

How much more do we expect and put the demand on Jesus?

Did you know that we are made in the image of God?

Like us, God has needs! Yes our Almighty Father has needs! He has desires and feelings. God has emotion and this is where we get ours from.

I wish above all that you prosper and be in good health even as your soul prosper! (A desire of God)

Did you know that God desires for us to hope for things with substance?

Not in material things but spiritual fruit. His fruit has substance and this substance in our lives turns into evidence day by day moment by moment, situation by situation that God is real and is very much alive.

> "But *now they desire a better country, that is, an heavenly where fore "God is not ashamed "to be called their God: for he hath prepared for them a city."* **Hebrews 11:16**

Wow!

God can be ashamed of us too?

How does that make us feel?

Now why on earth would God be ashamed of us?

Ever thought how it may feel to be the Holy of Holies and have your own child going and laughing at ungodly movies where men dress up like women or speaking in tounge one moment and fowl language the next in front of the same people we are supposed to be evidence in front of. When husbands had a bad day and come home fleshed out, maybe he lost the battle that day, but that's where your evidence must come into play to silently sometimes remind Him God is in control through our actions. We are to project kindness, love, meekness, and loyalty to them!

What ways do you have that may make God ashamed of you?

What ways make God proud to call you daughter?

Have you ever taken up for someone in a Godly way who was being picked on like someone who would not take up for themselves but kept dealing with abuse from a bully? If you have, this is an attribute given from our Father in heaven. This is a major part of God's person. He takes vengeance on those who abuse His sheep.

Note*Remember sheep are those who don't fight back.

Instead of us taking vengeance on people, God instructs us to pray His mercy on them and turn the other cheek while He takes care of the matter in His way in His own timing. Our Father pushes forth those unexpected by those around you. He'll use the one less popular. The person of God makes something out of nothing and makes it "very" beautiful.

If God chose the one expected then what glory would He really receive?

For example; He sings very well and has all chances to win. He's had singing lessons from the best and His talent is smooth, but when God enters into a situation He'll make that one that's less.....more. That one with no lessons at all. Look at *1 Samuel16:6*. Samuel went to anoint the next King from Jesse's house. Samuel, Jesse, and the young men all thought the same thing! The next king had to be one of them that had a strong posture. But David, that ruddy cutie pie in the field know one suspected.

When David was brought in God told Samuel to "arise"!

Arise not meaning to get or stand up because in verse 11 Samuel had already stated to Jesse to "*send and fetch him: for we will not sit down till he come hither.*" *So* when God spoke "*arise, anoint him,*" He meant *emerge: become apparent. Emerge meaning move out of or away from something and come into view.* The person of God wants us to see things the way He does and to Move from the way we see it and trust His views. Looking back at vs 7

> *"But the Lord said unto Samuel, look not on his countenance, or on the height of his statue; because I have refussed him: fit the Lord seeth not as man seeth; for man looketh on the outward appearance, but the Lord looketh on the heart."*

God get's the glory out of making the impossible possible! It's just how God works. His incredible uniqueness is beautiful. He's not limited to religion or the way people think about who's qualified and who's not. God does not call the qualified He qualifies the called! Yes! God's person is marvelous right! God also listens to the language of our tears and blood! These two things are very personal to Father. Jesus experienced these on the cross. Ever heard the song *"oh the blood of Jesus?"* Our sins are washed in the purified blood of Jesus. The term *"stabbed in the back?"* This did not just become a term for no apparent reason. Especially when this has not literally happened to you, but we use this term because in the given situation we feel a spiritual wound and we feel the blood pouring out of us possibly through hurt or anger and misunderstandings .God looks upon these situations and He reads them. He looks to see what's been done but more important why has this been done and He judges the situation righteously and by law. Tears are the same way. Our Father has an ear for tears! He does not approve of self pity tears but tears of faith and endurance, tears of hurt and misunderstandings and being misused. God has a reward for all who cry these tears, get up from praying to Him, and does not take vengeance in their own hands! (*Unforgivness is vengeance*) look at how loving and compassionate Father is,

> *"And He said, what hast thou done? The voice of thy brother's blood crieth unto me from the ground."*
> *(Gen 4:10)*

Did you ever know that blood could cry?

Drawing closer to Father we will begin to see and hear things the way He does. Things you would never dream that you could hear or see you will see! God knows when our tears are Unforgivness or bitterness or even resentment. He loves us so much until He wants us to get it right. When I say Father is the wisest of the wise He is! He has no time for bickering or arguing. I mean He's the King of kings so arguing would never ever reach the level of God. When Father does not agree you may just start to experience the silent treatment from Him, or if it's really important to Him you'll get different people telling you the same thing, or He'll allow you to just go around in circles until you get dizzy tired and surrender! On the other hand, for those that are not His and proudly make it known He's shown us through Jesus how a double question will shut the mouth of a nay sayer and leave them dumb founded. Look at this:

> And when He was come into the temple, the chief priests and the elders of the people Came unto Him as He was teaching, and said, By what authority doest thou these things? And who gave thee this authority? (They had come to try and trip Jesus up.) And *Jesus answered and said unto them, I also will ask you one thing, which if ye tell me, I in like wise will tell you by what authority I do these things. The baptism of John, whence was it? From heaven or of men? And they reasoned with themselves saying, if we shall say, from heaven; he will say unto us, why did ye not then believe him? But if we shall say, of men, we fear the people; for all hold John as a prophet. 27) And they answered Jesus, and said, we cannot tell. And he said unto them, Neither tell I you by what authority I do these things.*
>
> ### (Matthew 21:23)

Awesome! No arguing, just pure wisdom from our Father. When you fly with eagles, you just don't have time to cluck with chickens! Another wisdom that Comes from God's personality is asking a question you already know the answer to, but this question brings awareness to the other person! Like: when Jesus said in

> *"So when they had dined, Jesus said to Simon Peter, Simon, son of Jo-nas lovest thou me more than these? He said unto Him, yea Lord; thou knowest that I love thee. He saith unto him feed my sheep."*
>
> **(John 21:15)**

Jesus knew Peter loved him but He was trying to bring another level of awareness to Peter. Also, Jesus showed Peter mercy by allowing Peter to cancel out the three times he denied Jesus by saying I love you three times. Peter experienced redemption! And lastly notice Jesus said Peter, son of Jo-nas....this was to bring awareness to Peter also in this very instant that you have backslidden from the place of our Father by stating Peter's natural dad. He was bringing awareness to Peter and telling him to get back to his true Father's business! I have actually adopted many of these techniques and pleasure in them very much!

Many religious people today believe we must be like God spiritually while at church, but naturally free to be ourselves elsewhere. When the Spirit of God lifts off an individual God's character should always remain. That's the evidence of being a daughter in God! Being able to maintain when the spirit has lifted, and you've left church and you're doing your usual! This is how to know if we have spent time in the pasture or not. Or have we been traveling by bridge? This determines if we are truly His.

Can people see Jesus on you?

Another attribute of God is that He is also truthful without being dumb.

Ever known someone who was so detailed in telling the truth, even voluntary information that would get them fired, a behind spanking or a demotion?

(Brutally honest.) They may have been asked "why were you late to work?" They'll answer, "Well I mistakenly overslept.". They may say.

That's Okay but they feel no need to stop there! "After I woke up late I figured I might as well stop and get coffee which didn't take much time but after I pulled off I realized they had gotten my order wrong so I had go back so they could fix it." But while they are talking to much the boss is writing them Up! Another beautiful characteristic of God is to not reveal everything you know!

> "But when thou doest alms, let not thy left hand know what thy right hand doeth."
>
> **Matthew 6vs3**

Yes, right here Jesus is talking about alms but wisdom causes us to use this in other areas of our lives! check it out:

> *"And the Lord said unto Samuel, how long wilt thou mourn for Saul, seeing I have rejected him from reigning over Israel? Fill thine horn with oil, and go, I will send thee to Jesse the Beth-le-hem-ite: for I have provided me a king among his sons.* Check this out, *And Samuel said, How can I go? If Saul hear it, he will kill me. And the Lord said "Take an heifer with thee, and say, I am come to sacrifice to the Lord". 3)And call Jesse to the sacrifice, and I will shew thee what thou shalt do; and you shalt anoint unto me him whom I name unto thee."*
>
> **1 Samuel 16 vs 1 and 2**

Wow! The wisdom of God. Nosy people would say God just told a white lie. Wrong! They also say Half truth is a whole lie! Up....wrong again!

Have you all heard that before?

Father shows me that having wisdom is in fact not a sin and wisdom out weighs being a blabber mouth about all your business! In this case being a tell all would have cost Samuel his life.

God didn't lie, he just added the sacrifice to the journey of David being anointed king! Drawing Nigh to the personality of Father will give you a whole new character and way of seeing and doing things! Another thing Father loves is obedience. When He tells us to do things He wants us to be willing to obey. A lot of times we try to over compensate and sacrifice things like money, time, and good deeds in place of us choosing not to obey. We think this will make up for our strong wills and disobedience. It doesn't. The bible says *obedience is better than sacrifice. Father likes for His children to obey. (1 Samuel 15:22)* God loves also to give us things to do that seem impossible all to remind us that He makes all things possible to them that believe. Father is way more than a wishing well like many people believe. Father's the only one I know that will fire a person and let them keep working for a time like Saul.

What about Moses?

Moses had already crossed God more than once but because God played it cool Moses got cocky and forgot who he was dealing with! God told Moses to take his rod and go "speak" to the rock and water would come forth out of it. Moses went but he spoke to the people first and called them rebels. Moses is upset now. He then takes the credit from God and says must "I" fetch you water out of this rock? He smote the rock and water came forth.

Note * *Frustration will always bring one out of the presence of God and back into they way they see things!*

The way Moses saw things as a child was many sorcerers using demonic divine powers and heavily using witchcraft to get any impossible task done.

Question: *when Moses acted out of himself again why didn't Father just get him then?*

Answer: Because Father knew Moses would do this which is why He told Moses to take his rod in the first place! He let Moses fowl himself out from the promise land.. Moses had fowled out. Moses had crossed God long before but Joshua was still in the oven and not ready yet! But when the timer went off....ding ding. Moses had to go because Joshua was ready!

Turn, I never knew you is what Father will say to many people who's not willing to follow Him with a clean heart. These are also people that has been fired but still working.

Why else would they be expecting to get in?

Haven't we cast out devils and heal the sick in your name, they will say. Fired but still punching the clock. Father's the only one who can be cold blooded but still a hot consuming fire. A two edge sword He is!

He thinks generations down the road!

He has infinite wisdom!

Oh yes and please allow me to explain this about Father when it comes to relationships! If He really has His eyes on you, and He does, then relationships not ordained by Him or relationships out of season will be in foreclosure. Your will, emotions, and preference may be strong so you might bend over backwards and beyond trying to keep this person in your life but let me tell you, nothing you do will ever be good enough for that man. It'll always be something they feel you could have did more of or you did to much of or you may have that one thing that drives you crazy about him you just hate it but try to love through it. So you keep going back and fourth letting them back in with the attitude of "I'll do more ". I'll listen more. I'll try to understand more. I'll give more money, time, praise to this person and it works for a small while until that brick wall comes back and now the both of you are thinking and possibly saying I don't know what it is but it feels like a force that just will not let us get along know matter what I do or say or how I try to be. Often times we call it the devil and sometimes this is the case, but not all the time. When the devil tries to come in between a God relationship it's very obvious, their will be peace from God that will give you endurance or clarity as to why you are going through these things, and His plans of how much more mature you'll be in this area once you come out of this trial and how He will be able to use you to help others. Father has many relationships of ours that He does not approve of. Maybe He hasn't planned for the person to exist in your life for ever. Just for a season until He deals with the opposite person and gets them to a place where they are depending on Him and not you. But because we feel like we love people so hard we fight against Father without even knowing it. We fight and fight for this person to be apart of our lives even though they continue to hurt our feelings, mistreat us, destroy and slander our name and doesn't mind trying to mentally, emotionally, and maybe physically destroy us! This person could be a Pastor, friend, son, daughter, mother, Father, co worker or anybody. Anytime Father wants a relationship disposed of He has a way of getting it done. A lot of times this person is doing nothing but holding you back from growing, holding your church back from growth and full potential, and holding up your prayers. Let go and let God! It's not that you don't love them, it's that you don't want them to end up like Saul, dead, because if you keep choosing to go against Father and forcing relationships He doesn't approve of you'll put that person you love in danger! They will keep doing and saying things to you to hurt you and do you harm while crippling your growth and draining your oil. You won't ever be able to see God for always seeing stupidity in situations being done to keep you confused about them and confused about you and who you are in God and how God sees you and because of all the unjust evil being done God will keep allowing you to go through until YOU surrender! Just let go and let God. Even if you have a church where this person holds five different positions, if God says let go it's best to let go because He already has their replacement. God can have mercy on the person through your obedience. Disobedience mixed with love is a recipe for God's vengeance. Just let go....Now!!! Look at

1Samuel 19:9 Father was ready to elevate David, but David's loyalty to Saul was getting in the way. David wanted desperately to remain in Saul's kingdom peacefully and just be apart of the family but God had other big plans. David allowed love and loyalty to put him in deadly situations with Saul. God was done with this relationship and put it into foreclosure.

> *"And the evil spirit from the Lord was upon Saul, as he*
> *sat in his house with his javelin in his hand: and David*
> *played with his hand (David was a harp player) And Saul*
> *sought to smite David even to the wall with his javelin;*
> *but he slipped away out of Saul's presence, and he smote*

> *the javelin into the wall: and David fled, and escaped*
> *that night."*
>
> *(1 Samuel 19:9)*

When Father wants it over, He wants it over. If you find yourself in a relationship with someone and you know God is telling you and showing you that He's ready for this relationship to part ways ready for you to move so He can grow you and your faith and possibly that individual as well, but you two remaining together cause no growth and even decreasing in many areas. Just let go. Saul ended up dead and his son Jonathan too, because he could not bring himself to separate from the evilness of his dad. Don't end Up spiritually or naturally dead because you can't separate from someone with other intentions.

Is it really worth it?

Just let them go. Keep praying for them but let them go. You have to discern what's from Father and what the enemy tries to do. Father will make it clear to when He has placed foreclosure on a relationship you have. If you're having problems in your marriage seek God for counsel on what to do. Also seek someone seasoned in the Faith if need be and they can advise you on what to do according to the word of God! It's your job to trust and submit to His will! Father is so much more than what we try and pin Him down to be which is Someone paid by tithes and offering to protect us and our children. Father navigates through the law He has set in place in order to have mercy on us as satan goes and presents bad reports on us. Satan then has wishes for fatal destruction to come upon us. Second after this railing accusation Father even though He knows we broke fast after fast, not praying as much, and now has fallen into gossip but instead of going with satan's plan of evil destruction in the worst way, Father judges us righteously and He may allow satan to cause a broken foot or a burned down house, maybe that person may loose 200.00 dollars somewhere or was so close to getting that raise but now it fell through. These are types of punishments Father allows to happen when He is trying to still have mercy on us through our disobedience of choosing not to ask for forgiveness for things that's been done. Instead of us being grateful that satan wasn't able to go with his own plan which was fatality but had to go with the merciful plan of God, we complain.

> "Man why did this person have to sell that house to someone else. .crazy junk always happening to me. God must be against me. I'm tired of this crap."

Not knowing that Satan's plan was to do you in on this accident but God said no and had mercy. This is why *in all things we give thanks* because Father is always navigating through His word to find ways to show us mercy even when we don't deserve it! If you look at the last thing you went through and look closely you'll be able to see where Father navigated through His word to show you mercy in some way or another. Maybe it was to show you yet again that He does not approve of your unhealthy relationship instead of just getting rid of the whole situation with one airplane crash, one brutal robbery where nobody made it out alive, one drowning, or one explosion. Some of us make it very "very" hard for Father to find ways to show mercy, because Father dare not step off His word so we must look hard in the situation to see His mercy but it was there. Sometimes our kids go through because of something we do or did. Rapes and assaults on children. Make sure it's not because of something we parents has done in our lives to cause satan to have legal right to touch our children. Sometimes it's hard for hard headed people to see God's mercy because they tie His hands a lot of times with their ways and things they speak. If we are guilty of this we must do better! We must repent!

Another part of Father's person is goodness and mercy. Many people say;

> "I call on the angels of goodness and mercy to go before my family today, keep us and protect us in Jesus name amen."

This is okay, but one day I was praying for the people associated with the fire truck and ambulance screaming down the road in a frantic hurry one day, and I stretched out my hand to pray for them as usual and this time Father spoke to me and began to explain to me that He is goodness and He is mercy and the angels that He send out are His. He began to give me examples as a Father does. You are the mother of Paris, John, and Asia. David the son of Jesse. The Honda civic of Rashad Jamal. The angels of Goodness and Mercy. The angels of goodness and mercy. Goodness and mercy, which is Father, owns the angels. The angels are not named Goodness or Mercy. Angels are named Gabriel or Michael but calling on angel of restoration.....God is restoration and He sends angels out with that part of Him to restore the broken! When He finished explaining this to me I was blown away in a great way! I thought wow! All these years I was thinking the angels were named goodness, mercy, restoration, peace, etc. This may seem small but anytime Father takes time to explain something to us and you feel like you're sitting on His lap while He's doing so, so lovingly it's always a biggie! Father is a teacher! So I call on the angels of Father, who is Goodness and Mercy, to anoint our eyes with eye salve so that we may see God's desires for us to transform and prosper even as our souls prosper and our souls MUST PROSPER! *It's so much more to the person of God and I pray you are inspired to seek Him out and experience Him more on a more personal level because He loves us so much!*

I Pray we follow on to in our personal lives to achieve a more intimate and precise relationship with Father, getting to know His personality and that He has feelings. He will Love us for this!

Behind *The Veil*
_Offering Time

Uugghh it's time to pass the offering plate, or March up to the offering bucket. I don't have any money and my feet are screaming in these heels! I'm not going up there. I'm just not.

Have you ever felt this way before?

Some days you just feel like bla!
The Lord was dealing with me about this one day and was letting me know that touching the bucket is actually a faith thing. Many walk by without touching or don't walk up at all but when we see a car we really

want or a dress even if we don't have the money we want to touch and to feel the material or sit in that car and feel the wheel and seats because it's a desire that one day we will be able to drive this off the lot and park it in the yard. It's the same thing with giving an offering in church. If we desire to give then touching the plate even when we don't have money shows God that if He blessed us that our desire would be to give to the house! Touch the plate and believe that break through is coming!

CHAPTER 17

Higher Heights

Ever been to the Bahamas or the Cayman Islands or Maui and saw those crystal waters that look so much like a fairy tail but you didn't have any swimming attire to get into this majestic water? Ever walked the streets and smelled the delicious food they were cooking on the grills and in the smoke house but you didn't have money to part take? What about when you went site seeing.... All the historic and grand hotels towering the city that were lit up so bright but you had no finances to get a room. You're in this beautiful place. ...unprepared_

God's desire is for this_ not to be us when He brings us to higher heights and brings us to the place of being on His Holy Mountain where we hear Him so clear and respond with accuracy. He wants us to be prepared for pros and cons and the device of satan. God's desire for us is to be able to maintain this place with elegance, excellence, and finesse! The higher one goes in God, the thinner the air is. It's like flesh ascending upward. The heart says I want to go there.

> *"Who shall ascend into the hill of the Lord? Or who shall stand in His holy place? He that hath clean hands and a pure heart: who hath not lifted up his soul unto vanity, nor sworn deceitfully."*
> *(Psalms 24 3-4)*

Flesh wont be able to breath where you're trying to go. So we must make a continuous decision. Stay here where flesh can survive or ascend to our rightful places where flesh can't breath and it dies.

In this case the Father takes over because He needs your vessel in the earth and you need Him to breath on His holy mountain. This is the partnership! So now we're on His territory breathing His breath. We must have the mind of Christ in order to know how to function and survive breathing on His holy Mountain. Naturally we breath in and out, but spiritually we breath up and down, through our spirit man. God then teach us and show us when, where, and how to lower our spirits in order to reach those in a different hemisphere from us. When time to lower our spirits to minister on a level of understanding this is where we must be careful because pride awaits in the crowd. Arrogance and the heroic spirit of thinking it's us saving and healing, and not Christ in us.

We breath up and down spiritually like unto the angels ascending and descending. This is the breath of the spirit realm.

Ever was in a place with God but then stopped offering up prayers, stop offering dedication up, and offering up?

The spirit man begin to get chocked out because it can't breath.

Don't get cocky when your spirit has descended into a low place to reach out. If this happens and the heroic spirit attaches itself to us we'll begin to deny the timing and mindset of Christ and begin to lower our spirits just because somebody had a falling out and they want your wisdom, advice. Etc. If God has not sent you down don't come. Simple. Because coming away from Devine timing sets you up for demonic attack, distractions, and mind battles. Practice not coming down on self willed things.

Ex: Great aunt May wants to debate politics with you.

This is not a good reason to come down. We already know a disagreement is waiting near by. We loose power spiritually when we get cocky and step into our own time zone. We then get confused on what to do. We think it's time to pray and it's time to hush and meditate because God wants to speak. We think it's time to witness when God is saying I want you to self examine this week, Pay attention to what you're doing. We loose the timing of God.

Satan wanted Jesus to throw Himself down off the mountain* surly this was not of God. But to allow demonic attacks of our own self time zone we then get cocky.

"Let me show this devil something, I'll be back God." Just Cocky! Cockiness plays into the hand of the wicked one.

Sometimes it's God's will for you to play dumb. This is one avenue to keep us on the mountain until God says time to come down.

Gen 42:7 speaks of Joseph, how he saw his brothers and knew them but made himself strange.

> "He *spoke with his brother by an interpreter.*"
> **Gen 42:23**

The enemy expose himself and his agenda all the time, but our mouths are to busy running to hear it sometimes. Other times, God's will is for us to not listen. In one ear speeding out the other, because some information will mess you up. We can't afford to be contaminated and confused right now. Eyes focused, mindset clear, ear to the voice of God, armor on, ready to war in battle in divine timing and right alignment!

Staying in the Presence of God is like when a diver straps oxygen to himself. When he goes under water where he can't normally live or function he stays the amount of time given by his oxygen tank, and then he's up and out.

When born again our natural functions should become spiritual. God releases us for a certain amount of time to do assignment but we must report back in the correct time frame. Ever observed a minister when they finish ministering they go off to some place secluded or they may Neal and pray where they are because it's time to get back. The assassin demons await that minister who fails to get back into that place promptly.

Super means to place above or over. We think super natural to mean majestic or something. We should take it to mean extra.

It's Extra Natural For:

our bodies to need drinking water-
Babies to drink milk around the clock -
Us to have relationship with God -

One day last year, I was expressing myself to Father and letting Him know that I was heavy hearted that I didn't have any friends. He spoke to me and said

"You hang with the Supernatural!"

When I heard these words I was elated! My smile was big all day! What Father was saying to me was it's extra natural for me to talk with Him everyday! To eat with Him, to shop with Him. Heads up, shopping with Father is the best! He never let me walk out of the store with revealing clothing and He always allows me to find a good sale prices!

It's extra natural for us to operate spiritually on our jobs, in our homes or where ever we go because this ties to us being meek. You don't have to be the loudest one, or always have something to say. Everything doesn't have to be thus said the Lord. Spiritual fruits kicks in and the aura around you becomes Christ like.

Demon spirits around you wont like this and will fight you. Often times naturally but always spiritually.

Ever was around people at a gathering or church or something and you didn't do any bickering or debating but when you got home you were just so tired?

Often times we blame this feeling on our emotions but it's because your angels have been warring all day with your aunt tee Lucy demon angels and the other surrounding demon angels that wanted to put your light out. I'm talking about literal battle, so much until your spirit feels the tiredness, and the devil waits right by your mouth for you to confess that you're so tired and he assigns a demon by law on you and it's hard for you to get back up. We must wake up and focus! Next time this feeling comes upon you send strength to your angels and draw the blood line of Jesus Christ around yourself. Casting all spirits out: tiredness, tiredness, procrastination away from you into outer darkness. We must know how to war with the weapons God has given us.

It's not for you to witness to everybody! It's not for you to counsel everybody! We have to be led of God and stop opening ourselves up to devils that attach themselves to us. It's not for you to sew money into everybody. Super saints without the Super natural is bound for mistake after mistake. Because we go wild with bible instructions but no wisdom. God's about to send out well rounded individuals with equal balance! Ambassadors that represent Him well with integrity, being obedient, being servants, having an ear to hear, meek and quiet spirit, humble as a lamb, virtuous in prayer and having wisdom with finances! Two ways we have mistaken and charged God foolishly is in our time and our way. God is the maker of time and we consciously and unconsciously take it for granted. We take our breath for granted, our time for granted, and our way also.

> *"To every thing there is a season and a time to every purpose under the heaven. Time to be born, time to die, time to plant, time to pluck up that which is planted. Time to kill, time to heal, time to break down, time to build up, time to weep, time to laugh time to mourn, time to dance, time to cast away stones, time to gather stones together, time to embrace, time to refrain from embracing, time to get, time to loose, time to keep, time to cast away, time to rend, time to sew, time to keep silence, times to speak, time to love, time to hate, time to war, time of peace. Vs11 He hath made everything beautiful in "His" timing!*
>
> ***(Ecclesiastics 3:1)***

Question: Are you in your time zone or God's?

How can we ever look at a clock again and not see Jesus?

When I see Jesus on the cross I see time. 12;00,6;00,9:00,and 3:00.

These are the times I set my alarm to pray everyday. I realized it's importance to God because when I had started to work I couldn't have my cell phone on the floor but on many occasions people would walk right up to me out of the blue and ask me for the time and when I look at my watch or clock, it was one of my prayer times on the head! God enjoys when He has children that actually get to know Him and to know the parts not discussed by the masses. Breath, way, and time All link up to time in the judgment.

How did you spend your time while I was giving you breath?

How many times did I show you the proper way or send ones to show you the proper way?

How many times did I say in my word to love your neighbor, how many times did I Say forgive?

How many times did you go to church just to say you went?

Now it's your time to go.
It all boils down to time.

"But of that day and hour knoweth no man."
Matthew 24:36

When the bible says no man knows the day or hour it doesn't literally have to be a 24 hour day period. The bible speaks of two types of days and two types of hours. One type of day is in

"And God called the light Day and the darkness He called night, and the evening and the morning were the first day."
Gen 1:5

"And call upon me in the day of trouble: I will deliver thee, and thou shalt glorify me."
(Psalms 50:15)

"Behold the day of the Lord cometh and thy spoil shall be divided in the midst of thee. for I will gather all nations against Jerusalem to battle and the city shall be taken and houses rifled, and the women ravished; and half of the city shall go forth in captivity and the residue of the people shall not be cut off from the city(era)"

Zechariah 14

Hour_

This is the hour God is releasing inheritances to those making themselves ready.

"In that same hour said Jesus to the multitudes, are ye come out as against a thief with swords and staves for to take me? I sat daily with you teaching in the temple, and ye laid no hold on me."

Matthew 26:55

"He that is unjust let him be unjust still: and he which is filthy, let him be filthy still: and he that is righteous, let him be righteous still; and He that is holy, let him be holy still. God says behold I come quickly. In verse 13 God says I am Alpha and Omega, the beginning and the end, the first and the last."

(Revelations 22:11)

God in Kairos time interacts and controls His will in our lives as long as we are willing to receive this massive blessing. The Lord is always looking for ways to interrupt our Chrono's time with His Kairos time! Chrono's referring to chronological or sequential time and Kairos refers to the opportune time and/ or place that is, the right or appropriate time to say or do the right or appropriate thing. (Grammar.about. com>kairosterm) This speaks of being in the dead center of the timing of God. It signifies a period or season, a moment of indeterminate time in which an event of significance happens. Quantum Physics speaks of the eternal realm also. Quantum Physics allows for particles to be in two states at the same time!

One day I was on this long mile bridge headed to work and traffic was chaotic and bumper to bumper at a stand still. So I'm parked on this bridge and my mind started to wonder. What if theirs this massive angel holding up traffic by way of a small car accident, road work, or other incident while Father is going through judging each person in each car right now, and once He's done traffic slowly starts to move again? Nobody said you have to die naturally to be judged. People die spiritual deaths everyday. Some die out to God and others choose to take no place in life, which is God, so they ultimately choose death. Personally I don't believe Father would wait until the very end and be like us with all this work pilled up on our desk. God works smart. Once He's judged a person I believe He marks them then and there.

Why would He say He that is Holy be Holy still?

That person has already been judged they are now just waiting for God's kairos of timezone to call them home.

Ever heard the term seared with a hot iron?

"Speaking *lies in hypocrisy having their conscience seared with a hot iron.*
(1 Timothy 4:2)

Conscience means *an inner feeling or voice viewed as acting as a guide to the rightness or wrongness of one's behavior.*(Sense of right and wrong, moral sense, inner voice)

When Father sear a person, this person has had a part of judgement day and is now waiting to meet time/ creator of time, God. The books are opened and everyone get's a fair trial to know why Father has made that particular decision for their eternity. I call it "the play back." Just like a movie we are to look at our actions and motives, did we receive or reject the mission given to us.

John 14:6 -"Jesus said I am the way."

This is why you can't follow everybody because you haven't an idea who's just living and waiting to meet time. They've already been seared, so they can afford to play pretend Christian because their destination has already been determined. Follow Christ the hope of glory

> *"Nevertheless the foundation of God standeth sure, having this seal, the Lord knoweth them that are His. And let everyone that nameth the name of Christ depart from iniquity."*
>
> **2 Timothy 2:19**

When God says behold I come quickly, He'll already know who's His and who's not. We don't know which day or which hour God has picked to mark us His or not His. I'm convinced that every one that has died naturally was already marked before they met their God.

> *"And I saw the dead small and great stand before God and the books were opened; and another book was opened, which is the book of life; and the dead were judged out of those things which were written in the books, according to their works. And the sea gave up the dead and hell delivered up their dead which were in them: and they were judged every man according to their works. And death and hell were cast into the lake of fire, this is the second death. And whosoever was not found "written " in the book of life was cast into the lake of fire.*
> *Written meaning past participle of write. In **verse 13** says every man was judged according to his works and 14 says this was the second death."*
>
> **(Revelation 20:12-15)**

Is their two judgements? One where we are marked and seared and the second where we are to find out has our name been written?

> *"And the books were opened; and the dead were judged out of those things which were written in the books."*
>
> **Revelation 20:12**

Even people found to be guilty has a court case. God is just enough to give a trial. Many people await trial.

The third part God gives us of Him is the way.

> *"God gives His angels charge over us to keep us in all our ways."*
>
> **Psalms 91:11**

The highway, way of finances, the way of our emotions, the way of marriage etc. In everything their is a way even God gives us a way of escape.

> *"There hath no temptation taken you but such as is common to man: but God is faithful, who will not suffer you to be tempted above that ye are able; but will with the temptation also make a way to escape, that ye may be able to bare it.* Which means to endure it."
> **(1 Corinthians 10:13)**

<u>*How does God give me a way to escape but I still have to endure it?*</u>

Endure means *to suffer something painful or difficult patiently. Remain in existence; last, remain, and continue.*

<u>*So how can I have a way of escape, but I still have to endure or continue?*</u>

Remember God "is" the way and we ascend and descend in His timing like unto the angels. This is your escape. When your boss is chewing you out over something you didn't do you should just ascend spiritually!

In *Romans 12:19* God says *vengeance is mine I'll repay.* So this gives us the proper time of God to ascend. Walking in the Word gives us full awareness of God's timing to do things. When ascending we say few words, we listen. While listening satan will expose himself and what angle he's coming from, he'll expose his motives and his plan against you! Theirs nothing like knowing which way your enemy is coming. Saul even wanted to raise Samuel from the dead to find out! This shows us through Christ how to war a good warfare. So while enduring we learn the plan of satan also.

When we choose to just leave a situation without the timing of God we risk more demons attacking us from blind sides because we left without the blue print of satan fully exposing himself. This is when it's not God's time for us to leave. His "way of escape" is Him! He is the way the truth and the life! The bible says in *Matthew 7:14 Because strait is the gate, and narrow is the way* (talking about God) which leadeth unto life and few there be that find it.

Why will just a few find it?

Because He's hid in the secret place!(*Psalms 91)*this way is God and He is the way. When you have somebody with a loud mouth, loud spirit, and everything about them is loud, these are people who wont engage in the secret place.

Why would God let us shout on the bull horn where He is?

Of coarse not! We must become meek, quiet, humble. The strait gate- *strait* meaning *narrow.* God says many people choose the other path because this one cost to much. We must be spiritually fit to fit through the strait gate. All the fatness of flesh must be shaved off by the sword of the Spirit and crucified in order to get through. We must allow God to keep cutting away at us because Father knows the size we have to be in order to make it through. The three things we need to start sanctifying is our Breath, our Way, and our Time! This is why the enemy fight us so much dealing with these. Seems like it's not enough time in the day to get what I need done, forget about what God needs done.......this is our way.

How much breath do we misuse speaking negative words?

Why do we always get off on exists that seem right?

It seems right what our friends are doing so I'm just going to do it too.

"Their *is a way which seemeth right unto man, but the*
end thereof are the ways of death." This is the way of the
fallen angel.
Vs 14 says *"The backslider in heart shall be filled with*
"his own ways".

Proverbs 14:12

There are plenty people at your church filled with their own ways.
This is why we should look to Jesus/ Yahweh! We hear the word way in
Yahweh because He is the way, the truth, and the life.

"Examine yourselves, whether ye be in the faith!"

2 Corinthians 13:5

Let's sanctify these three areas and see God move mountains on
our behalf!

Behind The Veil
_Church Hurt Is Of God

Seems like these days you can't turn the corner good without over
hearing someone talking about what their ex pastor did to them the
reason they are no longer there. In some cases these people run whoever
they can down to talk about what their latest "father in the gospel"
has done to hurt them! Somewhere we have to stop and do a quick
regrouping. We must indeed realize that

Church hurt is a God thing and it's really for our protection!

<u>Do you know that if God didn't allow us to get hurt we would treat mortals
like an idol god?</u>

It's for our own protection in the long run. What's not God's will is for
us to always run from to church to church. When we do this it's because
we are either not getting fed simple things like how to live right and
make it to heaven (the simplicity of Christ) or we are looking for an idol
to worship!

News flash: Every last one of them will hurt you in some way or another because God designed it this way! Not that they mean to but the Word wars against the flesh 100%.

The pure word of God cuts in itself alone! Where do you think most rebuke come from. God use them to do it. In the long run God is thinking of you because you can't get into heaven with idol worship! Ever was apart of a ministry that actually taught you truth and righteousness? The preacher actually lived the best he could by the word and the elect Lady as well? But this preacher did something that you felt hurt you and so you left. More than likely it was not God's will for you to leave. It's God's will for you to cry to Him, get up, and turn from idol worship with forgiveness for that man or woman of God. In staying and sticking it out you have already experienced and know now that this man is not The Almighty and so now we hold God in His proper place while respecting His man of God but not treating this man of God like God! To run from church to church is to get hurt by each preacher. It's been a known fact since the beginning of time that you can't run from God! Church hurt IS of God! Take a deep breath, take your making, and see life differently. It's all g00d and it's all G0d!

CHAPTER 18

My Inheritance

God is in the mood of releasing inheritances to those who has and are continuing to make themselves ready and aligned with where He told us to be in this season!

Where has God told you to be?

What has He told you to do?

It's vitally important to have the right alignment in order to receive, but don't be anxious! God can't work through anxiety because it's not faith, it is unbelief. We must not be passive either, that's laziness. We must be found in the middle of these two words:

Anxious
Daughters of Zion
Passive

This is where faith is. Peaceful transition. God is ready to release inheritances and some of us are already feeling the first fruits of it. Congratulations in the Holy Ghost!!! You've leveled up!!!

For those of us that are still preparing for this phase, we can feel it in the air that something is about to happen. We don't know if we should be glad, sad, or scared; emotions are everywhere. It's because God is in the mood of releasing inheritances on/to His people. If you find yourself feeling spiritually sad sometimes it's because our spirit knows we're not spiritually dead enough to receive this amazing blessing and the enemy is trying to capitalize on waking the parts of us that we have surrendered under the blood, up! Those situations on your job, in your home, church house, or in other places you attend are to spark the flesh side of you. Anger, resentment, animosity, lustful feelings, and seductions are to wake your flesh up\to keep your flesh woke because he knows- In this case we must be spiritually dead to receive this inheritance. God isn't going to give His inheritance to someone who is taking Him for granted. Someone who bend to the enemy all the time or someone who yields to the voice of the enemy will not be selected, but someone who yields to His voice and has surrendered. Amen.

"But the meek shall inherit the earth ;and shall delight themselves in the abundance of peace."
Psalms 37:11

Meek meaning *quiet, gentle, and easily impressed on, submissive.- enduring injury with practice without resentment, not violent or strong moderate, mild, deficient in spirit and courage.*

Submissive means *yielding, obedient, complaint tamed, biddable, tractable, acquiescent, humble, deferential, timid, unprotesting, unresisting, like a lamb to the slaughter, quiet, mild, gentle, docile, lamblike, shy, diffident, unassuming, self effacing.*

Many equate meekness with weakness.

*An attitude to allow everyone to run over you because you are afraid of them is not meekness. This is simply not true. Some of the strongest men who ever lived were meek.(*Moses* in numbers *12 and 3*) (*Jesus in *Matthew 11:29*)

Meek in Greek word says : ***praus_***
used to *describe someone taking soothing medicine.*
Used by sailors to *describe a gentle breeze.*
Used by farmers to *describe a horse that has been broken.*

All of these descriptions have a common factor. They all describe great power under control.

"Blessed are the meek for they shall inherit the earth".
(Matthew 5:5)

"Knowing that of the Lord ye shall receive the reward of the inheritance for ye serve the Lord Christ."
(Colossians 3 23;24)

"Who *is that commanded? It's Christ that died, yea rather, that has risen again who is even at the right hand of God who also maketh intercession for us".*
(Romans 8 :34)

"Though *wilt shew me the oath of life in they presence is fullness of joy ; at thy right hand there are pleasures for ever more.»*
(Psalms 16:11)

We can't experience our inheritance/ pleasures at all without Jesus because our inheritance involves Him! He is the key to the lock.

Most often times inheritance takes place when one has died. Spiritually in order to be meek one must die to self allowing Jesus to reign. Once we have died to self, the way we think, the way we see things, and we take on the mind of Christ- then being totally surrendered to His will, we are able to actually claim our inheritance. The death to self has taken place but now God still need you physically to go, do, proclaim, speak out, and reach out -so now- you're operating your earth(body) lead by the Holy Ghost. You start to experience what you've inherited now; peace, joy, and the abundance of love.

I just want to encourage you to keep pushing because reaching inheritance status is in MUST!

Remember, it's impossible to receive our inheritance without Jesus.

When thinking of inheritance the natural mind thinks money, but this inheritance consists of the abundance of peace, fullness of joy, and pleasures for evermore FIRST! Yes money will come to but what truly matters is the inheritance money can't buy!

Most Billionaires don't have this! Many have died and went on never to experience what they wanted so desperately. The devil would have it that we chase after the emptiness that they had/have when our Father want to give us the fullness! The fullness of joy, and the abundance of peace.

How do we position ourselves and make sure we're in the right alignment with the Spirit of Grace?

"The *meek shall inherit the earth.*»

Psalms 37:11

We must inherit the earth in order to receive our inheritance. The earth being our temple, our bodies.

How do you inherit your own body?

We must become dead to flesh, dead to ourselves, dead to the way we view things, the way we respond, and the way we retaliate! *Retaliate* meaning we are no longer vindictive but now we invest in prayer chains!

What is a prayer chain?

A prayer chain is when your prayers meet each other in the spirit realm. When we constantly pray throughout the days forming a chain occurs. Each prayer is a link in the chain. Praying once one day and then again on the third or fourth day is not good. This will not achieve an effective prayer chain. Our prayer chain can break every illiterate chain of the enemy because it's way stronger and with power!

How do we inherit the earth/our temples   so that God can fill it with his inheritance?

*Death to flesh, because satan owns that part and works through that part of the flesh. If we surrender the flesh, crucify it spiritually then we inherit the form!

The heart, the lungs, the mind, the feet, the hands, the liver, the kidneys etc.- WE INHERIT WHAT GOD MADE! He then fills it because we took back what the enemy stole. He fills us with the abundance, and now we are walking witnesses that Jesus lives! We will become a walking billboard testimony that God does invest Himself in us! We become that manifestation of the sons of God!

But where are some believers now?

Some are at the place of *"give and take"*. This place is not uncommon and to be honest many believers have physically died in this place. They have followed this place of settling for knowing about the promise but not experiencing it. This place is called

"THE RENTER".

"The renter" can hold the keys to something but when payments are not made the repo man comes a knocking at the door. He wants his merchandises back.

When we don't have ownership of our earth/our bodies, satan owns it.

How do we get ownership?

- by killing the flesh spiritually- by surrendering to God and becoming meek_*the meek shall inherit the earth.* We don›t want to become like the person who buys their loved one a car. Yes, the loved one has the car but you're still making the payments on that car and as soon as you stop or can't afford to make the payments the repo man knocks at the door of your loved one! They don't care if your loved one has plans to go to work that day, plans to do business meetings that day, or graduation _the repo man DOES NOT CARE he just wants his merchandises back.

So yes, we give ourselves away to God!

"Take me Lord I'm yours", and we pray, fast, and give but as soon as we stop and we still don't hold the deeds to this old house, and trouble arise with situations that cause our flesh to act out/show out (attributes of the devil) then he comes and knocks on God's door and says, "please excuse me God, but that one needs to come with me. I have papers on her. They have some of me in them and I'm here to collect!"

God becomes remorseful and He's hurt but He will not go against His word and so we go with the repo man until we get our prayers up, our dedication back up_ just like getting the money up to get the car back to give the car back to your loved one to keep for a while until we are short on money again and well . . . yeah. It's like playing a game with our lives . . . we just hope we are In that place of still having the car when our name is called and time is up. My God!

The devil doesn't care if God had plans to send you out that day. Plans to break yokes off your mom and dad through you or off your children. The repo man don't care and so millions of believers grow old and die in this state right here. Never inheriting the earth and receiving the Inheritance which is that fullness that God wants to give us right now! God wont fill us with the fullness just for the devil to come and repo us and use it for his gain. We must come to the place where we can say the enemy comes and finds NOTHING in me.

God will only give the abundance of peace to those who has inherited their earth- the meek_ because when He has plans to send you out to just walk down the halls of the hospital and the spirit of peace just goes into every room and even settle upon the nurses, He doesn't have to worry about that knock at the door from the repo man. God can give things to us when we no longer stand in His way! His will then comes to pass.

WE MUST ELIMINATE THE REPO MAN and the only way to do this is to die to self! Become meek! We must have the deeds to this body!

In ending I'll leave this one last scripture and I pray that this book carries you to the place it has me where I'm sold out and bought with a price! Not affording anymore to care about life as America does but life as Jesus taught in the Holy scriptures!

> ***Romans 8:13***
> *For if ye live after the flesh, ye shall die: but if ye through the spirit do modify the deeds of the body, ye shall live.*

> *Amen*

Behind The Veil
-I Do

Sparkly, shinny, ridgetop or even antiqued, a lady loves a good quality ring that speaks volumes without her having to vocally say a thing! What is this bond with rings anyway? You have the:

Friendship ring
Promise ring
Champion ship rings
Engagement rings
Wedding rings
Class rings
Signet rings
Purity ring
Birthstone ring
Thumb ring
Toe ring

and might as well throw the onion ring in their! As always the human race takes things Father implemented and get carried away with them! In more dept., a ring has very sacred meaning to God. Their are two particular rings that God cherish so much! These two rings shows Him just who is all talk and no action and who really does love Him from the heart! We ladies wear rings for symbols of this and symbols of that but what about concerning God? Do we actually go shopping for hours to look for a ring that symbolizes our deep eternity filled love for Him? Honestly..no, we don't. Just to actually say something like this sounds a little crazy and over the top huh? When thinking of God, I don't think the word "ring" ever cross our minds! Maybe savior or healer but never .....ring. Truth be told, with our boyfriends and significant others the word ring pops up on day one! No serious lady wants to waist her time with someone she doesn't think she would like to marry one day. The ring pops up in our minds all too soon. That guy, on the other hand, may not ever think of the ring. Don't get me wrong, some are really serious and they do think and are looking for a potential wife! These fellas get that trait from Father! Father is always thinking of the ring and Who will say yes! Who will say I do and wear His rings? As a matter of fact He will not allow us to transform into Kingdom without them! Kingdom meaning God dwelling in us! God is not going to share habitation with someone He is not married to! God does NOT shack up ladies! These two rings are symbolic to our love for Him and His love for us! We can't become the bride of Christ without these two important rings God offers each willing vessel that will say "I do"! These precious rings are rejected by masses of people in the world because they bring the difference in between one just claiming to love God and one who is actually taking time out to become Kingdom for God to dwell in!

> *"For to be carnally minded is death; but to be spiritually minded is life and peace."*
> **Romans 8:6**

Carnally we look for rings that shine like the sun which is why the world could never receive these rings honestly offered to us from God.

> *"God is a Spirit: and they that worship Him must worship Him in spirit and in truth."*
> **John 4:24**

Since Father is a spirit of coarse the rings He offer us will be spiritual as well! (Nothing naturally shinny about this)

The first ring I would like to discuss that is very important to Father is the *suffer ring*!

Let's visit a variety of scriptures and then we will continue.

> "But *and if ye suffer for righteousness› sake, happy are ye: and be not afraid of their terror, neither be troubled. For unto you it is given in the behalf of Christ, not only to believe on him, but also to suffer for his sake."*
> **(1 Peter 3:14)**

> *"That I may know Him, and the power of God resurrection, and the fellowship of His sufferings, being made conformable unto His death."*
> (***Philippians 1:29***)

> *"For even hereunto were ye called: because Christ also suffered for us, leaving us an example, that ye should follow His steps"*
> **1 Peter 2:21**

The suffer ring is a ring we must retain! How can one claim to love in a world that is against real love, which is God,and not suffer? To not suffer in this world is to be in agreement to what they believe. They believe that houses, cars,land, and money are an exact proof of fruit that God is with you and His blessings are forever upon your life. God never labeled material things to be proof of fruit! It shows us in Galatians 5 22- 23 what is direct proof of the correct spiritual fruit from God. Check it out;

"But the fruit of the Spirit is love, joy, peace, longsuffering, gentleness, goodness, faith,

Meekness, temperance: against such there is no law."

Amen! Why does God have no law established for people abiding in these fruit? Simply because He knows this person has His characteristics and there is point blank no evil in them. This person has strived and is striving to become perfection which is to become His Kingdom!

Yes, the Lord wants us to have nice things. Yes, He loves for us to be blessed! The suffer ring could come in any given situations concerning forsaking all to follow Christ!

The rich young ruler in Mark 10:21 was very sad at heart when Jesus offered this ring to Him. What he did not understand is that this ring from Jesus comes with peace! Riches and fine things offer good feeling and great eye candy but no peace within!

> "Then *Jesus beholding him loved him, and said unto him,*
> *One thing thou lackest: go thy way, sell whatsoever thou*
> *hast, and give to the poor, and thou shalt have treasure*
> *in heaven: and come, take up the cross, and follow me.»*
> **Mark 10:21**

Why was it so easy for Jesus to just say you are "lacking" one thing, Go sell your stuff and give to the poor? I mean just like that I'm to sell all my stuff and give away the money? Say what? Our King is so beautiful! Jesus never meant For us to trust in riches, but He said seek ye first the Kingdom of God and everything else will be added! Why? Because now you know how to suffer and you know that your faith lay in Jesus! Let's squeeze this scripture together and sip on that "new wine"! We have been programmed by society, day time television, and false teachings that lack means to be without the wealth of material things! You don't have enough of this and you don't have enough of that! Webster's dictionary concurs with a definition stating the state of being without or not having enough of something.

In one form this is true but somehow between the natural and the spiritual mindset this definition got misconstrued spiritually. In all truth lack, to God, means being without HIM and not without money, cars, land and a five million dollar record deal! Jesus used also another deep word in this passage called "poor". The Word poor in this particular text has very rich meaning that we will dissect together!

Jesus told this man that He loved, that he "lacked" one thing and that was to go sell all he had and give to the poor. If all his material things caused him to lack with God then why was he directed to give it to the poor? Would not this cause the "poor" then to lack as well? The poor Jesus was speaking of in this text was those who has the mind frame of the world. Those who believe their material things are actually evidence that Jesus walks with them and they are walking in abundant favor. Those who believe that riches is where peace is. These people are in fact very poor to Father so give your old mindset and your old worldly fruit to them and come follow me that I may put these rings of true peace on you and show you what true riches are! Jesus always commanded that we "feed" the poor. These text mean actual poor people like in

> "For I was an hungred, and ye gave me meat: I was thirsty, and ye gave me drink: I was a stranger, and ye took me in."
>
> *Matthew 5 35*

Yes indeed one form of being poor is not being able to afford food but in another form(in another passage) it can also mean feed those in "poor" mindset,like this rich young ruler, the authentic gospel of Jesus Christ because they are in fact poor as well. Yet another form of in

> *Matthew 5* speaks of a «poorness « that we all must reach for and receive in order to even think about becoming Kingdom!
>
> **Blessed** are the poor in spirit: for theirs is the kingdom of heaven.
>
> *(Matthew 5)*

Really wanting to comprehend this I asked the Lord what does this passage mean? What do you mean by "poor in spirit"? He says "Naturally those that can never get enough food are always wanting more, and

Spiritually their are those that are always seeking me that can't get enough of *ME whom are poor in spirit and my Kingdom are for those!»*

Another example of this poor in spirit is **Matthew 5:6**

Blessed are they which do hunger and thirst after righteousness: for they shall be filled.(Poor in spirit)

<u>*Are you worthy of the suffer ring?*</u>

<u>*Would you give up all you had to follow Jesus?*</u>

This determined whether you really trust yourself of whether you trust Jesus! The question Is not, *is Jesus worthy enough for us to wear His ring.* The question is *are we worthy enough to wear the King's Ring? Never ever forget that the KING OWNS EVERYTHING! I'm very proud to wear His ring because it symbolizes that I belong to Him and nothing shall by any means harm me!*

> "Behold, I give unto you power to tread on serpents and scorpions, and over all the power of the enemy: and nothing shall by any means hurt you."
>
> *(Luke 10;19)*

I'm honored to have been bought with a price a long time ago and this type of purchase demands humility or/and massive chastening from the purchaser. It takes humility to purposefully and forcefully wear the suffer ring without taking it off. Jesus is worthy of it all! Jesus brings peace when our minds are stayed on Him. *Isaiah 26:3*

This peace is like no other feeling in the world or the universe! This peace from Jesus while wearing these rings are exhilarating! The very dynamic power of the word peace when expressing Jesus is not comprehensible! You could be in the middle of a back breaking storm, but with this ring God allows us to feel and experience the up most calmness! People all around you will think you have gone fool crazy because you are not pulling your hair out like them! It is an out of this world experience!

This same peace can be in acquaintance with us in earth with the seal of the rings offered to us by Christ!

Let's talk about the second ring! This ring is called the offer ring! Praise the Almighty God! Do you posses this ring? The story of Cane and Abel can explain this ring best! Let's take a look:

> *3 And in process of time it came to pass, that Cain brought of the fruit of the ground an offering unto the Lord.*
> *4 And Abel, he also brought of the firstlings of his flock and of the fat thereof. And the Lord had respect unto Abel and to his offering:*
> *5 But unto Cain and to his offering he had not respect. And Cain was very wroth, and his countenance fell.*
> *6 And the Lord said unto Cain, Why art thou wroth? and why is thy countenance fallen?*
> *7 If thou doest well, shalt thou not be accepted? and if thou doest not well, sin lieth at the door.*
> **(Genesis 4:3-7)**

We observe two men presenting offerings before the Lord! God has respect for one mans offering but not the other's. Why is this? Both of them gave to Him right? This is the reason we must posses the offer ring. Many people associated with/in the world offer things to God all the time. They offer their time, finances, prayers even their children, but they have not said yes to the offer ring which means God doesn't have their entire heart.

> "No man can serve two masters: for either he will hate the one, and love the other; or else he will hold to the one, and despise the other. Ye cannot serve God and mammon.»
> **(Matthew 6:24)**

The suffer ring and the offer ring from God allows us the being able to suffer and still offer pure praise unto God! Possessing these rings allow us to be suffering through hell but still offer pure love to our brothers and sisters in Christ Jesus! Having the deeds to this flesh and these two rings allow us to maybe not be financially confident but still offer that just amount of finances to the Lord with a cheerful heart! These two rings are the dynamic duo! God offers these rings to us. It Is up to us if we choose to walk in our rightful places. We must become kingdom!

Through this book we have learned simple things God cherish for us to know to become more developed and mature! Taking all these things into consideration, meditation, and prayer results in us oozing with Heaven's fragrance! When God sees that we are taking Him seriously He will be quick to impart more Kingdom things into us and transform us! Talk about moving to another level and another realm in God! On the other what single God fearing son of God wouldn't want to join hands with the King's daughter? A man who finds Kingdom...I mean a man who finds a wife finds a good thing! Being married is NOT our ultimate goal, but being Kingdom is! All these other thing important to us will be added unto us!

> *Thy Kingdom come and Thy will be done in earth (in me)*
> *as it is in heaven!*
> **Matthew 6:10**

As true daughters is Christ we walk by faith and not by site! Truly becoming Kingdom is a faith walk and we are just the ones to rise to the challenge and defeat the enemy for our families, our neighborhoods, cities, and regions! We,as the bride of Christ as a whole, shall be victorious! No spots, no wrinkles, no attitudes! We shall be as new!

Let's grab a hold of God and refuse to let go for anyone! God is counting on you! Start your journey with "It Is Written!"

~ He That Wins Souls Is Wise

I pray with all sincerity that this book has blessed you and that you will continue to walk in the shoes of becoming and then staying Kingdom! The small apparel collection that you observe are different designs Father gave me while giving me the material for this book! They are for sale along with many many more designs not listed! They come in all different colors and we supply men and children shirts and designs as well! The vision God has for these particular designs is that He wants us to branch out in the witnessing department. While wearing a T-Shirt one day that says "God can do all but fail," you are actually able to do none verbal witnessing while you're at a crowded bus station, in the mall, or just the super market! You may not be able to verbally tell "everybody" about the goodness of Father, but none verbally you will be! Some just don't feel like talking, some in despair, some In the middle of divorce, some about to face trial and jail time for something they didn't do and they look for encouraging words. These designs are a powerful tool in the Kingdom of God because people are so none personal now days! Do you have a prophetic saying that stirs your soul? Email it to us and let the world become inspired from what God gave you! With our gift of design and your vision let's make it a "God thing," in this dark world! Ever heard someone say, "Don't call just text me"? These designs are meant to plant seeds in the minds of people walking by! Those needing and wishing for help may get it through you!

"I have planted, Apollos watered; but God gave the increase."
(1Corinthians 3;6)

Talk about being a soul winner! How many people are waiting on you?

"30 The fruit of the righteous is a tree of life; and he that winneth souls is wise."
Proverbs 11;30

As we are becoming Kingdom let's represent Kingdom style! The world represents for satan in every way, shape, form, and color. Why must we continue to be silent in the way we believe and how we view this world! We are not from here! It's time for us to, to learn the power of speaking without speaking!

"Then saith he unto his disciples, The harvest truly is plenteous, but the laborers are few»
(Matthew 9:37)

All this work to be done. My beautiful mom, Lady Elect Darlene Cook, would tell us girls to "work smart not hard"! God gives us wisdom so let's use it a defeat the dark Kingdom! If you find interest in these designs and want to purchase them or see loads of other designs to help you advance Kingdom you can contact me through email at

Contact: *Carrier66@mail.com*

We are here to service you!

Join us in being a carrier of the gospel of Jesus Christ!

Behind The Veil {Exit}
_Warning To The Bride of Christ

Life is so full! From the time we wake up to the time we go to bed people are depending on us to do something. After all this depending on us We often times go our own way thinking on things important to us but not how Father may be feeling! It is a delighting thing for Father when we ask Him how he feels and it makes him feel loved. Ask Him is it somethings about you that displease Him. We, as daughters want to at least be found trying to do better. The Lord expressed some things to me that bothers Him as a whole and told me to heed the warning to Leaders and Sheep as well! Today we have female in leadership and this must be spoken. These things deal with:

The overwrite
The Disrespect
The Nasty Attitude

I will future expound on these titles in their entirety. We also must take a dose of reality and realize that a baby disobedience from us will lead to a grown up hell.

The Lord desires for us to stop over writing His presence with what we call the schedule or program which is also boring. We call it the order of service because we actually think it's our house and in some cases it is our House because God does NOT show up anymore.

2 Corinthians 11:14 says <u>And no marvel ;for Satan himself is transformed into an angel of light.</u>

One example is Moses in **Numbers 20:8-12**

God gave simple instructions to Moses which were: Go out and speak to the rock before the people's eyes. He spoke that the rock would bring forth water, and give the people and there beast to drink. Moses using emotion lifted up his hand, and with his rod he smote the rock two times instead.

Verse10)<u>Moses said to them Hear now,ye rebels; Must we fetch you water out of this rock?</u>

He Over wrote the presence and the very appearance of God, because of what he thought was necessary. What HE wanted to do.
Overwrite *means to write on top of other writing.*
God is the Word and the Word is God! When we choose to do our own thing once God's presence come so thick in our church houses, we are then participating in over writing God and we wonder why the church house is so messed up! While Leaders are very much so of a necessity Leaders are not the only ones God move through.

We think this way often times because we are so used to God speaking through us.

Now that we choose to have our own schedule we start to refuse to acknowledge when God has come into the house through a song of somebody, or through a worship dance or poem. Instead of having respect and shortly after taking the microphone and instructing the people to enter in «Right now» because God has come and right now is the time to get your healing, your deliverance, and break through, we tell God to sit down on the front row, it›s not your time yet.

How do we do this?

By our Programs! Okay now we're scheduled to do this, and now that, then preacher bring the word and you may every blue moon have an altar call .

Do we ever wonder why this method is rarely to none effective?

Why?

Because God came through the song of a young man singing or through another creative way and we failed to capitalize on His entrance! We didn't treat Him with royalty! We didn't reverence. We over rode Him and told Him to sit down and wait His turn. Then we proceed to try and reinvent the presence through preaching or through the rest of or schedule and it doesn't happen.

Evidence: No change in people's hearts! Change on the outside but none of substance on the inside!

The disrespect is another area to be addressed! A lot of people whom call themselves daughters and sons of God are very very disrespectful and have no clue how to honor and respect a King! We have become Confused by Moses and his actions in Exodus 32:14 which reads,

And the Lord repented of the evil which he thought to do unto His people.

Why do we get so overwhelmed with joy over this? "Moses made God repent"!

Clear message to the nation: We are Not saved by grace through Faith if this delights us!

Our motives are not pure at all if we joy in this. Why must we always try to find fault in something God has said or that God has done? Are we impostors? Are we? The truth is that our flesh glory in this because we feel like Moses made the Almighty God repent, but never look at the disrespect in this case as Moses told God, "you gone make me look bad and become a laughing stock to the Egyptians". Let's look a verse 12:

verse 12)*__Moses told God to turn and repent.__*

He told GOD that!

Vs 13 Told God "you said" you would multiply thy seed as the stars of heaven. The "you said" was to get God to change His mind and yes God repented. It's not that He can't go against His word, it's that He wont go against His word. His word is

Matthew 5:25 says ***agree with thine adversary quickly!***

Adversary means *one's opponent in a contest, conflict, or dispute.* "God you said"!

So why are we so proud of Moses that we make him an Idol?

Subconsciously we look for little ways to contest with God. Religious people think Moses brought God back to His senses. Religious people also think the great Moses saved God from lying. Religious people think Moses, by contesting with God, saved the seed of Abraham, Isaac, and Jacob! Religious people think Abraham, by contesting with God saved Lot and his family. Religious Folks!

The truth of the matter is Moses told God he didn't want Him to destroy the people. "The Egyptians will laugh at me ". Somehow Moses took himself right down the mountain and destroyed a lot of these same people with the precious law God had taken His time and written himself. This is a very good example of over writing. Oh yeah

verse 10 says__ **God said I will make of thee a great nation.**__

So God knew what He was doing! God was willing to present Moses this great nation. That wasn't good enough for Moses. In consequence He let these same people he chose cause him to take God's glory and strike the rock instead of speak to it! They still didn't enter the promise land and neither did Moses, but The kids did! So do we go follow Moses? Somebody whom the devil himself showed up for to take his soul after he died? The remnant will appreciate all of Moses good works but follow Jesus! Abraham learned quickly not to contest with God. After his first time doing this, Lot's wife ended up a salt statue for birds to sit and stool on and Lot ended up in a cave fathering his own grandchildren! God came to Abraham again and told him to sacrifice his son! Abraham *"Did Not"* question God this time! Even to the very time when he was about to strike his son and the angel had to quickly intervene! Abraham was so into the zone of obedience until after being stopped by the angel he didn't even grab his son and rock and cry and say "Thank you God "!!! He was yet looking for another offering to please the King with!

Abraham's thoughts: Okay you don't want him? I can find something else!

This is when Abraham could have contested but "Did Not"!! And he's now the father of many nations!

*Religious people say "we don't know how long it took Abraham to make up his mind to take his son to be sacrificed. Why do they say this? Because THEY always questioning God about every little thing and they want to feel justified! No faith at all.

Disrespect

God "you said" is one of the most disrespectful things you can say to God! He wants me to let you know that he's had mercy since the beginning of time on men's ignorance of not knowing how to respect Him! For years God has had hurt feelings by people claiming His name! God says for centuries, many have treated Him like He is a liar. Many many have disrespected Him because they choose the path of Moses to contest and disrespect.

How long will we put God on the witness stand hollering

"you said you wasn't a man that you would lie"

"God you said you would never forsake me that you would be with me to the end".

In the moment we use these scriptures what are we going through in our lives? Did you ask God for something and have not gotten it yet? Are you naturally hungry without food, and now trying to passively utilize a spiritual scripture on your natural situation? In other words we secretly call God a lie or insinuate that He lied or try to use manipulation that if God don't do it He will in fact have lied! So we, not the devil, try to bully God with "you said " like a lawyer trying to intimidate and some of us try to get a jury on God, so we holler across the pulpit, gymnasium, or on our jobs if He don't do it, He aint God. A person like this is not saved and need to repent. God don't have to watch over our foolishness with His word! Let me go ahead and bust another bubble since I have the knife, none of God's benefits apply to us if we not in the process of looking like Him! We must stop trying to activate something that doesn't belong to us. Then go around with our ungodly jury hollering God You said thinking we gone bully God into doing something for our sinful nasty hearted selves. Sit down religious people please!

For those who like to say God remember you said this and that and I'm holding you to your word "we dead wrong. God wants me to tell those guilty of this that we're wrong. We are acting like prosecutors and instead of using ammo on the devil we're using friendly fire on Him and has been doing this for decades! We look at the children of Israel in disgust but we had no idea we were looking like the replica of them.

For example, God you said you was going to give me a store remember? Remember you said that and you can't lie!

The Nasty Attitude

When things don't necessarily go our way, why do we find others to point our finger at?

This reminds me of Adam who tried to put the blame back on God!

God, the woman "you" gave me.

Adam, God didn't give you a "woman" He gave you a female who was named Adam. You out of your excitement renamed her woman and now you're not happy because she's being a woe-man unto you!

Woe meaning great sorrow or distress, things that cause sorrow or distress ;troubles.

God NEVER asked you to rename what He had already named! Adam, God gave you an animal naming anointing and now you name this lady and she starts talking to snakes. Women can't get enough of animal prints! Animal print rug, animal print clothes,and animal print car interior to name a few. My God. Be careful what you prophecy on your wife Adam because it will come to pass.

Matthew 19 verses 4 - 6 states

And he answered and said unto them, Have ye not read, that he which made them at the beginning made them "male and female " 5)And said, For this cause shall a man leave father and mother, and shall cleave to his wife: and they twain shall be one flesh? 6)wherefore they are no more twain, but one flesh, what therefore God hath joined together, let not man put asunder.

Wow! Jesus repeated the exact prophecy of Adam but Did Not add in that "rename to woman" Jesus said He which made them male and female. Adam that little blunder is on you now and forever more. Wow! I feel a lot lighter now! Daughters, it's up to us to become greater than a name!

"Remember you said"

God has never needed our memory to help Him remember anything. So you got prophesied to twenty years ago about owning a store, your life comes up before God everyday and if it's not speaking your faith in having this store then guess who's not getting a store? Why faith?

Because your faith will make you walk right, talk right, treat people right, and treat God right! We can holler "you said" all day long we not going to bully God into doing nothing! He remember things just fine and have never been strike with Amnesia or Alzheimer's!

Exodus 2:24 And God heard their groaning and God remembered his covenant with Abraham, with Issac, and with Jacob. 25:And God looked upon the children of Isreal, and God had "respect" unto them!

Did you know that God has respect for children who actually act like children? -Some teenagers start to get grown and smell themselves thinking they can raise up at their parents "you said " you was going to take me to the game! "You said " you would buy me a pizza for me and my friends! God remembered the children of Israel because they at the time were acting like He told them to act! Pray without ceasing, cry out, moan, weep, groan, and before Him speaking in Holy language edifying the spirit. God chose to remember them and had respect for them!

I tell you something else God chose to remember that religious folk don't talk about and that is, He remembered Moses broke those tablets!

Exodus 34:1 And the Lord said unto Moses, Hew thee two tables of stone like unto the first: And I will write upon these tables the words that were in the first tables "which thou breakest"

You better believe He remembers!

Remembering is a choice when it comes to God! He chooses to remember or He chooses to turn His face from it. Depending on our life! What is your life saying? God wants us to bring these offenses in check because He's in the mood to stop winking on ignorance! Amen.

Good To Know ~Trees~ One of the very famous things God created in this world are trees! Middle sized ones, small ones, and ones that take up your whole back yard! Trees are magnificent but have you ever thought of yourself being as a tree? Doesn't this sound a little silly? I know but it's true. Let's take a closer look at what the Lord has to say about us being as trees and the symbolism He gives us on this subject! {**Genesis 1: 11**} And God said, Let the **earth** bring forth grass, the herb yielding seed, and the **fruit tree** yielding fruit after his kind, whose seed is in itself, upon the earth: and it was so. * Let me tease your brain a little. Are we not earth and as fruit trees yielding spiritual fruit? Have you ever heard a man use this term concerning his child? *"This is my seed right here".* What he has to reproduce with is inside of him already. Have you ever heard anyone say, *"you're just like your daddy!" (Seed after his kind)* *Remember *St John 10 and 4 _* Jesus said *"abide in me and I in you. As a branch cannot bear fruit of itself, except it abide in the vine; no more can ye, except ye abide in me".* How about this term, when you're angry with your kid and then someone else comes along and says to you, *"The fruit don't fall to far from the tree."* We talk like we are as trees all the time. My daddy said, not to long ago concerning one of his grandkids, *"You can still bend a young tree."* (Meaning shape them to do right) You ever wonder why we as a people try to keep up with the seasons? Like trees, we want to actually appear spring, fall, summer, or winter by the colors we tend to shop for. In summer we want nothing but summer colors! We never think twice about it. To us it's normal. Maybe more normal than we know! *Trees are green.* The color green represents growth. As sons and daughters of God we should all be growing- weather growing more roots which can't be seen by others or branches that can. (Sometimes we're just in a root season) It may not look like you are physically growing sometimes because roots grow under ground but are very important. *Trees has to have water.* (Ephesians 5:26) says Jesus wants to cleanse us with the washing of the water by the word. What does this mean for our tree? Without the word, our tree will die. Jesus is the living water! (Side note) Ever thought about how selfish the flesh really is? We disconnect flowers and such things from life just to experience having them in our homes on our counters looking beautiful for a short time! We to at some point in our lives get disconnected from our source of life, but we must connect back to the true vine,which is God, to experience life again! (*St John 15*) *Trees bare fruit.* Every spiritual tree should bare fruit. Not apples, pears, Kiwi, and coconuts but love, joy, peace, long-suffering, gentleness, goodness, meekness, and temperance! *Let's talk property value_ Trees in general can raise property value by up to 10%.

Fruit trees won't necessarily bring more or less than that, but if they are well maintained the fruit trees can make a property "stand out" *more* than a common tree would. What am I saying? We as property of God should stand out more than the average tree because of our fruit. *Trees stand through every season.* Even through winter when no pretty leaves are present to reflect growth and good works, they still stand because seasons change. *Trees worship when they sway in the wind.* We to, should worship even more when the storms of life come to test and try us! *Trees have roots.* Roots are very important. It's the life of the tree. Would you say spiritually, that a person's branches reflect their roots? I personally believe it's a mirror image. What's in our roots will definitely show up on our tree for everyone to see! It's a very serious thing to renounce the hidden things! Spring is coming up... *Trees have sticky bark.* Should we have something sticky about us? I would say yes! Jesus had people following Him many places. Even people that hated Him followed. Something about Him caused people to want to be around Him. *Birds rest on tress,* but can a person rest their problems on our shoulders without us tipping over? What I mean by tipping over is spreading people's business to other people or receiving second hand hatred from someone. What's second hand hatred? It's like second hand smoke. Someone else is doing it but you receive the hazardous chemicals and bad doctors report because of association. Don't let other people talk about folks to you. *Trees provide shade.* (Psalms 121 5&6) says *"The Lord is thy keeper: the Lord is thy shade upon the right hand. The sun shall not smite the by day nor the moon by night."* We should be protectors as well. *Trees release oxygen.* Who else releases oxygen? Our Father which art in heaven gives us breath everyday! We are to release oxygen to others as well by sharing the word of God which is life.(Isaiah 61 1-3) Says "The spirit of the Lord God is upon me; because the Lord hath anointed me to preach good tidings unto the meek; he hath sent me to bind up the brokenhearted, to proclaim liberty to the captives, and the opening of the prison to them that are bound; To proclaim the acceptable year of the Lord,and the day of vengeance of our God; to comfort all that mourn; To appoint unto them that mourn in Zion, to give unto them beauty for ashes, the oil of joy for mourning, the garment of praise for the spirit of heaviness; that they might be *called trees of righteousness,* the planting of the Lord, that He might be glorified". Astounding! (*Mark 8 23-25*) says "And he took the blind man by the hand, and led him out of the town; and when he had spit on his eyes, and put his hands upon him, he asked him if he saw ought. And he looked up, and said, I see men as trees, walking. After that he put his hands again upon his eyes, and made him look up: and he was restored, and saw every man clearly." Restored in this verse means_ back to your original state. Restored meaning return (someone or something) to a former condition, place, or position. When Jesus first touched him, it wasn't that the miracle didn't work, it was that Jesus healed him and he began seeing in the spirit realm! He began to see as Jesus saw. (Men as trees) Then Jesus returned the man's eye sight back to it's original state. My prayer is for more than restoration but to restore me like unto Christ. Last but not least I would like to introduce to you a type of tree that bends so far to the ground through the storms and rains of life but after the storm is over this tree is almost Always still standing! This tree is the Palm Tree!

(Jeremiah 17;8) For he shall be like a tree planted by the waters, and that spreadeth out her roots by the river, and shall not see when heat cometh, but her leaf shall be green ; and shall not be careful in the year of drought, neither shall cease from yielding fruit.

This scripter makes me think of the Palm!" Most palms are distinguished by their large, compound, evergreen leaves, known as fronds, arranged at the top of an unbranched stem. However, palms exhibit an enormous diversity in physical characteristics and inhabit nearly every type of habitat within their range, from rainforests to deserts. They have been important to humans throughout much of history. Many common products and foods are derived from palms, and palms are also widely used in landscaping, making them one of the most economically important plants. In many historical cultures, palms were symbols for such ideas as victory, peace, and fertility. For inhabitants of cooler climates today, palms symbolize the tropics and vacations. Palms bare fruit! The fruit is usually a single-seeded drupe (sometimes berry-like) Some Palm genera (e.g. Salacca) may contain two or more seeds in each fruit. Palms thrive in moist and hot climates but can be found in a variety of different habitats. Their diversity is highest in wet, lowland forests. Members of the palm family with human uses are numerous.

The type member of Arecaceae is the arecapalm, the fruit of which, the areca nut, is chewed with the betel leaf for intoxicating effects (Areca catechu).Carnauba wax is harvested from the leaves of a Brazilian palm (Copernicia).Rattans, whose stems are used extensively in furniture and baskets, are in the genusCalamus.Palm oil is an edible vegetable oil produced by the oil palms in the genus Elaeis.Several species are harvested for heart of palm, a vegetable eaten in salads. Sap of the nipa palm Nypa is used to make vinegar. Palm sap is sometimes fermented to produce palm wine or toddy, an alcoholic beverage common in parts of Africa, India, and the Philippines. It is also drunk, fresh, as neera, and is a refreshing drink that is consumed until sundown, after which it starts to ferment. Palmyra and date palm sap is harvested in Bengal, India, to process into gur andjaggery.Dragon's blood, a red resin used traditionally in medicine, varnish, and dyes, may be obtained from the fruit of Daemonorops species. Coconut is the partially edible seed of the fruit of the coconut palm (Cocos nucifera).Coir is a coarse, water-resistant fiber extracted from the outer shell of coconuts, used in doormats, brushes, mattresses, and ropes. In India, beekeepers use coir in their bee smokers. Some indigenous groups living in palm-rich areas use palms to make many of their necessary items and food. Sago, for example, a starch made from the pith of the trunk of the sago palm Metroxylon sagu, is a major staple food for lowland peoples of New Guinea and the Moluccas. This is not the same plant commonly used as a house plant and called "sago palm". Palm wine is made from Jubaea also called Chilean wine palm, or coquito palm Recently, the fruit of the açaí palm Euterpehas been used for its reputed health benefits. Saw palmetto (Serenoa repens) is under investigation as a drug for treating enlarged prostates. Palm leaves are also valuable to some peoples as a material for thatching, basketry, clothing, and in religious ceremonies (see "Symbolism" below).[12] The palm branch was a symbol of triumph and victory in pre-Christian times. The Romans rewarded champions of the games and celebrated military successes with palm branches. Early Christians used the palm branch to symbolize the victory of the faithful over enemies of the soul, as in the Palm Sunday festival celebrating the triumphal entry of Jesus into Jerusalem. In Judaism, the palm represents peace and plenty, and is one of the Four Species of Sukkot; the palm may also symbolize the Tree of Life in Kabbalah". (Wikipedia Palm Trees) *We are as trees and should* : Bare fruit, have a healthy root system, be able to survive in dessert places, have sharable fruit, provide oxygen for others, not be moved through the storms of life!

#Did You Know:

~ Not all Pastors live what they preach, but YOU can live what they preach and become something beautiful in God! ~ The devil abides in the word of God so he is blessed. He's blessed enough to bless those in connection with him. So your cars, houses, acres to land, and money in the bank don't necessarily mean you have the Holy Ghost living in you! ~ "The church" is actually you. You then bring your church to church to fellowship and learn more things to make sure you are all the time preparing for the coming of our King! ~God is a quality God and not a quantity God? Don't feel bad that many has left and chosen other doctrine of Satan. If God loved to be around people so much He would not dwell in the secret place. He would have allowed more than 8 on Noah's ark. He cares nothing about having the masses around Him and popularity. He cares about that one who really does have a pure heart and a right spirit! ~ After repentance a change should take place! ~ Heaven is not a VIP club. You can't use someone else's name to get in! ~People think hell is not that bad because they say they go through hell on Earth. These people have not met the "lake of fire" yet! ~Less is more! The less you want, other than God, the least the devil can tempt you with! Thy will be done Lord! ~People spend all their lives trying to become something great instead of serving a great God! We were put here to serve and worship. ~Children are the closest people to God's heart because they exercise true forgiveness. ~ Treating your enemies the right way will cause your perfection! ~ Love is addicting! ~ The fruits of the spirit actually have a beautiful smelling scent to them. All the scents joined together makes a nice Melody ~The things you say on the inside of your heart matters a great deal! Sarah laughed within herself and was called out about doing it. ~There is power in femininity! Remember the road of the weaker Vessel Is sweet! ~ Jesus used food for spiritual reasons and purposes in the Bible, not just to indulge! ~ It's not more so your gift to God as much as it is your delivery! Give with a cheerful heart! ~ You can actually hang around people that will draw the wrong things out of you or resurrect things in the flesh that you have taken time to kill! Be careful. Association is deadly. ~Being a slave to an old ungodly mentality of yours is the worst form of slavery!

~ God never judged people by the color of the skin but the content of the heart! ~ Living to please a person is not living to please Jesus! ~ Salvation without redemption is spiritual retardation! ~God loves you so much! He gave His only son that we could be forgiven of sins and be free! Father made men in His image and men are CRAZY about their sons!!!! So God loved His son to but He unselfishly gave Jesus for us! ~Jesus lives and is very much alive!

I pray that this book reaches every hand that Father desires to have it! The journey to becoming Kingdom is not a bed of Roses but Father being along side to hold our hands makes the journey worth while! Be blessed.

FROM
PROCESS
TO
PROMISE
CARRIER66

LETTUCE
PRAY

IT'S
HEALTHY
CARRIER66

PRESSURE
MAKES
FLAWLESS
DIAMONDS
CARRIER66

VOTE
HE
DO IT

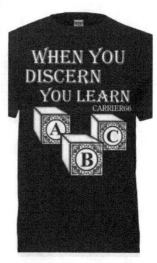

WHEN YOU
DISCERN
YOU LEARN
CARRIER66
A B C

PATIENCE
CARRIER66

NO
MORE
APRONS

SINCIRITY
A+
LEVELED UP
CARRIER66

IF I PERISH,
I PERISH

CARRIER66
ESTHER 4:16

PRAY
A
B
OUT IT
CARRIER66

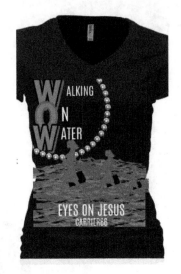

Printed in the United States
By Bookmasters